"Dr. Kupers gives us a front-row seat to America's tragic experiment in mass incarceration and one of its most devastating, cruel, and painful practices: solitary confinement. Kupers's unflinching insight into the hidden world of prisons exposes America at its darkest, but at the same time offers concrete solutions and hope for a safer, more effective, and humane criminal justice system."

—Amy Fettig, Deputy Director, American Civil Liberties Union National Prison Project

"Terry Kupers's wisdom, humanism, and generosity have helped advocates and litigators across the United States—not to mention countless prisoners— seeking to curb solitary confinement. His commitment to the well-being and dignity of every person behind bars has shaped his work and immeasurably enriched the prison reform movement. We are all in his debt."

—Jamie Fellner, former Director, US Program, Human Rights Watch

"The most prominent psychiatric expert witness in prison solitary confinement litigation is now the most important author in the field. The analysis is powerful and fits within a dramatic narrative of actual cases: inmates broken by the terrifying isolation that is solitary confinement."

—Fred Cohen, Professor Emeritus, University at Albany, State University of New York, and Executive Editor, *Correctional Law Reporter*

Solitary

Solitary

THE INSIDE STORY OF SUPERMAX ISOLATION AND HOW WE CAN ABOLISH IT

Terry Allen Kupers

UNIVERSITY OF CALIFORNIA PRESS

University of California Press, one of the most distinguished university presses in the United States, enriches lives around the world by advancing scholarship in the humanities, social sciences, and natural sciences. Its activities are supported by the UC Press Foundation and by philanthropic contributions from individuals and institutions. For more information, visit www.ucpress.edu.

University of California Press
Oakland, California

Library of Congress Cataloging-in-Publication Data

Names: Kupers, Terry Allen, author.
Title: Solitary : the inside story of supermax isolation and how we can abolish it / Terry Allen Kupers.
Description: Oakland, California : University of California Press, [2017] | Includes bibliographical references and index.
Identifiers: LCCN 2017002267 (print) | LCCN 2017008047 (ebook) | ISBN 9780520292239 (cloth : alk. paper) | ISBN 9780520965737 (ebook)
Subjects: LCSH: Solitary confinement—United States—Psychological aspects. | Prisoners—Mental health—United States.
Classification: LCC HV9471 .K86 2017 (print) | LCC HV9471 (ebook) | DDC 365/.33—dc23
LC record available at https://lccn.loc.gov/2017002267

Manufactured in the United States of America

26 25 24 23 22 21 20 19 18 17
10 9 8 7 6 5 4 3 2 1

CONTENTS

ILLUSTRATIONS

ACKNOWLEDGMENTS

I am blessed to have worked on jail and prison litigation with some of the very best constitutional lawyers in the country, who care deeply about the prisoners and families they serve. Without public interest attorneys, the rights of disempowered people would never see the light of public notice. Here is a partial list, with much gratitude: Terry Smerling, Don Specter, Mike Satris, Allyson Hardy, Sarah Norman, Steven Fama, Sid Wolinsky, Jody Owens, Alesha Judkins (senior advocate), Margaret Winter, David Fathi, Gabe Eber, Steve Berlin, Eric Balaban, Elizabeth Alexander, Amy Fettig, Carl Takei, Alan Mills, Steve Hanlon, Warren George, Peter Eliasberg, Dennis Cunningham, Don Lipmanson, Anita Arriola, Ernest Galvan, Charles Carbone, Michael Bien, Luther Orton, Keith Wattley, Jane Kahn, Sanford Rosen, Bob Fleischner, Staughton Lynd, Alice Lynd, Jules Lobell, Alexis Agathocleous, Carol Strickman, Carol Travis, Marilyn McMahon, Anne Weil, Sharon Dolovich, Sunday Rossberg, Eric Olson, Nick Straley, LaRond Baker, Emily Cooper, Margaret Chen, Sarah Dunne, Erin Sullivan, Deborah LaBelle, Molly Reno, Patricia Streeter, Sarah Kerr, Betsy Sterling, Nina Loewenstein, Sandy Girard, Cynthia Chandler, Peter Cubra, Ken Falk, Margo Schlanger, Millard Murphy, Richard Goff, Bret Grote, Catherine Campbell, David Lew, Azadeh Zohrabi, Harold Hirschman, Ben Salk, Nancy Alisberg, Robert Navarro, Sonia Mercado, Sam Paz, Barry Litt, Ron Kaye, David McLane, Marilyn Bednarsky, Caitlin Weisberg, Lindsay Battles, Ellen Barry, Eva DeLair, Mark Donatelli, Andree Larose, Jennifer Giuttari, Michael Pitt, Mark Vermeulen, Sarah Chester, and Michael Mushlin.

It's terribly unfortunate that most people think those who dwell in our jails and prisons are heinous criminals. Most prisoners today ran afoul of the law because they were using or selling drugs. To be sure, we don't want to foster a black market in illicit substances. But are long prison terms the answer? I find that prisoners are fairly ordinary people: that is, when I first meet them, I sense that, if not for fortune, they might be part of my community or my personal life.

Once prisoners go to jail, they are trained to acquiesce. "Do not argue with a correction officer," they are told. If you do, you can be beaten or carted off to a solitary cell. So with this level of intimidation, how do prisoners gather the courage to sue the state or federal government that incarcerates them? When I sit in the federal courtroom in Detroit and hear the testimony of women prisoners who have been sexually abused by prison staff, I am awed. These women have been taught they should be ashamed, yet they stand up in court and protest that their rights have been violated. And I am awed by the jailhouse lawyers, and the ten prisoners who were brave enough to sign on as named plaintiffs in the *Ashker v. Brown* class action lawsuit. Ultimately, prisoners (and ex-prisoners) are the heroes in this struggle. I will name a few, but there are many others: Mumia Abu-Jamal, Dan Pens, Willie London, Raymond C. (Chuck) Walen and the legal team at Michigan Prisoner Legal Services, Willie Russell, Steve Czifro, Dolores Canales, Hank Skinner, Danny Murillo, Brian Nelson, Five Mualimm-ak, Donna Wilmott, Linda Evans, Penny Schoner, Luis "Bato" Talamantez, Dorsey Nunn, Manuel La Fountaine, Robert King, Daisy Benson, O'Neil Stough, Claud Marks, Ed Mead, Rita "Bo" Brown, Donny Donaldson, Stephen Donaldson, Diana Block, Tom Cahill, Sarah Shourd, Shane Bauer, Paul Wright, the leaders of the California hunger strikes of 2011—13, and the named plaintiffs in *Ashker v. Brown*: Todd Ashker, Danny Troxell, Ronnie Yandell, Ronald Dewberry, Lewis Powell, Paul Redd, James Williamson, Arturo Castellanos, Alfred Sandoval, George Franco, Antonio Guillen, Jeffrey Franklin, George Ruiz, Gabriel Reyes, Richard Johnson, and Luis Esquivel.

Activists in the broad movement to reshape the criminal justice system share the memory of their horror when they were introduced to the gruesome reality of our jails and prisons. Once they went in and looked about, they could not return to llife as usual without speaking out and trying to end some of the horrors they had witnessed. Without the activists the class action lawsuits would not be effective and change would be unlikely. There are too many committed activists to name, but I will begin with these: Jamie Fellner, Angela Browne, Corey Weinstein, Judy Greenspan, Angela Davis, Ruth Gilmore, Craig Gilmore, Helen Grimes, Laura Magnani, Ron Ahnen, Dorsey Nunn, Ida Robinson, Esther Lin, Don Sabo, Sandrine Ageorges,

Karen Shain, Jody Sokolower, Tom Quinn, Kiilu Nyashi, Barbara Becnel, Joanne Mariner, Lovisa Stannow, David Kaiser, Matt Lowen, Helen Grimes, Georgia Shreiber, Bonnie Kerness, Keramet Reiter, Mike Castell, Patricia Hilden, Terry Day, Miranda Bergman, Felix Shafer, Rose Braz, Leslie DiBenedetto Skopek, Naneen Karraker, Joyce Miller, Dylan Rodriguez, Cassandra Shaylor, Nancy Stoller, William "Buzz" Alexander, Noel Hanrahan, Heather Rice-Minus, and Rev. Markle Downton.

I have learned a lot from my fellow experts, including Hans Toch, Craig Haney, Stuart Grassian, Eldon Vale, Joe Goldenson, David Lovell, Carl Fulwiler, Bart Abplanalp, James Austin, Vincent Nathan, Pablo Stewart, Ed Kaufman, Raymond Patterson, Robert Walsh, Jeff Metzner, Brie Williams, Steve Martin, Martin Horn, Brenda V. Smith, Edward Kaufman, Lindsey Hayes, Kathryn Burns, Barbara Owen, Michael Puisis, Sheryl Kubiak, Paul Good, Marc Stern, Kathy Wayland, Madeleine LaMarre, and Bobby Cohen. Fred Cohen is in a category of his own, having provided rigorous and brilliant descriptions and critiques of prison litigation over decades.

Journalists have played an important role in exposing harsh conditions and abuse in the jails and prisons. There are many, and I much appreciate their work. I will mention a few who stand out. Jean Casella and James Ridgeway direct the website Solitary Watch, far and away the best source of information about what goes on in supermaxes. Lance Tapley, Michael Montgomery, Mark Arax, Erica Goode, and others have provided powerful stories about what goes on "Inside."

I have been blessed to work with truly outstanding editors and publishing staff. Maura Roessner stands out: she has offered immense support and wisdom in the evolution of this book. The entire editorial and production staff at University of California Press have been invaluable, including editors Chris Lura, Elisabeth Magnus, and Jessica Moll, as well as editorial assistants Jack Young and Sabrina Robleh.

I could not have done the work and written this book without immense love and support from my family and friends, especially my wife, Arlene Shmaeff, who passed away in 2013. It is a great gift to have Harriet Charney by my side.

Introduction

THE TERM *SOLITARY CONFINEMENT* (or *supermaximum security confinement*) "is generally used to refer to conditions of extreme (but not total) isolation from others." It has been defined as "segregation from the mainstream prisoner population in attached housing units or free-standing facilities where prisoners are involuntarily confined in their cells for upwards of 23 hours a day . . . , given only extremely limited or no opportunities for direct and normal social contact with other persons (i.e., contact that is not mediated by bars, restraints, security glass or screens, and the like), and afforded extremely limited if any access to meaningful programming of any kind." There is no such thing as total isolation in prison, and some prisoners in solitary confinement may have a cellmate, but even those with cellmates are "isolated from the rest of the mainstream prisoner population, deprived of even minimal freedom of movement, prohibited from access to meaningful prison programs, and denied opportunities for any semblance of 'normal' social interaction."[1]

When I am called on as a forensic psychiatrist to tour a supermaximum security prison facility, I see and hear of very harsh things. I see cells where prisoners spend nearly twenty-four hours a day alone, in a cell containing a bunk, a sink/toilet appliance, and little else. They eat their meals alone in their cell and have little or no opportunity to be productive (often they are not even permitted paper and pen). Some facilities have windows in cells so prisoners can look out—usually onto concrete buildings capped by razor wire—but many have no windows in cells. Some permit phone calls home, but again, many do not. Some of these facilities will put a few prisoners in a recreation yard together, but most make them exercise alone, often in a small fenced area that prisoners refer to as a "cage" or "dog run."

Details vary, but during tours of supermax isolation units in fifteen states I frequently hear of extreme and excessive punishments. For example, I hear about "cell extractions" where a group of officers in riot gear spray a prisoner with immobilizing gas and then rush into his cell and violently subdue him; I hear about prisoners being unable to gain the staff's attention for urgent medical and psychiatric needs; and I meet prisoners who have been viciously beaten or raped. However, despite the unacceptably high prevalence of these occurrences, the general public does not know about them. I am witness to these things only because, as a forensic psychiatrist, I am regularly called on to serve as an expert witness in class action lawsuits brought by civil rights and human rights attorneys on behalf of prisoners. The lawsuits challenge unconstitutional prison conditions that violate the Eighth Amendment of the US Constitution's prohibition against cruel and unusual punishment or violate the Americans with Disabilities Act. As a result of the litigation, prison authorities are ordered by the courts to provide me with a tour of the prisons so I can investigate and prepare expert testimony. After touring supermax security prisons around the country and presenting expert testimony in over forty cases, I feel the need to speak out about what I have observed taking place in these facilities.

When I testify in court, I am often asked: "What is the damage of long-term solitary confinement?" In response, I recite a long list of prisoners' frequently reported symptoms, including anxiety, panic, paranoia, memory problems, and despair. Many prisoners were already suffering from serious mental illness when their stint in solitary began, and for these prisoners solitary tends to exacerbate the preexisting mental illness and to worsen their disability. The high suicide rate in solitary confinement is also a cause for serious concern. But the long-term damage from solitary confinement does not always take the form of a traditional mental illness. Many prisoners emerge from prison after years in solitary with very serious psychiatric symptoms even though outwardly they may appear emotionally stable. The damage from isolation is dreadfully real.

In an article published in 2016, Five Mualimm-ak—who had moved with his family from his native Ethiopia to the United States at the age of twelve, entered a New York prison in his early twenties, and spent five of his twelve years behind bars in solitary confinement—described his experience in solitary:

After only a short time in solitary, I felt all of my senses start to diminish. There was nothing to see but grey walls. In New York's so-called Special

Housing Units, or SHUs, most cells have solid steel doors, and some don't have windows. You can't even tape up pictures or photographs. . . . To fight the blankness, I counted bricks and measured the walls. I stared obsessively at the bolts on the door to my cell. There was nothing to hear except empty, echoing voices from other parts of the prison. I was so lonely that I hallucinated words coming out of the wind. They sounded like whispers. Sometimes I smelled the paint on the wall, but more often, I just smelled myself, revolted by my own scent. There was no touch. My food was pushed through a slot. Doors were activated by buzzers, even the one that led to a literal cage directly outside of my cell for one hour per day of "recreation." Even time had no meaning in the SHU. The lights were kept on for twenty-four hours. I often found myself wondering if an event I was recollecting had happened that morning or days before. I talked to myself. After a while, I began to get scared that the guards would come in and kill me and leave me hanging in the cell. Who would know if something happened to me? The space I inhabited was invisible to the outside world, just like I was.[2]

While there certainly is a need to maintain order in the prisons, we too regularly accept uncritically the notion of "Lock 'em up and throw away the key." And our willingness to close our eyes means that the degradation and the physical and psychological abuse of prisoners that occurs on a regular basis will be unseen and off limits to reporters, legislators, and families alike.

MY PATH TO SOLITARY

I was not focused on the harm of solitary confinement during the first half of my career as a forensic psychiatrist. Crowding, sexual abuse, and the quality of correctional mental health treatment in prisons and jails were more at issue in the class action lawsuits where I served as psychiatric expert witness in the 1970s.[3] That would all change in the late 1980s as uncontrollable prison violence and the presence of high numbers of prisoners suffering from serious mental illness set the stage for a boom in supermax prison construction that has lasted for over three decades and brought with it the placement of a large number of prisoners in solitary confinement.

I first became an expert on prison conditions and correctional mental health care in the 1970s following a work-related visit to the Los Angeles County Jail. While still in my residency training as a psychiatrist, I was already a licensed physician, so I was qualified to work after hours and on weekends as the primary care physician at a free clinic in the community, the

Bunchy Carter Free Clinic in South Central Los Angeles. The clinic was run by the Black Panther Party as part of their community service program, and the patients were community members who lacked other resources for medical care. My clinical caseload also included members of the Black Panther Party. Meanwhile, the Los Angeles Police Department and the FBI had joined forces in the COINTELPRO collaboration,[4] a national project created by J. Edgar Hoover in the late 1950s. On December 9, 1969, in the early hours of the morning, the Los Angeles Police Department SWAT Team, the FBI, and other COINTELPRO-affiliated law enforcement agencies surrounded the Black Panther headquarters in Los Angeles armed with heavy military equipment. It was a few days after the Chicago Black Panther leader Fred Hampton had been shot to death in his bed by a COINTELPRO-coordinated law enforcement raid on his home. The second floor of the building at Fortieth and Central in South Central Los Angeles was the headquarters and living space for the Black Panthers, while the ground floor contained the Bunchy Carter Free Clinic. It was only because an urgent call went out via telephone tree and a large number of social activists showed up to stand and witness the event that the law enforcement team was unable to entirely destroy the building and kill the Black Panthers sleeping inside. Eleven Black Panthers were wounded, arrested, and carted off to jail.

At that time the law provided that if one was sent to jail one's physician was permitted to visit and participate in medical assessment and treatment. The L.A. Panthers were on the jail ward of Los Angeles County Hospital, so I went there to see my patients. The Sheriff's Department did not want to permit my access, but civil rights attorneys were present with me at the entry point and successfully argued that my patients had a right to a visit from their physician.

The horrifying scene that I witnessed that day was one of the initial catalysts in my long journey to becoming an investigator of the treatment of prisoners in America. I found my patients lying in hospital beds on a ward, handcuffed and chained to their beds, with a large number of armed police and sheriff's deputies standing around. Many of their intravenous setups were not functioning properly, some with blood backed up in the tubing, and several patients were experiencing severe pain. The wounded men told me that some officers would hit them with an elbow in the area of their wound as they passed their bed, and they were not getting adequate treatment, mostly because of the concentrated police presence on their ward. I complained to the physicians, left the hospital, and spoke to the press about their treatment. There were headlines, there were protests, and their treatment did subsequently improve.

Several years later, after years of complaints about the treatment of prisoners, the American Civil Liberties Union of Southern California launched a class action lawsuit against the Los Angeles Sheriff's Department alleging unconstitutional conditions at the Los Angeles County Jail and asked me to be their psychiatric expert witness. By that time, I had undergone training in forensic psychiatry, but I had not spent much time in jails, and I told the lead attorney that I did not feel very expert about jails. But he was aware of the reports I had made previously on the conditions that my patients from the Black Panther Party had been subjected to earlier, and he noted that nobody else was yet very expert on the subject. "It's a novel kind of litigation," he said. "We just want you to go into the jail and report on any deficiencies of treatment or abuses you witness." Eventually I agreed.

I studied the research literature that existed about jail and prison conditions and correctional mental health treatment. When I toured the Los Angeles County Jail in 1974 in preparation for testimony in the ACLU's case (called *Rutherford v. Pitchess*), I found the harsh conditions and deficiencies in medical and mental health treatment so glaring and obvious that they hardly needed an expert: all I had to do was report to the court precisely what I had observed.

The jail was a complete mess. For example, the pods containing the cells and dayroom where prisoners congregated were massively overcrowded. There was almost no floor space to walk across the dayroom because prisoners were lying on the floor or, if they were standing, had to turn sideways to squeeze by each other. In the cells, men were lying on the upper bunks, others on the lower ones, and several on the floor. There were metal tables in the dayroom with benches on each of their four sides, and the tables and benches were bolted to the floor. Men were sitting or lying on the tables, and others were sitting or lying on the benches. Bedding material was strewn around everywhere, and the noise in the pod was deafening. I asked some of the men to explain the situation to me, and they told me how the tougher prisoners were on the top bunks or on the table tops, less tough guys were on the lower bunks and lying on the benches, and the not-so-tough prisoners had to sleep on the floor. They all stayed in the pod all day and all night, and that was why I was seeing so much bedding thrown around. The prison offered no activities outside the pod, no exercise or recreation, and no group therapies or rehabilitation programs. And many quite psychotic prisoners were wandering about. I went back to the court and reported what I had seen.

FIGURE 1. Prisoners living in a gym converted into a dorm at Mule Creek State Prison, August 2008. The words on the left wall read, "No Warning Shot Is Required." This photograph was appended to the majority decision in *Brown v. Plata* (2011).

The court ruled in favor of the prisoners, and Los Angeles County was required to reduce crowding and upgrade medical and mental health services. The county appealed the case all the way to the US Supreme Court, and the trial court's order was upheld. As a result, Los Angeles County built the Twin Towers section of the jail, where mental health treatment would take place.

Later, in the years that followed, I would testify in several lawsuits in California counties about the harm of crowding and the harm of inadequate mental health services when a growing number of prisoners in the jails were suffering from serious mental illness.[5] In addition to providing testimony in court about the conditions in jails, I would be called on to serve as an expert witness in prison litigation. Unlike jails, which are local detention facilities where individuals await trial or serve sentences up to a year in length, prisons are administered by states or the federal government and contain convicted prisoners serving sentences greater than a year. When I toured California prisons in the late 1970s, I was shocked by the degree and ramifications of crowding and inadequate medical and mental health care. The prison crowding did not match—in sheer concentration of bodies within a confined space—what I had found in the Los Angeles County Jail. But in many ways the harmful effects of crowding in prisons were even worse than those I was discovering in jails.

In California prisons I saw crowds of idle men in the yard and in the dayrooms, and when I would enter the gymnasium, a structure built for basketball and other athletic events, I would see bunk beds, three-high, in rows, where 150 to 250 prisoners were housed. Many men would be milling about the gymnasium in the middle of the day or lying on their bunks. Along one wall of the gymnasium were makeshift urinals, toilets, and shower stalls, and along another wall were a few pay phones. I found the officers, four or five of them in charge of supervising the dorm, sitting around a desk near the door. As I looked around the gymnasium with the rows of bunks three-high and blankets and clothes hanging from many of them, I was impressed by how little I could actually see from any one spot. But the officers seemed to have very little interest in what was going on with the prisoners. Several prisoners whom I interviewed later told me that a fight or a rape could take place on the far side of the gymnasium/dorm and the officers would have no idea it was happening.

A HISTORIC WRONG TURN

Most of the central issues in class action lawsuits of the 1970s and 1980s arose from jail and prison crowding, which created harsh conditions of confinement that violated the US Constitution's Eighth Amendment prohibition against cruel and unusual punishment. The War on Drugs and increasingly harsh prison sentences were causing the prison population to swell precipitously. Crowding became so severe that gymnasiums were converted to impromptu dormitories, and in the jails four or six prisoners were crammed into cells built for one or two. Education and rehabilitation programs not only failed to expand to fill the need but were reduced because conservative politicians were making a concerted effort to dismantle such programs, on the assumption that they "coddled" criminals. Meanwhile, with the deinstitutionalization of state psychiatric hospitals and subsequent budget cuts in community mental health programs, large numbers of individuals suffering from serious mental illness found their way into jails and prisons. So a lot of idle prisoners, many suffering from serious mental illness, were crammed into small spaces, and too often the result was mayhem. The entire scenario led to a fateful historic wrong turn.

On October 22, 1983, two officers were stabbed to death at the maximum security federal penitentiary in Marion, Illinois. The staff did not know for certain who killed them, so they decided to "lock down" the prison. All prisoners were confined to their cells for nearly twenty-four hours per day, they were fed in their cells, and almost all rehabilitation programs were canceled. Prison lockdowns usually last a few weeks or months, long enough for the staff to regain control of the prison and solve the crime that precipitated the lockdown. But at Marion the lockdown became permanent and continued for the next twenty-three years, essentially relegating a large proportion of the prison population to solitary, whether or not they had been found guilty of a rule violation or were determined to be affiliated with a gang. The locked-down prison seemed more quiet, peaceful, and easy to manage than it had been when the prisoners were in the general population.

Many states began building cellblocks or entire prisons dedicated to solitary confinement, and the entire trend was known as the "Marionization" of the prisons. The age of the supermax had arrived. The Federal Bureau of Prisons proceeded to build a new, state-of-the-art supermaximum security prison, the ADX (administrative maximum facility) in Florence, Colorado. Supermaximum security units are also known as Security Housing Units or SHUs, the California acronym that has become synonymous with supermax confinement around the country. A supermaximum security unit or SHU is a cellblock or prison made up entirely of isolation or segregation cells. In these cells, where the prisoners are confined nearly twenty-four hours per day and eat meals alone (or, in some cases, with a cellmate), idleness and isolation are severe.[6] Few if any rehabilitation or education programs exist in super-maxes. Most states and the federal government built them, and an unprecedented proportion of maximum security prisoners were consigned to some form of long-term segregation.

As a result, in the late 1980s, the focus of prison litigation changed. No longer would crowding be the main issue when I testified in court, though the crowding problem still prevailed as a backdrop to what would happen next. The new issue was solitary confinement. It is estimated that one hundred thousand prisoners are in solitary confinement in the United States today, and I believe that figure is a gross underestimate (for example, it does not include the number of prisoners on lockdown). And the number of prisoners in solitary confinement at a given moment is only a small fraction of the number of prisoners who spend significant time in solitary confinement or segregation during their prison tenure. The Bureau of Justice Statistics recently released a report showing that 20 percent of prisoners in federal and state prisons and 18 percent of those held in local jails had spent time in solitary confinement during the previous twelve months.[7] Since there are currently well over two million prisoners in American jails and prisons, that means that over four hundred thousand current prisoners have spent time in solitary, and that number does not include all those who are no longer behind bars.

But over the past few years, consensus has been building that solitary confinement is both ineffective and cruel.[8] In 2015 Supreme Court Justice Anthony Kennedy testified before Congress that "this idea of total incarceration just isn't working—and it's not humane. The federal government built—what do they call them—supermax prisons, with isolation cells. The prisoner we had come before our court a few weeks ago . . . had been in an isolation cell according to the attorney—I haven't checked it out—for 25 years. Solitary confinement literally drives men mad."[9] The attorney and scholar of correctional law Fred Cohen concurred in 2016 that the practice of holding inmates "indefinitely in tiny cubicles without review and without social stimulation . . . is torture, in my view, and there are no procedural solutions to the imposition of torture."[10] And President Barack Obama joined the chorus, stating in a speech before the National Association for the Advancement of Colored People (NAACP): "Do we really think it makes sense to lock so many people alone in tiny cells for 23 hours a day, sometimes for months or even years at a time? . . . That is not going to make us safer. That's not going to make us stronger. And if those individuals are ultimately released, how are they ever going to adapt?"[11]

Correctional administrators and policy makers once believed that by putting "the worst of the worst" in long-term solitary confinement they would resolve the problem of prison gangs and reduce prison violence. They were wrong: the gang problem continues unabated and the violence continues to flare. Meanwhile, solitary confinement is causing immense human damage, reflected in the degree and chronicity of serious mental illness in the prisoner population and in rising recidivism rates and parole violation rates. It is time for a comprehensive overhaul of our criminal justice system. The approach of devising ever harsher punishments—three strikes, life without parole, solitary confinement, further privations within solitary confinement—has been a failure.

As I and many other experts counseled from the beginning of the explosion in supermax construction, there are much better ways to confront increased violence and disorder in our prisons. We need to drastically downsize the prison population by ending the War on Drugs and reversing the trend toward stiffer sentences for just about every variety of crime. This would address the problem of prison crowding. With fewer prisoners, the staff would be able to spend more time devising effective management plans for even the most difficult prisoners, so that solitary confinement would be unnecessary. We also need to provide more and better mental health treatment both inside and outside our prisons. Finally, we need to expand and enrich effective rehabilitative programs. As I report in this book, I have seen many such programs. Each prison system has a corner where creative and enterprising staff construct rehabilitation programs that work, such as a class

FIGURE 2. A pod at Pelican Bay State Prison SHU with metal grid doors and cell-fronts. Photo by Monica Lam, working with journalist Michael Montgomery and the Center for Investigative Reporting, 2012.

on parenting skills, a substance abuse treatment program, a group on anger management, or a large garden where prisoners learn to farm. With greater opportunities to gain an education and learn a trade, far fewer prisoners would feel they had "nothing to lose" and nothing to keep them from joining in the violence. In short, we need to be certain that what we do to people when they are behind bars decreases rather than increases the likelihood that they will resort to illicit substances and crime after they get out of prison, since 93 percent of prisoners do eventually go free. We need to replace the culture of punishment with a rehabilitative attitude.[12]

THE ORGANIZATION OF THIS BOOK

This book contains three parts. In Part I, I explore the harsh reality of solitary confinement. Chapter 1 traces the history of solitary confinement from the early penitentiaries at the beginning of the nineteenth century to the modern supermax. It provides an in-depth look at the conditions of confinement and the quality of life in supermax units and facilities today, including the SHU at California's Pelican Bay State Prison, where a significant proportion of my own research and litigation has focused. But solitary confinement or isolation is not limited to units designated supermaximum security. I briefly describe as well other locations of solitary confinement that go under other names.

In chapter 2 I explore the culture of punishment that prevails in correctional facilities. Prisoners who break the rules receive harsh punishments in the form of ever tighter controls, culminating in confinement to one's cell for nearly twenty-four hours per day with little to do. Even during the brief periods when prisoners are taken out of their cells they may be restricted to small cages on the recreation yard or confined in individual, phone booth–like cages if they are assembling for group psychotherapy or a class. And even in solitary confinement, worse punishments are inflicted for continuing misbehavior. The rationale for ever tighter controls revolves around the staff's fear that unrestrained or unbroken prisoners would be difficult to manage and potentially dangerous. Actually, the opposite is the case. In their attempts to isolate and control prisoners correctional staff exacerbate one of the most disabling symptoms caused by long-term solitary confinement: anger. The culture of punishment and control is not very conducive to efforts at treatment and rehabilitation.

Chapter 3 is about race relations behind bars. Prison reproduces the trends of society at large, meanwhile amplifying their toxic repercussions. A disproportionate number of young African American men are arrested and sent to prison. In prison, African Americans are more likely than their white counterparts to be sent to solitary confinement and less likely to win positions in desirable prison jobs and rehab programs. Racial tensions among prisoners mean that when trouble erupts, prisoners gravitate to others of their own race for safety's sake. And I hear many reports of racial discrimination by staff. I will explore prison racial dynamics, which shape to a great extent prisoners' experience of solitary confinement.

Part II is about the human damage wrought by long-term solitary confinement. In chapter 4 I review the well-known symptoms associated with even a few months in solitary. They include anxiety, panic, disordered thinking, paranoia, memory and sleep problems, compulsive acts such as pacing or cleaning one's cell six times per day, despair, and suicidal thoughts. In the *Ashker v. Brown* class action lawsuit I was asked if any additional damage was done by longer-term solitary confinement of a decade or more. Indeed, at the Pelican Bay State Prison I discovered more serious and lasting emotional problems in prisoners who had been in solitary confinement for over a decade. They reported intense cravings for isolation even beyond the exigencies of solitary confinement, as well as severe emotional numbing: many said they felt like the walking dead. The most destructive consequence of long-term solitary confinement is great and lasting disability in the realms of personal relationships, work, and the enjoyment of life. Solitary confinement decimates life skills. This violates the Eighth Amendment prohibition against cruel and unusual punishment and also constitutes torture. Solitary confinement damages prisoners in ways that make them less likely to succeed when they are released and more likely to resort again to illicit substances and crime.

In Chapter 5 I examine the interface of solitary confinement and mental illness behind bars, revisiting themes I explored in my 1999 book *Prison Madness*. I discuss the trend in recent decades to criminalize mental illness by providing so little in the way of a social safety net in the community that an unprecedented number of individuals suffering from serious mental illness wind up behind bars. There are ten times as many individuals with serious mental illness in our jails and prisons as there are in our psychiatric hospitals.[13] But the budget for mental health treatment has not expanded commensurately with the enlarged population. The result is inadequate treatment and a tendency for prisoners suffering from serious mental illness to spend an inordinate amount of time in solitary confinement. Solitary greatly exacerbates serious mental illness, and the tragic result is a growing population of individuals with very severe disabilities and dire prognoses.

Chapter 6 is about the plight of women in solitary confinement. Women who go to prison tend to have quite a great deal of trauma in their histories before they went to prison. In prison they are traumatized anew with cross-gender strip searches, sexual abuse, and solitary confinement. Quite often the traumatic events they suffer behind bars reenact their past traumas. And when they are sexually abused in prison, they are reluctant to report the abuse because they fear they will be transferred to solitary "for their own protection."

Chapter 7 is about youth, who are entering adult prisons in unprecedented numbers. The proportion of juveniles tried as adults and sent to adult prisons is growing. Too often, fearing sexual assault but not wanting to be perceived by other prisoners as weak or a "snitch," the juvenile in an adult prison hits an officer so he can be sent to solitary, an honorable action according to the prisoner code. But in solitary juveniles suffer even more severe emotional damage than adults.

Chapter 8 is about what I call SHU postrelease syndrome, a constellation of symptoms that a significant number of prisoners experience when released from a long stint in solitary confinement. Such prisoners are likely to become withdrawn and feel that their emotional life is flat. If released to a general-population setting within prison, they spend an inordinate amount of time in their cell, and if they leave prison they stay in their room or their house, avoiding social contact and becoming anxious when in proximity to people they do not know. Often they are not capable of seeking employment.

In Part III I set out alternatives to harmful isolative confinement, including a community mental health model in corrections as well as a strategy for working with "disturbed/disruptive" prisoners, and I describe an attitude that is the common denominator in all the successful rehab programs I have visited. Chapter 9 is about this "rehabilitative attitude," which provides a much-needed alternative to the culture of punishment and must be shared by all staff if prisoners are to have a decent chance at success after their release. Staff who adopt a rehabilitative attitude envision and take as a goal a positive future for the prisoner, such as a happy marriage, a successful role as parent, and a meaningful job. By doing so they can encourage the prisoner to focus his or her energy on life after release by learning social skills that will lead to success as a partner and a parent and by developing the capabilities that foster satisfying paid work. Prisoners who "keep their head out of prison and keep prison out of their head," by staying connected to loved ones while doing time and envisioning a future at home and in the community, are very likely to stay out of trouble in prison and to take advantage of educational and job training programs. Staff's rehabilitative attitude pays off in more peaceful prisons and prisoners' greater success at going straight after release.[14]

Chapter 10 is about mental health treatment, a high priority in jails and prisons if only because, as a society, we have elected to consign so many individuals with serious mental illness to jails and prisons. Nobody makes that consignment consciously. More often there is this series of events: the person with serious mental illness does not have the means to purchase treatment in the private sector; public mental health clinics and hospitals are underfunded and do not offer enough in the way of treatment; the person falls into homelessness and possibly substance abuse, then is arrested for a crime and placed behind bars. Of course, the best plan would be to keep individuals with serious mental illness out of jail and prison. This would require beefing up public mental health services and substance abuse treatment (recovery) in the community and having a large proportion of individuals with mental illness who commit crimes participate in mental health and recovery programs as an alternative to incarceration (this is called diversion and is usually supervised in a mental health court). But in the meantime, we have many individuals suffering from serious mental illness in correctional settings. Their treatment is too often abysmal, and they spend an inordinate amount of time in solitary confinement, where their condition deteriorates. I will address this problem and explain how failure to maintain quality mental health programs behind bars inevitably leads to harmful solitary confinement for this vulnerable subpopulation.

Chapter 11 is about a uniquely difficult group of prisoners to work with, those whom social psychologist Hans Toch describes as "disturbed/disruptive." Corrections staff have typically distinguished between the "Mad" and the "Bad." When mental illness—for example, hallucinations commanding the prisoner to break a rule or hit someone—drives unacceptable acts, the prisoner is deemed mad and sent for more intensive mental health treatment. But when the rule violation or assault is considered willful, the prisoner is sent to "the hole"—solitary confinement. Toch argues that very troublesome prisoners are likely to be both Mad and Bad, that their madness and badness exacerbate each other, and that it makes very little sense to sharply distinguish between madness and badness in determining the cause of unacceptable behaviors. Rather, a comprehensive treatment and management plan is needed. If prisoners with mental illness are to be effectively excluded from solitary confinement on account of the harm it does to their condition, an intensive mental health treatment program at a high level of security must be available to meet their needs.

In chapter 12 I address the stark choice we face today between isolation and rehabilitation. Jails and prisons must replace the culture of punishment with rehabilitative approaches. But the alternative to solitary confinement is not to be found entirely in the prisons, or even in departments of correction. It is also important to step back and look at the bigger picture, the larger social arrangements, starting with sentencing laws. The call for harsher punishments that accompanied the "law and order" boom of the 1970s led to the crowding of jails and prisons, which in turn led to increased prison violence and disorder that triggered the foolhardy notion of "locking up" in solitary "the worst of the worst." And the public outcry for harsher sentences did not occur in a vacuum. By the 1970s, many people who had relied on social welfare assistance to keep their heads above water, including those suffering from serious mental illness, were vastly overrepresented among those falling into homelessness and eventually finding their way into jail and prison. It is as if society were hiding its shameful record of inadequate housing and public mental health services by disappearing the very people who were left adrift as the social safety net was taken away from them. Dostoevsky famously warned, "The degree of civilization in a society can be judged by entering its prisons."[15] Prison reforms including an end to solitary confinement are not enough: they must be combined with large changes in our social arrangements if we are to improve this society's degree of civilization.

A NOTE ABOUT CONFIDENTIALITY

When I conduct a forensic examination I begin with an explanation to the interviewee of the lack of confidentiality involved in the process. In my clinical psychiatric practice I strive to maintain full confidentiality within the limits of the law, but in a forensic examination the material uncovered in my interviews may be utilized in court and may even find its way into newspaper articles. At the same time, in my jail and prison investigations I function under a strict agreement about my privileged access to confidential information. Much of the information I obtain that names individuals or provides details that could identify them is to go no further than the legal forum where I will be presenting my findings and opinions. I present quite a bit of case material in this book. I have made every effort, in the context of very public litigation, to maintain the confidentiality of the prisoners I have interviewed. All prisoner stories I relate are true. I learned the facts from the prisoners or from documents. Where the prisoner's story has not been made public, I make up a first name for him or her, leave out the location and name of the prison, and alter personal details enough to support confidentiality but not enough to distort the data. Where my report in a case has been made public, for example in newspapers or on the website of the legal group representing the plaintiff(s), I include here only the personal information that has already been made public. And where the prisoner has given me permission to tell his or her story or has published the story, I quote the story and cite the reference. In other words, I try my best at all times to balance the interest of confidentiality and the need for accuracy. I admire the prisoners whose stories I discuss for their courage in letting their stories be told in the courtroom and in print. Most of them believe that telling their story in the context of class action litigation will help improve the situation of many other similarly situated prisoners.

PART ONE

Harsh Prison Conditions

_____

ONE

Supermax Isolation

SOLITARY CONFINEMENT HAS BEEN part of American correctional practice since the birth of the nation. The idea of isolating prisoners for their own good was supported in the final years of the eighteenth century by such prominent figures as Benjamin Franklin and his friend Benjamin Rush, the pioneering psychiatrist. During that era, many Quakers viewed crime as a moral lapse and jail as a place where prisoners would be left by themselves in a cell and would be expected to search their souls about their errant ways and be "penitent" (thus the origin of the word *penitentiary*). But over the years, prison funding could not keep pace with a growing prison population, so this kind of solitary confinement for the general population of prisoners was abandoned as too expensive to construct for or to maintain. Where solitary was retained, its original rehabilitative rationale was stripped away; it was now openly used merely as a dreaded punishment and deterrent within the prison and as a convenient means of separating out, for months, years, even decades, individuals whose inclusion in the general prison population might pose problems for prison management.

THE LONG HISTORY OF SOLITARY CONFINEMENT IN THE UNITED STATES

The first correctional facility in the nation to consign prisoners to single cells was the Walnut Street Jail in Philadelphia. It was originally built in 1773 to handle the overflow of prisoners from the nearby, massively overcrowded High Street Jail. There were simply too many debtors, paupers, prostitutes, thieves, and ex-slaves going to jail for the jailers to find the space to house them. When Walnut

Street Jail opened, it contained very large rooms with high ceilings where prisoners were crowded and left to shift for themselves. They received little attention from staff; there were fights, thefts, and sexual assaults; the cellblocks were filthy; and there was absolutely no attempt at rehabilitation. But fifteen years after the Walnut Street Jail opened, the Quakers, in collaboration with other religious groups, succeeded in opening a wing of the jail, the "penitentiary house," where each prisoner would have a room of his or her own, a notion very popular in the religious community. The small, clean single cells were arranged in a way that prevented the inhabitants from having contact with each other. They had windows high off the ground, and the window coverings prevented prisoners from looking out upon the surrounding streets. The prisoners in "separate confinement" were left alone in their cells and, at the beginning of their sentence, were not given work to do because the designers felt that they needed to be idle to properly reflect on their criminal ways and correct their life course. Later, however, the prisoners would be given handicraft materials and required to work alone in their cells—for example, repairing boots. An important feature of this "Pennsylvania System" for reforming criminals—one that at least to some degree may have mitigated the pains of isolation—was that the warden would visit each prisoner individually on a daily basis to check on his or her progress.[1] By the 1830s, with a continuing crowding problem in the Philadelphia jails, the single cells were converted to house two prisoners each, the warden's visits became less frequent, and the conditions deteriorated until the penitentiary house at the Walnut Street Jail became as crowded and as nonrehabilitative in its aims as the group cellblocks that had preceded it. The Walnut Street Jail was finally shuttered in 1835. But other prisons, including Eastern State Prison in Philadelphia and Trenton State Prison in New Jersey, were built according to the "Pennsylvania System" that had originated there.

Eastern State Prison, established in 1829, also in Philadelphia, continued the effort begun at Walnut Street Jail to keep prisoners separate so that they could be penitent and to stress rehabilitation over punishment. Like the Walnut Street Jail, Eastern allowed some degree of prisoner labor carried out in solitude.[2] The facility's architecture featured a central guard tower with multiple long hallways radiating out from it like the spokes of a wheel. The concrete cells had a high ceiling in the middle that contained a skylight, as if the "eye of God" were upon the penitent prisoner. There were small individual exercise areas outside the cells, but prisoners were not permitted to go to their exercise area when a neighbor was in his outside area. That way, the prisoners remained starkly separate. As at Walnut Street, the warden was, at least initially, required to visit and talk to each prisoner frequently. Apart from that, total silence was enforced, any form of communication between inmates was forbidden, and prisoners wore hoods when they were taken out of their cells so that they would never see the faces of other inmates or of guards. To deepen the silence, guards had to wear socks over their shoes, and the wheels of the food wagons were covered with leather.[3] This was the second installment of the "Pennsylvania System."

Charles Dickens and Alexis de Tocqueville both visited Eastern State Prison while the Pennsylvania System was being implemented and wrote about what they saw.[4] Dickens had this to say about Eastern State Prison in 1842:

> In the outskirts (of Philadelphia), stands a great prison, called the Eastern Penitentiary, conducted on a plan peculiar to the state of Pennsylvania. The system here is rigid, strict, and hopeless solitary confinement. I believe it, in its effects, to be cruel and wrong. In its intention, I am well convinced that it is kind, humane, and meant for reformation; but I am persuaded that those who devised this system of Prison Discipline, and those benevolent gentlemen who carry it into execution, do not know what it is that they are doing. I believe that very few men are capable of estimating the immense amount of torture and agony which this dreadful punishment, prolonged for years, inflicts upon the sufferers.[5]

As prisoners repeatedly broke rules in attempts to resist the isolation and monotony of this regime, attempting to escape, communicate with each other, or harm their captors, prison officials and guards improvised new punishments, including dousing prisoners with ice-cold water during winter or strapping prisoners so tightly into makeshift restraint chairs that they could not move at all and leaving them there for hours or days. Such abuses led to investigations. By 1913, the solitary confinement model was abandoned because of proliferating abuses, difficulties of finding work for prisoners that could be accomplished alone and in a small cell, and the high cost of housing prisoners separately. Prisoners were again housed in groups, and solitary was retained solely as a punishment rather than as a condition for all prisoners. But by the 1960s the prison had become so overcrowded that it was merely warehousing its inmates, and the building itself had deteriorated to such a degree that in 1970 Eastern was closed.

In 1816, in Auburn, New York, a large new prison opened utilizing a somewhat different model of isolation as rehabilitation, the "Auburn System."[6] Auburn Prison is still operating, and its facade looks much as it did in the nineteenth century. When I visited the facility in 2007 while preparing to testify in a statewide lawsuit about the adequacy of mental health services in prisons run by the New York Department of Correctional Services (DOCS), the very high, intimidating wall, which bordered the street, seemed to convey the utter separation and seclusion of prisoners that the regime was originally intended to enforce.

All of Auburn's cells were very small and single occupancy. They were arranged in two rows down the middle of the building and stacked in five tiers. Cell doors faced the outer walls, whose grated windows provided indirect light but no view of the outdoors.

Auburn Prison initially introduced solitary confinement in 1821 by imposing absolute isolation and idleness on prisoners, but according to Alexis de Tocqueville and Gustave de Beaumont, nineteenth-century French writers who visited the United States and toured the prison in 1832, this experiment had horrifying results: "In order to reform [the prisoners], they had been submitted to complete isolation; but this absolute solitude, if nothing interrupt it, is beyond the strength of man; it destroys the criminal without intermission and without pity; it does not reform, it kills. The unfortunates, upon whom this experiment was made, fell into a state of depression, so manifest, that their keepers were struck with it; their lives seemed in danger, if they remained longer in this situation."[7] Some prisoners died, others attempted suicide, still others went mad. So in 1823 the system was modified to what became known as the Auburn System: prisoners were confined to their cells at night but were brought together in the daytime to take meals and to labor in prison industrial shops where products were manufactured for sale on the market. Even in these group settings, however, staff attempted to enforce absolute silence and noncommunication among inmates that would maintain their separation. Yet as de Beaumont and de Tocqueville note, "In observing silence, [prisoners] are incessantly tempted to violate its law,"[8] and additional punishments, even more severe punishments and restrictions had to be devised to prevent this and other infractions. Consequently, abuses—flogging, icewater baths, restraint positions—proliferated just as they had at Eastern State Penitentiary.

But the Auburn System, despite its critics, spread beyond the walls of Auburn Prison, informing especially the architecture, the use of isolation, and the work programs at Sing Sing Prison just north of New York City as well as prisons in other states. The Pennsylvania model effected at Walnut Street Jail could not be extended up above a single floor because it required a small outdoor area for each prisoner. But as prisons grew in size, that model would prove too expensive. The five stacked tiers of Auburn Prison proved more economical.

By the 1860s and 1870s, however, overcrowding and abusive staff practices had tarnished any reputation for effective rehabilitation that the Auburn System had once possessed. Like the Pennsylvania System, it gradually gave way to and was superseded by other approaches for the general prison population. Auburn today is a maximum security prison with little in the way of programs for education, work, or schooling, and with a solitary unit used for disciplinary purposes.

Thus all three experiments had as their starting point a Quaker vision of reform in which a prisoner would have the opportunity to introspect and reconsider his criminal ways, in a clean and quiet space, while being shown kindness and given counsel by visitors and officials who would guide his penitence. Even so, the system proved to be ineffective and cruel and to generate escalating abuses. Today solitary confinement has entirely lost its claims of rehabilitative purpose and has become merely a means of enforcing discipline and removing from the general prison population inmates considered to be dangerous or in any way problematic. The result is that these inmates are warehoused in deteriorating isolation cells, where they may be neglected for years.

According to the social historian David Rothman, this trajectory is replicated in larger historical trends.[9] Reviewing publications by psychiatrists of the period, Rothman tracked the optimistic expectations that accompanied the construction of a new generation of mental hospitals and prisons under the Jacksonian reforms in the late 1820s and demonstrated how the initial optimism of clinicians and warders faded as ex-patients and ex-prisoners they had declared cured or reformed, and had released from the institutions, returned a few years later in a deteriorated state. Rothman concludes that by the time of the Civil War prisons and asylums had once again become mere crowded warehouses for incorrigible criminals and lunatics—the same fate as the Walnut Street Jail, Eastern State Prison, and Auburn Prison.

By 1890, when the US Supreme Court considered an appeal of the sentence for murder of Mr. James J. Medley, the expectation that solitary confinement involved penitence and provided rehabilitation had entirely disappeared, and the practice was seen as what it really was, harsh punishment.[10] Mr. Medley had been sentenced to death by the Colorado District Court for the 1889 murder of his wife, Ellen Medley. The court also sentenced him to be consigned to solitary confinement at Colorado State Prison for one month prior to his hanging. Hearing an appeal of the case, the Supreme Court opined that solitary confinement was an additional punishment beyond execution, one that they called "a further terror and peculiar maker of infamy." The issue the Supreme Court justices were interested in was not the death penalty, which they thought was fair, but the *ex post facto* quality of the additional sentence to a month in solitary confinement at the state prison prior to the hanging. The state of Colorado had passed a new law making legal a period in solitary confinement at the prison, but that law was passed after Mr. Medley killed his wife, so he was being punished *ex post facto*. In its ruling, the Court referenced an entry in the *American Encyclopedia* that included this passage about solitary confinement:

> The peculiarities of this system were the complete isolation of the prisoner from all human society, and his confinement in a cell of considerable size, so arranged that he had no direct intercourse with or sight of any human being, and no employment or instruction. . . . But experience demonstrated that there were serious objections to it. A considerable number of the prisoners fell, after even a short confinement, into a semi-fatuous condition, from which it was next to impossible to arouse them, and others became violently insane; others still, committed suicide; while those who stood the ordeal better were not generally reformed, and in most cases did not recover sufficient mental activity to be of any subsequent service to the community.

The site of solitary confinement that is perhaps most well known to the public is the Alcatraz Federal Penitentiary, nicknamed "the Rock." It was built on an island in San Francisco Bay and was opened in 1934. The most dangerous prisoners in the federal prison system were sent there, and security was very high. One of the famous inhabitants of Alcatraz was Robert Stroud, "the Birdman of Alcatraz," played by Burt Lancaster in the 1962 film of that name. The penitentiary was composed of four cellblocks, A, B, C, and D, with the rowdiest prisoners consigned to D. D-Block was the site of varying degrees of solitary confinement: its prisoners would eat their meals alone in their cells and not be permitted to work or to have contact with other prisoners. At the end of the dark and dank hallway of D-Block were cells 9 to 14, which were called "the hole." Those cells had no light and were colder than other cells. Then, for prisoners who were especially incorrigible or disliked by officers, there was a basement under D-Block where the dark, cold cells contained a hole in the floor in place of a toilet. Prisoners were sometimes chained to the walls in the dark in "the dungeon" under "the hole" in D-Block. Needless to say, unfathomable other abuses and suffering went on in "the hole" at Alcatraz. The Rock was closed in 1963.[11]

Another infamous solitary confinement unit was the "Adjustment Center" at San Quentin Prison, a large state prison jutting out into the San Francisco Bay from its northern shore in Marin County. It is California's oldest prison, having opened in 1852. The aging facility has a design capacity of more than three thousand prisoners, and until the 1980s it was the highest-security prison in California. The Adjustment Center at San Quentin was the site of stark solitary confinement, where political radicals of the 1960s, among others, were held in extreme isolation and very tight security. George Jackson was a black revolutionary leader who joined the Black Panther Party in the 1960s and wrote poignantly about race relations in America and why so many young black men found their way into the prisons.[12] He was shot and killed by guards while housed in the Adjustment Center at San Quentin, allegedly while trying to escape. It remains unclear what happened on August 21, 1971, but it is known that George Jackson was gunned down by guards, that two other prisoners and three guards died, and that afterwards there was brutal retaliation against radical black prisoners in the Adjustment Center.[13] The Adjustment Center, which is still in operation even though San Quentin is no longer the highest-security prison in the state, served as one of the models for the Security Housing Unit or "SHU" at Pelican Bay State Prison, which would open nearly two decades after the killing of George Jackson. Both the Adjustment Center at San Quentin and the SHU at Pelican Bay were premised on the notion that if "the worst of the worst" were locked away in solitary the problems of prison violence could be controlled.[14]

THE MODERN SUPERMAXIMUM SECURITY PRISON

As noted in the Introduction, the modern love affair with supermaximum security began with the 1980s experience of a long-term lockdown at the federal penitentiary in Marion, Illinois, and came into its own, nationwide, during the 1990s, when many of today's supermax facilities were built, including the state-of-the-art federal supermax, the ADX (administrative maximum facility). Sharon Shalev, a London-based criminologist and human rights advocate, in her 2009 book *Supermax: Controlling Risk through Solitary Confinement,* points out that although solitary confinement is far from a new development the modern supermax's use of advanced technology to maximize security also maximizes human damage. Over forty state departments of correction as well as the Federal Bureau of Prisons contain supermaximum security solitary confinement units.

In supermax units, prisoners are held alone, or less often with a cellmate, for approximately twenty-three hours a day in a cell that lacks natural light and does not permit much in the way of meaningful activities. They are fed in their cells. They have little or no physical contact (or, for that matter, verbal contact) with anyone except an officer who passes them their food trays through a slot in the door and accompanies them in shackles when they leave their cells to go to the shower, the recreation yard—which is usually a very small enclosure with insufficient room and equipment to exercise large muscles—or a medical appointment. In many supermax units where cell doors are solid metal, the only way for the prisoner to see outside the cell is to stoop down and look out the food port when it is briefly opened for food delivery. In others, the cell doors have bars, and in still others a perforated metal grid partially obstructs the view through the cell door. Some supermax units have on the outside wall a small window, which usually does not open. Other units do not even have a window, so the prisoner is isolated all day in artificial lighting, with no view of the sky or the natural world outside.

Some supermax prison facilities are built as separate units within a larger prison complex. In this case, the supermax occupies a single cellblock or even a separate building. For example, at the new Montana State Prison that opened in 1979 near Deer Lodge, Montana, the Max Unit (which is actually supermaximum security) occupies a separate building in the maximum security portion of the prison. A-Block is a small special detention unit within the supermax that is designed for extra disciplinary punishment above and beyond standard solitary confinement. If a prisoner receives a serious disciplinary infraction he is sent to Max for "administrative segregation" or solitary confinement, but then if he gets into more disciplinary trouble while in segregation he is placed on A-Block and his activities are even more severely restricted. At Montana State Prison, inmates in A-Block receive only the bare necessities and cannot have visits or phone calls until they go for a full year without further disciplinary infractions. The cells do not have windows to the outside, so no natural light enters. There is a single light fixture in the ceiling, and staff control the lighting. The light remains on twelve to sixteen hours a day. No recreation yard time is allowed for inmates in A-Block, and they are permitted to keep in their cells only paper and pencil and a few books. I will discuss in chapter 2 the experiences of two prisoners with serious mental illness who were consigned to A-Block, Edward Walker and Raistlin Katka.

Other supermaximum facilities, such as the Northern Correctional Facility in Connecticut (NCI) and the Upstate Correctional Facility in New York, fill an entire prison complex. The architecture of the NCI is distinctive. There are six, essentially identical units, each with fifty cells, arranged in an upper and lower tier. Doors are controlled remotely by an officer in a control center, and video cameras are installed throughout the institution but not in the cells. There is a speaker system between the cells and the control center, and there are buzzers in the cells. The thick concrete walls lack decorations for the most part. Cells have no windows, and their furnishings are very sparse. The effect is an oppressive sense of enclosure. The cells measure seven feet by twelve feet and are identical throughout the institution, with a few exceptions. The doors are solid metal with a horizontal food port below waist level and a nonopening vertical transparent panel at approximately eye level. Most of these "boxcar doors" slide on a track, remotely controlled. A few cells in the Administrative Segregation Program are designated "In-Cell Restraint," and prisoners are assigned to these stripped-down cells as a consequence of a disciplinary procedure. Prisoners can talk to their neighbors only through a vent or by screaming, but this is discouraged by staff.

The Supermax Correctional Institution (SMCI) at Boscobel, Wisconsin, is built entirely of isolation cells. It was the focus of the class action lawsuit *Jones 'El v. Berge* (2001), brought by the ACLU National Prison Project. As a psychiatric expert witness in *Jones 'El*, I was provided access to this state-of-the-art supermax prison.

Two architectural features of SMCI still stand out for me as I recall the case. One was the solid metal "boxcar door" to each isolation cell, which featured a small metal food slot in the middle of the door and a small port near the bottom of the door through which leg irons or shackles were affixed. The other was a feature of the Alpha Unit cellblock where the most troublesome prisoners would be consigned, a place the prisoners described as "the hole within the hole." On Alpha Unit, cells did not open onto the hallway where officers would move about; instead, pairs of cells opened onto a small chamber that was separated from the hallway by another door, so that the inhabitants of those cells would not even have the experience of seeing officers walk up and down the hallway across from their cell.

Rule-breaking prisoners with serious mental illness were disproportionately consigned to the superisolative cells on Alpha Unit. Colin, a thirty-two-year-old African American man, had spent over two years there by the time I met him. He had entered prison ten years earlier after first being adjudged incompetent to stand trial, and then when he was subsequently declared competent again he was seriously considered for an insanity defense. But he was found guilty and received a twenty-year sentence. In prison, he was diagnosed as having major depressive disorder with psychotic features and was prescribed Haldol, a strong antipsychotic medication, along with an antidepressant medication. He was consigned to solitary after assaulting a correction officer when a hallucinated voice commanded him to do so. He had spent most of his term in solitary in the Alpha Unit.

Almost immediately after entering Alpha Unit he began attempting suicide on multiple occasions by cutting himself or by ingesting an overdose of pills. Each time he made a suicide attempt he would be transferred to a small observation cell in the infirmary where he would remain for a few days, or until he told staff he was no longer feeling suicidal, and then he would be returned to his cell on the Alpha Unit. He said of the extreme isolation, "It makes me feel like I'm in a coffin." Only video visits were permitted for prisoners on the Alpha Unit, so visitors would be in a room on the other side of the prison and would be visible to the prisoner only on a monitor. Colin refused visits and told me why: "How do I know they are not faking the images?" He did not know the date or time of day, and no watches or clocks were permitted on the unit.

Colin admitted that he heard imaginary voices, and when I asked if the officers knew he was hallucinating he said, "The doctor told them I hear voices, but still they punch me and spray me [with pepper spray]." Colin told me with tears in his eyes that as soon as he was placed in a solitary cell the voices became louder and more insistent and he became extremely anxious; that was when he started trying to kill himself. He felt he was stuck forever on Alpha Unit because transfer to a less restrictive environment would give him access to a television, and staff were very concerned that he might break the television and use some of its metal parts to kill himself. By the time of our interview Colin had been issued disciplinary reports multiple times while in the Alpha Unit for destroying state property, the pieces of metal he used to cut himself. In my report about the SMCI for the *Jones 'El* litigation, I strongly recommended that he be removed from isolation and transferred on an urgent basis into an intensive mental health treatment program. The lawsuit was eventually resolved, with part of the agreement being that prisoners with serious mental illness would no longer be consigned to the SMCI.

In all facilities, the profoundly deleterious effects of this type of solitary confinement on individuals are pervasive. A significant number of individuals in supermax units commit suicide along the way or are driven by conditions to commit a crime while in prison that gains them a longer prison term; but in the end most are released, very damaged, back into the community.

For those interested in viewing a supermax isolation cell in more detail, the *Guardian*, along with the prisoner rights organization Solitary Watch, a

FIGURE 3. Solid metal cell doors on pod of administrative segregation unit with evidence of fires set by prisoners desperate to have officers pay attention to their needs, Eastern Mississippi Correctional Facility, 2014. Photo by ACLU National Prison Project and Southern Poverty Law Center.

FIGURE 4. A prisoner exercises by jumping off a toilet in the cage-like "yard" in administrative segregation at San Quentin State Prison. Photo by Lucy Nicholson, Reuters, 2012.

Web-based project "aimed at bringing the widespread use of solitary confinement out of the shadows and into the light of the public square," has created a virtual reality experience of a solitary confinement cell with links to interviews with individuals who have spent time in solitary confinement.[15]

PELICAN BAY STATE PRISON AND
THE STRUGGLE FOR DECENT CONDITIONS

I first visited the SHU at Pelican Bay State Prison in 1992, two years after it opened. I drove toward the high-tech prison through the lush, green forest that surrounded it, then entered a clearing containing what looked like large concrete bunkers surrounded by glistening gravel on the bare ground. As it turned out, what I had taken for bunkers were the surprisingly low prison buildings. I soon learned that much of the SHU had been constructed below ground level. And officers who accompanied me on my tour explained that the gravel surrounding the supermax unit made it more difficult for prisoners to escape without being seen—as if anyone could escape from that grotesque concrete and steel labyrinth.

The purpose of my visit that first time was an investigation in preparation for expert testimony in *Coleman v. Wilson* (1993), a statewide class action lawsuit claiming substandard mental health treatment and consignment of inadequately treated prisoners with serious mental illness to solitary confinement, where their condition would predictably deteriorate dramatically. I interviewed prisoners who had been in the SHU for up to two years and determined that the extreme isolation was exacerbating their mental disorders, whether they suffered from schizophrenia, bipolar disorder, major depressive disorder, or another condition. I heard stories of terrible abuse from guards, and I witnessed the despair on the men's faces, their conviction that they would never get out of the hell where they found themselves and would die alone inside those concrete walls. For a long time after that 1992 visit, I could not get out of my mind the image of human beings dwelling alone with nothing to do in windowless cells made of concrete and steel.

Pelican Bay State Prison, a maximum security correctional facility located near California's coastal border with Oregon, opened in December 1989. Its sprawling, interconnected buildings are arranged in the shape of an X. The prison has a design capacity of approximately three thousand prisoners, and out of that number approximately 30 to 35 percent (1,000–1,200 prisoners) are consigned to the SHU. The SHU contains twenty-two housing units of six pods each; each pod contains eight cells, four on the lower tier and four on the upper tier. Thus there are 1,056 cells. Cells are eight feet by ten feet; they contain a metal toilet/sink appliance, a concrete slab designed to hold a mattress, and a sliding metal door covered by a sheet of metal with perforations that permit the occupant to walk up close to his door and peer out through the metal grid to gain a distorted view of a blank wall across from his cell. Doors are opened and closed by remote control. An armed officer in a control booth looks out over the six pods that project radially from the control booth, and at the far end of each pod is the recreation area or "yard."

Prisoners are released from their cells for sixty to ninety minutes, five days per week, to go alone (or with a cellmate) to "the yard," a room-sized space with walls twenty feet high that is devoid of equipment except for a pull-up bar and a small ball.[16] A Lexan sheet covers over two-thirds of the ceiling area of the yard, so that only the remaining third permits a view of the sky. Prisoners say that if they see a bird, a bit of nature, fly over the uncovered ceiling of the recreation area they feel they are having a good day. When they leave their cells, they are searched and escorted in handcuffs and, if they are considered especially dangerous, in even more metal restraints. There are no areas designated for congregate activities. Prisoners are permitted showers where they are locked into a shower stall for a short period.

To a visitor, the hallway in the pods looks deserted. When you walk up to a cell door and peer in, you see a man, usually in white T-shirt and boxer shorts, sitting on or lying in his bunk or pacing in circles in the very small floor space he is allotted. It is always jarring to stand in an empty, fluorescent-lighted hallway, to walk up to a cell door covered by a perforated metal sheet, and to discover a man alone in the very small space behind it. Sometimes it is even difficult to discern the race of the man in the cell because the years with no exposure to natural light have made very pale the complexion even of men who once had a lot of pigment in their skin. Michael Montgomery, a journalist who wrote a series of articles about his visits to Pelican Bay State Prison during the hunger strikes of 2011 to 2014 and was a major source of information about developments there, wrote, "The monochrome landscape seemed to permeate even the faces of the inmates here; men I encountered (mostly through the perforated metal cover of a cell door) had a pasty, ghostly pallor."[17]

FIGURE 5. A view of a pod at the Pelican Bay SHU. Photo by Monica Lam, working with journalist Michael Montgomery and the Center for Investigative Reporting, 2012.

No matter what mental condition a man is in before entering solitary, in my experience it is rare that he does not emerge in demonstrably worse mental and physical condition. A Mexican American prisoner from Southern California who had been in the Pelican Bay SHU for seventeen years told me he was lucky to sleep four or five hours at night. He was hearing voices when nobody was talking to him and believed that this was caused by SHU confinement. He was overweight (240 pounds, when he should weigh 170). He knew he should exercise, but he felt so listless all the time that he did not have the initiative or the energy to do that or anything else. He experienced a lot of headaches. The unfairness of his long-term isolation, his lack of recourse, and the dull-colored walls and monotony of life in the SHU all caused him to feel depressed and hopeless.

An African American man who had been in SHU for thirty-six years at the time of our interview told me about the anxiety he was experiencing all the time, so intense that he was sweating even without exertion. He reported frequent "weird violent dreams," a strong startle reaction especially to the sound of doors opening, perceptual distortions that he attributed to the lack of windows in his cell and the odd experience of looking at the wall across from his cell through the small holes in his metal cell door, a sense of losing the ability to feel things, wide swings in emotion, a tendency to constantly

FIGURE 6. Inside a windowless cell at the Pelican Bay SHU. Photo by Monica Lam, working with journalist Michael Montgomery and the Center for Investigative Reporting, 2012.

FIGURE 7. The yard at the Pelican Bay SHU. Photo by Monica Lam, working with journalist Michael Montgomery and the Center for Investigative Reporting, 2012.

misplace things, an inability to concentrate, memory loss, irritability, and worries about becoming more unkempt and disorganized. He described irregular sleep with frequent waking whenever he heard the sound of doors opening and closing. He explained that loud noises made him jump or induced panic attacks because he was afraid officers would come into his cell and beat him. He admitted to being hyperaware, even paranoid. In chapters 4 and 5 I will have much more to say about the symptoms and emotional damage that are typically brought on by long-term solitary confinement.

One reason that solitary confinement has been allowed to proliferate so much in the modern era is that the general public has very little knowledge about what is occurring inside the prisons. The California Department of Corrections has a "gag order," a policy prohibiting journalists from talking to prisoners without the department's specific prior approval. The policy was supposedly put in place to prevent prisoners from using press contacts to foster personal fame or business pursuits, but the effect of the prohibition has been to greatly limit the public's knowledge about what is going on inside the prisons.

To the extent that the public—including researchers and journalists—have learned about what is happening in supermax units, the breaking news has tended to come from reports of prisoners' family members who have found a way to visit or to hear about the prison's day-to-day reality and then to return to the community, and legislators, to talk about the abusive conditions they witnessed. But rules for visits are very strict, especially for prisoners in solitary confinement. Moreover, supermaximum security units tend to be located far from population centers, and many relatives and friends drop off the visiting rolls because of the long distances. Visits with prisoners become less common. This is not a positive development because, when the statistics are run, prisoners who sustain quality visits with loved ones throughout their prison term have a much lower recidivism rate than prisoners who are cut off from family while doing their time.[18] In the absence of robust public awareness of the problems associated with solitary confinement, its use has unfortunately spread in ways that are not even officially considered solitary confinement.

ISOLATION BY ANY OTHER NAME

There are varied rationales for prison isolation techniques. The discussion so far has mostly been about isolation as punishment for rule violations or for gang affiliation. But isolation is also used for other purposes. For example, a prisoner deemed suicidal may be placed in an "observation cell," a setting that can be virtually the same as solitary confinement.

The observation cells for suicidal and acutely psychotic prisoners in Unit 42 at the Mississippi State Penitentiary in Parchman demonstrate the problem. When I toured the unit in preparation for testimony in the *Willie Russell v. Epps* and *Presley v. Epps* class action lawsuits, Unit 42 was functioning as the prison infirmary. There were several observation cells for suicidal and acutely psychotic prisoners along one hallway. The cells were relatively large. Some had a window to the outside and some did not, and all cells had a solid metal cell door with a small window at eye level through which the prisoner could look out onto the hallway. Prisoners were cell-fed. They were given no therapy sessions, no congregate activities of any kind, not even time out of the cell for recreation. Psychiatric patients could spend many months in one of these cells. They were permitted fewer activities than prisoners in supermax isolation and did not receive much mental health treatment except, perhaps, psychotropic medications. Many prisoners transferred to the unit told me they would prefer being back in a segregation cell to the numbing isolation of "Observation." Why would anyone think such a situation might prevent further decline in the mental health of a person who felt suicidal?

There are numerous other examples of solitary confinement by another name. Most prisoners on Death Row are restricted to their cells inside a supermaximum security isolation unit. In my view, there really is no sound reason for this. I suspect it is done as a public relations ploy: it helps convey the impression that the corrections mission is the management of extremely dangerous people who can be contained only by extreme measures.

Or consider a lockdown on the basis of race. Let's say there has been a violent incident, such as a knife-wielding prisoner's attack on an officer. There is no reliable identification of the assailant, but several officers report that he was African American. The warden orders that all African American prisoners are on lockdown status immediately until further notice. The men in lockdown are cell-fed. They may be alone in a cell or have one or several cellmates. They get no phone calls and no out-of-cell programming. Though in theory they are allotted five hours per week on the recreation yard, often so many prisoners are on lockdown and so few officers are available to guard them that many of their allotted recreation periods are canceled with no prior notice and no explanation. These locked-down prisoners are in solitary confinement, and not for anything they have done, only for the color of their skin.

Then there is "protective custody."[19] I interviewed a young man in an administrative segregation unit of a maximum security prison in a western state who entered adult prison at seventeen and was almost immediately raped by an older prisoner. When he reported the rape to officers they demanded to know who had done it. He suffered from schizophrenia and was having trouble thinking clearly, yet he had to decide whether to snitch on another prisoner to an officer. The stakes were very high: if he snitched and word got out, there would be certain retaliation, perhaps lethal retaliation. In any case, he was consigned to solitary confinement "for his own safety," where he had to remain for months while the investigation into the alleged rape proceeded.

A trans woman prisoner may also be put in solitary, simply because her sexual identity has created a quandary for the classification officers and because they have no appropriate housing situation for her.[20] In solitary, they believe, she will at least be safe until some other solution can be found.

All prison systems have a classification system that serves to separate members of rival gangs and prisoners who have enemies. But separation must not entail isolation. According to all standards, prisoners who need to be separated from the general population because of their vulnerabilities or their enemies must be transferred to another setting where they will not be isolated in a cell and where they have all the freedoms and amenities, including access to all the jobs, educational opportunities, and vocational training programs, that their classification level permits.[21] The distinction between separation and isolation is very important. Similarly, the prisoner who is at high risk of acting violently must be separated from those with whom he is likely to become violent, but that does not justify his isolation. In many situations what is needed is separation, not isolation.

Solitary confinement is also the preferred form of housing for people captured during wartime who are being interrogated or tortured. Mohamedou Ould Slahi, a Mauritanian, was in Al Qaeda fighting against the Russians in Afghanistan in the early 1990s and much later was picked up by the United States and brought to Guantanamo.[22] Although he maintained that he had had no further connection with Al Qaeda, he has been kept a prisoner at Guantanamo since soon after 9–11. Slahi's gruesome description of his years of confinement and interrogation at Guantanamo are emblematic of the torturous experiences of individuals in solitary confinement:

> When I entered the block, it was completely empty of any signs of life. . . . In the block the recipe started. I was deprived of my comfort items, except for a thin iso-mat and a very thin, small, worn-out blanket. I was deprived of my books, which I owned, I was deprived of my Koran, I was deprived of my soap. I was deprived of my toothpaste and of the roll of toilet paper I had. The cell—better, the box—was cooled down to the point that I was shaking most of the time. I was forbidden from seeing the light of the day; every once in a while they gave me a rec-time at night to keep me from seeing or interacting with any detainees. I was living literally in terror.[23]

Correctional authorities might protest that Mr. Slahi was not in "solitary confinement" because there were military intelligence officers interrogating him. But the interrogation did not include any trace of human understanding or meaningful communication, and after being interrogated, he would always be returned to an isolation cell.

Solitary confinement is commonplace in jails or local detention facilities. Jails contain a variety of different types of housing, but often the prisoner is in a cell by himself. A number of jail commanders have reported to me that if a prisoner seems to have a significant mental illness they will do their best to keep that prisoner in a single cell because mixing him or her with others is too risky. But although placing such individuals in isolation is meant to protect them from other prisoners, it also forces them into a type of solitary confinement that will almost certainly damage their mental health.

Another area of concern is the use of solitary confinement on detained immigrants. US Immigration and Customs Enforcement (ICE) has contracts with private companies to run detention centers. These companies reap profits by lowering their budget for staffing as much as possible, and on average immigration lockups are very poorly staffed. As a result of this, undertrained and overworked staff tend to consign to solitary immigrant prisoners who seem troublesome in any way. Moreover, because the rest of the prisoner's family are frightened that they too might be arrested if they appear anywhere near immigration officials or police, they do not visit and do not complain about the horrendous conditions where their kin are confined, such as in a solitary confinement cell.[24]

Solitary confinement is quite simply the fallback option for any number of difficult scenarios in corrections today. Rowdy prisoners? Lock them up! A prisoner wants to cut his wrists? Lock him up in Observation! Violence on the yard? Lock down the racial group that seems involved! Not enough staff to move prisoners in isolative confinement to recreation? Leave them in their cells twenty-four hours per day!

There is a growing consensus in corrections circles today that solitary confinement facilities were overbuilt in the 1990s and that solitary confinement can be very counter-rehabilitative and countertherapeutic.[25] The advent of the supermax certainly signaled the demise of robust prison rehabilitation and the expansion of an ever harsher culture of punishment in prisons.

TWO

———

A Culture of Punishment

A FEW YEARS AGO I TESTIFIED as a psychiatric expert in federal court about the supermax unit at Mississippi State Penitentiary at Parchman.[1] The prison, built in 1900 on a large plantation, is known as Parchman Farm. It covers several square miles. Between its buildings are lawns and fields where cotton and other crops are grown. Prisoners in striped garb work in the fields, supervised by officers on horseback, with shotguns across their laps. The scene is reminiscent of a pre–Civil War plantation. One unit on the grounds, Unit 32, was a state-of-the-art supermax facility, opened in 1990 to hold the "worst of the worst" in solitary confinement. There were one thousand cells, most for prisoners serving a sentence in administrative segregation but a few for lower-security prisoners who had jobs cleaning the supermax or performing clerical functions. Doors were remote-controlled, and prisoners were confined to their cells almost twenty-four hours per day. Death Row, holding approximately ninety men, was located inside Unit 32. The conditions for its inhabitants were repugnant. Cells had a small window on the outer wall, but most of the screens were broken. Prisoners had to either open the window and suffer mosquito bites or close the window to keep the mosquitoes out and suffer the heat and humidity of the Mississippi Delta. The toilets tended to back up in one cell when flushed in the next, and the cells were filthy but the prisoners were not provided any cleaning materials. When prisoners misbehaved in that setting, they were consigned to even smaller special punishment cells with no light.

Just prior to my testimony I toured a supermax pod. I walked along the hall between cells and could talk to the prisoners through the bars of their cell doors. Many of the prisoners were asleep with their lights off, but some were standing at their cell door and very willing to talk. They reported to me that one particular officer on the evening shift would spitefully shoot pepper spray through their food ports if they angered him. After spraying the prisoner, the officer would keep on walking down the tier, leaving the prisoner coughing and choking from the toxic gas. Mississippi Department of Corrections (DOC) policy mandated that whenever officers resorted to immobilizing gas, they had to write an incident report, get the prisoner checked and treated by medical staff, and get the cell decontaminated. This officer did not write reports, did not notify the medical staff, and did not make provisions for decontaminating the prisoners' cells. His behavior constituted excessive force and violated Mississippi DOC policy. Sadly, I have to report that it is far from unusual for officers to resort to excessive force and violate policy in solitary confinement units. In fact, with the advent of supermaximum solitary confinement there has been an alarming escalation of force used against prisoners, especially prisoners with serious mental illness. We need to understand the dynamics of excessive force in solitary confinement units, and we need to end it. An important part of any effective remedy for abuse by prison and jail staff is to create a zero-tolerance attitude toward all forms of abuse by properly screening potential correctional staff to exclude individuals who are prone to bullying and abusing others, by giving staff intensive and ongoing training with close and professional supervision, and by establishing effective recourse for prisoners who believe they have been abused.

RULES AND PUNISHMENTS

In the supermax isolation unit, punishments become the main mode of intervention for custody staff, and prisoners' misbehavior is the trigger and rationale for these measures. Rules are detailed, pervasive, and controlling. A comprehensive analysis of the grievance process in the California Department of Corrections and Rehabilitation (CDCR) in 2015 points out that there are rigid rules for just about every aspect of prison life. As the authors note: "In prison virtually all behavior is 'played in the key of law.'"[2] In maximum security prisons, for example, the rules include waking on time and standing at attention during "count" (the times when prisoners are counted by officers); returning food trays on time; not walking beyond lines drawn on the floor; following officers' every order; when ordered, putting your arms behind your back and your back up to the food port of your cell door so officers outside your cell can apply handcuffs; not speaking to other prisoners as you walk down the hall with wrists handcuffed behind your back; not using foul language when addressing staff; not being found with "contraband" or items not allowed by the rules in your cell; wearing only prison-issued garb; and not having too many books in your cell. The list goes on. Violation of a rule leads to punishment.

"Tickets" are rule violation reports or disciplinary infraction notices written by officers when a prisoner breaks a rule. There is a hearing, and in well over 90 percent of cases the prisoner is found guilty of the infraction cited. Prisoners also have a right to appeal, and as the 2015 report explains, "Prisoners' willingness and ability to name problems and file grievances must be seen within this context of prison not only as a total institution but as a conspicuously legal one where explicit rules govern every aspect of behavior."[3] Because they have little hope of a fair hearing, prisoners hesitate to appeal even when they believe a ticket was unfair.

Confinement in a supermaximum security cell is a severe form of punishment, usually meted out by a hearing officer for a serious rule violation: fighting, lighting a fire, possessing a weapon, attempting to escape, or assaulting an officer. Minor violations, like having outdated or too many anti-inflammatory pills in one's cell, or possessing prison-brewed alcohol ("pruno" or "juice"), receive lesser punishments, usually the loss of privileges like going to the yard or watching television (if television viewing is permitted) or having phone calls. There are administrative segregation units for short-term sentences to isolation, and then there are supermax units for prisoners with longer segregation time to serve. States, in their prison systems, and the federal government in its Bureau of Prisons, have different policies that determine when a prisoner is sent to supermax and for how long. For example, in the CDCR it was once common for prisoners to remain in solitary for decades, or until they died. But beginning in 2011 prisoners went on hunger strikes, and in 2012 they filed a lawsuit claiming, among other things, that indefinite consignment to SHU and a lack of legal recourse violated the Eighth Amendment of the Constitution's prohibition of cruel and unusual punishment. The settlement of the *Ashker v. Brown* federal class action suit prohibited the CDCR from sending prisoners to solitary confinement for the remainder of their lives simply because they were allegedly gang members. Now a prisoner has to commit an unlawful act worthy of the punishment of being placed in a solitary unit, and the term of that punishment has to be finite, or determinate, and limited to a year or a few years.

Once a prisoner has been placed in long-term solitary confinement, staff face a dilemma if he continues to break rules. The prisoner is already being punished with the most severe sanction in the department, extreme isolation and enforced idleness. Still, pursuing the logic of control in the prisons, when a prisoner already in isolation breaks more rules, new punishments need to be devised. In the solitary unit, this creates a situation where every misbehavior on the part of the isolated prisoners triggers even more harsh punishment.

As a number of researchers have noted, the logic of control in solitary, where staff's options are narrowed to the infliction of punishment as a singular and automatic response, has become more characteristic of the culture of prisons generally.[4] In this kind of culture, relations between staff and prisoners become colder and more formal. Everybody knows that the officer will write a disciplinary ticket at a moment's notice, so why act as if the relationship involves caring and goodwill?[5] Just a few decades ago, prisoners at every level of security spent more time out of their cells and in public spaces at work or on the yard or in a dayroom, interacting informally with staff. But today officers have essentially forgotten (or have never learned or practiced) how to interact with prisoners informally and in too many cases are actually frightened of interacting with prisoners. Is it any wonder that staff who once "walked the line" and chatted with their wards are now afraid to be in a room with prisoners who are not in total restraints? Staff who are inclined to focus almost exclusively on punishment for prisoners become even less inclined to get to know the prisoners and to talk with them in a friendly, nonpunitive context. Many prisoners tell me that their contact with officers is limited to the officers silently passing their food tray through the slot in their isolation cell door, or yelling orders at them and swearing they will punish them for one misstep or another.

Before the 1970s, when incarceration included much more rehabilitation, officers were more likely to see themselves as teachers, mentors, even Big Brothers for the prisoners under their care. John Irwin and James Austin provide useful historical perspective on how the role of officers has changed in their 1994 book *It's About Time*.[6] Pre-1970s officers could be tough and would take part in a violent melee if they had to, but they also saw themselves as role models for the prisoners and tried to help them gain skills that would make them more likely to succeed after release. Their interactions with prisoners were quite varied. While officers had to enforce prison rules and be tough enough in the process to gain the prisoners' respect, they could also be kind to prisoners and talk with them about the value of living within the law or writing to a child.

In supermax facilities, officers are much busier enforcing rules. It might seem a daunting challenge to invent new and harsher punishments in that context, but alas, over the last several decades prison staff have been very innovative and often extremely cruel in inventing new and ever more complicated punishments.

MORE SEVERE PUNISHMENTS

Typically the progression of punishments begins with simple things. In some solitary confinement units, including the one at Pelican Bay State Prison, prisoners are not permitted phone calls at all. But in other solitary units, the average prisoner is permitted phone calls, so when a prisoner misbehaves, phone privileges can be taken from him. Denying prisoners phone calls, or taking them away when the prisoner misbehaves, is foolhardy. Prisoners need quality contact with loved ones if they are to endure their prison term and if they are to succeed in the community after they are released. In a psychiatric hospital, the more out of control a patient becomes, the more important phone contact and visits with family will often be (assuming there is no toxic or abusive family situation). The reason is that the aggressive misbehavior is frequently related to issues in a person's social or family life—in the case of a prisoner, maybe a spouse who is threatening divorce or a child who is in trouble at school—and if the prisoner is allowed contact with family members in order to give or receive support there is a chance that these issues can be resolved and the prisoner can settle down. But after interviewing hundreds of prisoners in solitary confinement I can only conclude that taking away phone privileges as punishment for unacceptable acts is counterproductive and usually leads to even more misbehavior.

Other punishments for prisoners in solitary that remove privileges include taking away a prisoner's commissary (i.e., he or she will not be able to purchase things from the prison store or commissary). If he or she has a television or radio, that can also be taken away.

Harsher punishments—which corrections officials will sometimes even deny are actually punishments—are also frequently employed. For example, staff might leave a prisoner alone in an unlighted cell. Restraints can become extreme, including shackling of all limbs, the abdomen, and even the head and neck.

There is also the cell extraction, with or without immobilizing gas. A prisoner in solitary who refuses a direct order to return his food tray or to back up to the food port so officers can apply handcuffs is very likely to be the target for immobilizing gas sprayed through his food port, and a "cell extraction" where five or six officers in riot gear burst into his cell and take him down. Officers say the use of immobilizing gas and the cell extraction are not punishments but security measures necessary for maintaining order. But a number of states now explicitly prohibit the use of immobilizing gas and cell extractions as punishment. For those that do permit them, they are—at least in theory—a last resort to restore order in a chaotic isolation unit. But policy and daily practice can be very different, and prisoners in different facilities all across the country almost universally tell another story: that officers will utilize the threat of immobilizing gas and cell extractions to make prisoners compliant and that officers will often use these brutal interventions to punish prisoners who have angered them.

Immobilizing gas and cell extractions constitute "use of force," and in general there is a line beyond which the use of force is considered "excessive." The standards of the American Correctional Association, as well as courts that rule on whether there is a violation of the Eighth Amendment, are continually drawing a line between the appropriate use of force and excessive force. Usually that means that officers must resort to force only after all less restrictive interventions have been tried and exhausted, and then the force must be the minimum required to accomplish the restoration of order. But anyone who has worked in a prison knows that abuses of those guidelines occur frequently. Some of the abuses are by policy, and some violate the policies. As Lorna Rhodes has noted in her ethnographic study of supermaximum security facilities and what goes on inside them, "Officers can sometimes be very clear about the surplus power generated at the cell door, insisting on the value of self-control in the face of provocation. A young sergeant remarked, 'Inmates feed on making you mad, it's like negative energy. If you do get mad, you don't belong here.' . . . But some prison workers cannot or do not want to resist the excess of authority made available to them, using their position to launch aggression of their own—gratuitously, pre-emptively, or in retaliation, openly or covertly."[7]

ABUSE BY POLICY

Some punishments that are clearly abusive are mandated by official policy. Yet as the criminologist Steve Martin argues, the fact that prisoners in solitary confinement are called "the worst of the worst" does not give officers a green light to inflict excessive force upon them.[8]

One chilling example of excessive use of force by policy is the Montana Department of Corrections' Behavior Management Plan (BMP), which came to public attention when a prisoner with serious mental illness who had been subjected to it in isolation eventually sued the state claiming cruel and unusual punishment. Edward Walker, a prisoner at Montana State Prison, had long been diagnosed as having bipolar disorder. He had served a prior prison term in Colorado and had been treated for it there with lithium. In the Colorado DOC, with lithium treatment, his bipolar disorder went into remission, and he received relatively few tickets for disciplinary infractions. When he was admitted to Montana State Prison, the psychiatrist decided he was malingering mental illness and needed no treatment. Off his medications, he soon suffered a relapse of his mental illness and, while experiencing severe mood swings, proceeded to get into a lot of trouble. Consequently he was given a record number of disciplinary tickets. He was sent to solitary confinement as punishment for rule violations, and there his psychiatric condition deteriorated even further. With each inappropriate behavior, he was punished more severely, and still he was not prescribed lithium, even though his clinical chart documented his successful treatment with lithium in the Colorado DOC as well as the fact that on lithium he evidenced no behavioral problems.

Eventually, Mr. Walker was put on a series of BMPs in solitary confinement. BMPs are management tools to force behavioral compliance. While not specifically a psychiatric intervention, they are claimed to effect behavior change and are typically administered by the prison's mental health staff.

Mr. Walker, like others on BMPs, was stripped naked and fed cold sandwiches instead of regular hot prison food. His bedding and mattress were removed, so he had to sleep naked with only a blanket on a concrete slab in his cell. The water and sewer lines for his cell were turned off, and he had to ask officers to turn them on when he wanted to use the toilet. While the Montana DOC policy stated that BMPs were "designed to last 24 to 48 hours," if the prisoner continued to misbehave the BMP could be extended by additional days.

Mr. Walker did not respond well to the BMPs. He was placed on them five times over several months because of disruptive behavior. The first BMP was extended, because of his very poor reaction to the stressful regimen, to last five days. The second lasted eleven days, the third six days, the fourth two weeks, and the fifth nearly three weeks.[9] The disruptive behavior that earned him longer than usual stays under these abhorrent conditions tended to intensify the more he was restricted. The behaviors included screaming for days and nights on end, throwing food, smearing ketchup and mayonnaise on the walls of his cell, disobeying orders, purposely flooding his cell and the pod, and attempting suicide three times. The Montana Supreme Court eventually ruled that the BMPs applied to Mr. Walker were unconstitutional and tantamount to torture.[10]

In numerous other cases as well, abusive policies have been challenged in the courts and sometimes revised. For example, in 1989 the class action lawsuit *Gates v. Deukmejian* in California, which concerned the quality of mental health treatment that prisoners with serious mental illness were receiving at the California Medical Facility (CMF) in Vacaville, was resolved by a consent decree that required the CDCR to adhere to new, stricter guidelines.[11] The CMF had been designed as a major innovation in prison mental health care and had even been cited by the pioneering psychiatrist Karl Menninger in his 1968 book *The Crime of Punishment* as a model for how quality psychiatric care could be provided in prison.[12] But with massive overcrowding of the prisons the care at the CMF deteriorated drastically over the years. After the consent decree was issued, the magistrate held periodic hearings to determine whether the CDCR was carrying out its provisions in good faith. Part of the settlement involved restricting the use of tasers, a supposedly nonlethal measure against prisoners who were out of control. A taser is a gun that fires a dart connected to the gun by a wire and, once the dart is affixed to the prisoner, administers an electrical shock through the wire that knocks the individual out or at least incapacitates him with intense pain. Three prisoners had died after being shot with tasers at CMF.

As a psychiatric expert witness in the *Gates* litigation, I had been called before the magistrate to discuss the taser deaths, all three involving prisoners with serious mental illness. I explained to the court that individuals with serious mental illness are at heightened risk when shot with a taser because the antipsychotic medications they are administered lower their seizure threshold and interfere with the electrical conduction in their heart that regulates their heart rate. The sudden burst of electrical activity that is sent through their body by the taser dart can cause a grand mal seizure or a heart arrhythmia or both, and the result can be death. The magistrate ruled that tasers cannot be used with prisoners suffering from serious mental illness unless a psychiatrist signs off on their use after considering the risk. Policies at the CMF were changed accordingly and the matter was closed.

A few months later I was called to testify before the magistrate again in one of the most bizarre court events I have ever been part of. It seems the CDCR had responded to the magistrate's ruling by instituting, in the very close quarters of a prison segregation pod, the use of riot guns that have the shape of a rifle and fire blocks of wood or hard rubber with a very loud bang. Riot guns of this kind are designed as a nonlethal weapon in the hands of police for crowd control. They are fired at demonstrators on the street, typically at a distance of one hundred or two hundred feet. I was asked whether a prisoner with serious mental illness in a segregation pod would be at any heightened risk of harm if an officer standing in the hall outside the prisoner's cell fired a riot gun into the cell. Commanders from the CDCR assured the magistrate that the riot gun would not be pointed at the prisoner but would be fired into his cell to frighten him and make him comply with orders. I testified that in a six-foot-by-eight-foot cell (the cells in California's old prisons were very small) the ricochet effect of the riot gun would in many cases cause the pellet to hit the prisoner and cause physical damage, for instance knocking out his eye or, if it hit him in the head or abdomen, causing brain or organ damage. There would also be a very high risk of psychological harm. The firing of a riot gun in such close quarters could constitute a serious trauma for the prisoner being shot as well as for prisoners in neighboring cells and would likely exacerbate anxiety, paranoia, and possibly acute psychosis.

Instead of accepting my testimony as rather obvious, given the extremity of the situation when a riot gun is fired at close quarters, the assistant attorney general defending the department asked me if I could cite any research published in a scientific journal to back up my testimony. I had to answer that I had never heard of a punishment as grotesque as firing a riot gun in the close quarters of a segregation pod, so no, the practice was entirely unprecedented and therefore no research had yet been conducted on its outcome. The magistrate issued orders to cease and desist. But at the time I fully expected that some new and even more abusive and bizarre use of force would be written into the CDCR's policies. Sure enough, the next round has involved shooting prisoners with immobilizing gas, usually "O.C.," also known as "pepper spray." Attorney, researcher, and human rights advocate Jamie Fellner describes the practice in a 2015 Human Rights Watch report entitled *Callous and Cruel: Use of Force against Inmates with Mental Disabilities.*[13] As far as I know, the more toxic gas mace is not utilized in American prisons, but I would not be surprised to hear of exceptions. Meanwhile, I am called upon to testify in prisoner abuse lawsuits and to offer my opinion on the use of pepper spray on prisoners suffering from serious mental illness as the initial step in cell extractions.

ABUSES IN VIOLATION OF POLICY

We can debate the humanity of shooting prisoners with riot guns or immobilizing gas, but these practices are typically covered by policies within a department of corrections. Beyond these are all too many dangerous violations of policy. For example, while I was investigating in preparation for expert testimony in *Coleman v. Wilson*, a class action lawsuit about the adequacy of mental health services to prisoners in the CDCR, I reviewed incident reports for a single weekend of sixty cell extractions that had occurred in the SHU at Pelican Bay State Prison. I was shocked to discover that the misbehavior that was cited as the reason for the cell extractions in most of the cases was the prisoners' refusal to return their food trays. Let's be reasonable here. There is no safety issue, the prisoners are in their cells, they are merely disobeying an order to return their food trays. If nearly sixty prisoners in a solitary confinement unit are refusing to return their food trays on a single weekend, there must be some type of problem or protest. Perhaps the food was rotten or infiltrated by vermin. One would think a commander would come to the unit to ask the large number of prisoners why they were refusing to return their food trays. If a commander did that, he or she would be exhibiting respect toward the prisoners, they would likely complain about the rotten food, the commander could say he would look into the matter, and the incident would be over. Instead, the officers on the unit formed cell extraction teams and sprayed the sixty prisoners, one by one, with immobilizing gas, then burst into their cells to take them down and retrieve the food trays. There were many injuries.

Immobilizing gas can be used inappropriately, even if its use is covered by policy. I have encountered situations, especially when the prisoner suffered from serious mental illness, where officers would spray him or her with immobilizing gas repeatedly, each burst following the previous one by a minute or even less. The operating instructions for the immobilizing gas, and the policies guiding the use of gas in prison settings, clearly state that the officer should spray the prisoner and then wait for several minutes to see if the prisoner is now willing to "cuff up." If the prisoner takes the spraying as a warning of worse to come and decides to "cuff up," there is no need for further spraying or for a cell extraction. A special problem with prisoners suffering from serious mental illness can be that they do not understand that the spray of immobilizing gas is a warning and a precursor to a cell extraction. In other words, paranoia or a disordered thought process may keep the prisoner from understanding the intention of the spraying. So he or she stands in a daze and does nothing. Then the officers spray the prisoner again. Jamie Fellner's 2015 report on excessive force utilized on prisoners with serious mental illness, like so much prior research, reaffirms how frequently severe punishments are meted out and how inhumanely prisons manage prisoners suffering from serious mental illness.

The day I told the story in federal court in Mississippi about the officer who sprayed prisoners he disliked with pepper spray without writing an incident report and without initiating decontamination, the commissioner and the deputy commissioner of the Mississippi DOC were in the courtroom. They were contrite: they quickly disciplined the errant officer and ordered all officers henceforth to follow policy regarding the use of immobilizing gas. But this unfortunate incident illustrates how the culture of punishment so often gets out of control in solitary confinement and supermax units. Once the staff buy into a culture of punishment, the only tools they have in the face of further unacceptable behaviors are enhanced forms of punishment. In the process of escalating punishments, abuses become more frequent and tend to become more arbitrary and vicious. The rogue officer in Mississippi was violating policy by spraying prisoners with immobilizing gas and not following the required procedures. But there is considerable room for discretion on the part of officers, and a policy can be misused and become abusive.

The Stanford mock prison experiment, conducted in 1971 in the basement of the Psychology Building at Stanford University, presents a graphic picture of how abuse evolves in a prison setting. Philip Zimbardo, Craig Haney, and their team revealed in this classic experiment in social psychology how ordinary people are capable of abusing their peers whenever one group is given total control over another.[14] The experimenters at Stanford enlisted as experimental subjects students who were randomly assigned to act the role of guard or prisoner. The experiment was planned to last for two weeks but had to be called off after six days because the "guards" had so disrespected, humiliated, and denied agency to the "prisoners" they were put in charge of, and the abuses had reached such a dangerous level, that the experimenters feared that the students who were acting as guards would cause serious and lasting psychological harm to the students who were acting as prisoners. For real prisoners, however, especially those consigned to solitary confinement, who are actually under the total control of officers, the "experiment" continues and the cruelty escalates. And this does not need to be the case: there is no legitimate "penological objective" in denying prisoners respect and agency while they are doing their time.

Shane Bauer, an award-winning investigative journalist, spent four months working undercover as a correction officer at Winn Correctional Center in Winnfield, Louisiana, the oldest privately run medium security prison in the United States. The Winn Correctional Center is run by the Corrections Corporation of America. The other trainees, who were mostly young men from the rural vicinity of the prison, were much less educated than Bauer. For them, a job as a prison officer was quite attractive, even though the wages were only $9 per hour. Bauer describes how arbitrary and unprofessional officers' attitudes and behaviors can be.

> A fellow cadet [trainee to become an officer] asks in training class what he should do when he sees two inmates stabbing each other. Another cadet offers, "I'd probably call somebody." A veteran guard attending the training says, "I'd sit there and holler 'stop.'" The trainer points at the veteran and agrees, "Damn right. That's it. If they don't pay attention to you, hey, there ain't nothing else you can do." The trainer continues, "Somebody's go' win. Somebody's go' lose. They both might lose, but hey, did you do your job? Hell yeah!" The classroom erupts in laughter. The trainer continues: "We could try to break up the fight if we wanted, but since we won't have pepper spray or a nightstick, (I) wouldn't recommend it. We are not going to pay you that much. The next raise you get is not going to be more than the one you got last time. The only thing that's important to us is that we go home at the end of the day. Period. So if them fools want to cut each other, well, happy cutting."[15]

These individuals, minus Shane Bauer, went on to complete their training program and are now working as corrections officers at the Louisiana prison.

THE BLUE CODE

Since I regularly express indignation about officers acting abusively toward prisoners, people often ask if I am "anti-officer." They ask me why I don't spend more time pointing out instances when officers act benevolently, even heroically. Of course officers act benevolently and even heroically sometimes. I have heard many stories from prisoners about how a certain officer was kind to them, mentored them, and helped them get through the hell of their years in prison. But officers' abuses are the focus of lawsuits where I testify as an expert, and those abuses cause great harm, so that is where my focus goes.

I believe most correction officers have benevolent motives for going into the profession. But my forty years of experience as a forensic psychiatrist have shown me that there is a very real risk for more brutal and cynical officers to gain influence and authority over the others. Philip Zimbardo's research in the years since the Stanford mock prison experiment has documented this kind of process and detailed the group dynamics involved.[16] And all too often, as a minority of officers abuse the prisoners, the other, more caretaking officers who end up witnessing the abuse fail to complain about it. The situation is especially toxic when overt racism is involved, an issue that I will take up in the next chapter.

In prisons across the country, there regularly exists an implicit—or sometimes explicit—pact between officers to not inform on their peers about inappropriate or illegal behavior, a sort of "don't snitch on your colleagues" policy.[17] It is widely known as "the Blue Code." The Blue Code is extremely harmful in the context of supermaximum security facilities, as it provides cover for inappropriate and sometimes illegal activities, while preventing any progress toward badly needed therapeutic or rehabilitative approaches. What prisons should be advancing in its place is an honorable system of peer review where professional officers who follow policies and who treat prisoners with respect are encouraged to speak out when they see other officers beat or sexually assault a prisoner, sell drugs to prisoners, or steal a prisoner's possessions.

The Blue Code came up as an issue when President Bush signed the National Prison Rape Elimination Act (PREA) into law in 2003. The standards of the Prison Rape Elimination Commission, which oversaw the implementation of the act, require correctional managers to show "zero tolerance" toward the sexual abuse of prisoners. This sounds like a good idea, but like other good ideas it runs into problems in practice. For staff, zero tolerance of sexual abuse requires staff to report other staff they see violating the rules. But informing on colleagues would break the Blue Code. This is not a small issue. Prison staff often experience serious stress in their work—not only from the complexity of handling prisoners but also from contradictions between policy and practices, which, unfortunately, are common. As a result, prison officers have a very high rate of burnout, and as a group they register relatively high rates of substance abuse, domestic violence, and even suicide.[18] Most custody staff respond to the contradictory expectations of mandated policies and the Blue Code by remaining silent: for example, only a relatively small minority of those who witness sexual abuse of prisoners by one of their colleagues carry out their responsibility under PREA and inform on other officers.[19] When they do, the price they pay is ostracism and sometimes violent revenge by their peers. The experience of the Prison Rape Elimination Commission with "zero tolerance" is an important precedent to consider as we search for a way to replace the culture of punishment with a prison environment that fosters inmates' emotional stability and rehabilitation.

THE PRISONER'S CHOICES

To evaluate the effectiveness of punishment systems in prisons, we need to see how prisoners respond to them. For example, if prisoners want to conform their behavior to the rules in response to a relatively minor punishment for rule breaking, then one hopes that they will be able to do so, that their obedience will be followed by an appropriately positive response from officers, and that they will avoid any additional, more severe forms of punishment, such as the removal of personal items or the use of force. But too often, especially if they suffer any degree of mental illness, prisoners will exhibit an almost automatic resistance to punishments. For example, the prisoner with mental illness who is ordered to return his food tray, or to put his hands through the food port so officers can apply handcuffs, refuses. When the officers threaten to come into his cell and take him down, he stands up straight, puts up his dukes in a mock fighting stance, and says something like "Come on in if you think you can handle me." Of course, this is irrational bravado on the part of the disturbed prisoner; he knows the officers will assemble an "extraction team" who will spray him with immobilizing gas and then burst into the cell and shove him into a wall and secure him.

There are a variety of reasons why a prisoner would resist like this in the face of overwhelming force. I have asked prisoners why they do it when they know they will be outnumbered, the officers will physically overwhelm them, and they can be hurt badly in the process. Typically the answer I hear is, "Sometimes you just have to stand up for yourself." In other words, the prisoner has been subjected to more and more forceful and brutal recriminations and punishments for unacceptable behaviors, so that finally, when the officers return to threaten him with even more severe punishments, the prisoner decides that enough is enough and that he is going to stand up to his assailants.

Prisoners universally tell me that the need to demonstrate self-respect in this type of situation is a big part of the equation. But there can also be motivations that are more subtle and more basic emotionally. Couples counselors know well the scenario where one member of the couple gets irrationally angry at the other, and the partner receiving the anger is surprised at how quickly their conversation descends into loud arguments. When the therapist is able to calm the two and explore what happened, it frequently emerges that one partner was feeling deprived of emotional connection with the other and started an argument over basically nothing, simply to create a moment of emotional contact. The partner who was quick to anger explains: "I don't like arguing, and what I really want is loving closeness, but I will take the emotional connection that comes from an argument over not having any moments of emotional connection with my partner at all." Similarly, a prisoner may find himself disobeying an order or inexplicably screaming at an officer when really all he wants is for the officer to interact with him a little longer than it takes for a food tray to be slid through the slot in his cell door. The prisoner is so starved of human contact that he'll start an argument with an officer—knowing that it will lead to further punishment—merely to extend his engagement with others and break the crushing monotony of silence and isolation.

INCREASINGLY BIZARRE RESISTANCE

As psychiatrist Karl Menninger cautioned in his 1968 appraisal of the prison system, *The Crime of Punishment,* harsh punishments lead to resistance and acting out from prisoners, not constructive change.[20] The proliferation of rules, the incrementally intensifying forms of punishment, the defiant reactions of prisoners, and the effects of conditions such as solitary confinement all add up to create violent and chaotic situations.[21] For example, Rodney G. (I leave out his last name for confidentiality reasons), a twenty-four-year-old man imprisoned in the solitary housing unit at the Special Offenders Center (SOC) of the Monroe Correctional Complex in Washington, was on trial for felony assault on a corrections officer when I was enlisted by his attorneys in 2000 to examine him and render an opinion about his state of mind at the time of the assault. He had been in prison for four years, the last two in the supermaximum segregation unit at Monroe Correctional Complex, and for the two months prior to the offense he'd been kept in four-point restraints twenty-four hours per day. Four-point restraints are straps to the wrists and ankles to tie a person down. Standards and protocols in psychiatry require this extreme form of restraint to be utilized only when less restrictive measures have been tried and failed and only for very short periods, a few hours. At Monroe, clinicians in the special psychiatric unit assumed that long-term restraints would cool down Rodney's rage and halt his rule breaking. But the psychiatrist visited Rodney for only a few minutes once a week and didn't have a clear grasp of the situation. The restraints actually exacerbated Rodney's feeling he was being disrespected, and his anger grew. Somehow he got loose from the restraints and proceeded to assault the next officer who entered his cell. In my interview with him, he told me that he didn't know how he'd gotten loose, that he had nothing against that particular officer, and that he didn't remember the whole event. He was prosecuted for felony assault on an officer of the law.

During Rodney's trial, I testified that prolonged isolation was diminishing his capacity to think and act rationally. I explained he suffered from the "SHU syndrome" (a term then in use to encompass the panoply of symptoms secondary to long-term confinement in isolation) and that the restraints he had been placed in had enraged him and driven him more and more mad (in both senses of that term). He had also been disoriented by massive sleep deprivation: the officers had been waking him every hour to adjust the restraints, the lights were always left on, and he was never permitted to sleep for extended periods of time. In short, I testified that prison officials had been torturing Rodney, in violation of all corrections and medical standards regarding seclusion and restraint. I testified that the defendant, in that state of mind, could not have formed intent. The jury agreed, stating that it was not fair for a prison system to drive people over the brink of insanity and then try to add time to their sentences for the crazy acts they were driven to commit. The jury hung 9 to 3 in favor of acquittal. The DA decided not to seek a new trial.

Rodney's disciplinary record sheds some light on whether supermaximum units cause violence or constitute a necessary measure to control an increasingly violent population of felons. During the first year of his incarceration, Rodney had 3 disciplinary infractions. In the second year he had 6, including the one that led to his transfer to the supermaximum unit. During the next year, in punitive segregation, he had 63 infractions, and in the year leading up to the assault he had 139. When asked why he had so many infractions, Rodney responded: "Once they put me in a strip cell, I don't know what happens, I just keep getting in trouble. . . . They never told me what I could do to get out, I believed I'd be in there forever." A few days after the assault, Rodney was transferred to another facility where the staff had no beef with him and where the associate superintendent took the time to listen to him talk about the ways he had felt disrespected by officers at the other prison. He was then placed in the general population. Tellingly, he proceeded to have no infractions for the subsequent year. The fact that the defendant received no further write-ups after being transferred out of the SHU suggests that he, like so many others I have examined, was capable of getting along and programming successfully as long as he was not kept in an emotionally devastating environment.

A CYCLE OF HOSTILITY

Once a culture of punishment takes hold and the staff feel that they need to respond to each new unacceptable behavior on the part of prisoners with further punishments, and once the interactions between staff and prisoners become predominantly punitive in nature, the punishments become more severe and the effect too many times is more emotional harm to the prisoners, in many cases including suicide. In supermax, it is not uncommon for prisoners to spit, throw food, or throw urine and feces. Then there is extreme self-harm: instead of directing their rage outward toward their captors, they direct it against themselves. I have reviewed cases where prisoners have cut themselves on all parts of their bodies, have cut off their ears, have cut off their penis, and have cut open their abdomen so that their bowels fall out. Each case of bizarre and extreme self-harm has been preceded by many incidents in which the prisoner has been put in restraints, sprayed with immobilizing gas, or been subjected to violent cell extractions.

This pattern of escalating violence is so often repeated and so predictable that special cells have been constructed in the most extreme isolation facilities. For example, I toured Tamms Correctional Facility in the Illinois Department of Corrections in 2004 as part of my preparation for expert testimony in a class action lawsuit. The prisoners were suing the state because they were denied adequate mental health treatment: for example, there was no inpatient psychiatry facility in the department of corrections, so floridly psychotic prisoners would be left to yell and smear feces on the walls of their solitary confinement cells. I examined several very disturbed prisoners whom

I would consider severely damaged by their confinement in that stark solitary setting. One of the officers leading the tour took me to see a couple of "special cells" that had recently been constructed, precisely to reduce the trouble very disturbed prisoners caused staff. He showed me an isolation cell that, like all the other cells at Tamms, was made of concrete with no functional window to the outside (there was a small rectangular "window" high on the outside wall that could not be opened, and the prisoner would have to stand on his bunk to see through it). The special cells were painted with a thick, shiny and slippery material that resisted both liquids and dirt, the floor was sloped higher at the far wall and lower at the wall containing the door, and just outside the cell was a channel that would carry fluids or excrement away from the cell into the sewer. The officer proudly told me that troublemaking prisoners like the one I had just examined could be consigned to that cell; then, even if they smeared blood and feces on the walls, staff could simply hose down the cell and it would quickly be clean again. The efficiency of the cleanup after the prisoner had been driven to such extreme acts reminded me of the efficiency of the death camps in Nazi Germany.

The more totally human beings are disrespected and disappeared, the more creative they become at declaring their presence. Recently I witnessed a bizarre and horrific situation in the solitary confinement units at Eastern Mississippi Correctional Facility (EMCF), a prison in an unincorporated area of Lauderdale County near Meridian. This "special-needs" prison, opened in 1999, has space for 1,500 prisoners and is run by a private corporation, the Management and Training Corporation of Utah, on contract with the Mississippi Department of Corrections. Prisoners with serious mental illness within the Mississippi Department of Corrections are consigned to the EMCF for treatment. The National Prison Project of the American Civil Liberties Union and the Southern Poverty Law Center filed a class action lawsuit in 2013 alleging horrible human rights abuses there, especially in its supermax isolation unit, Unit 5. The legal complaint described the facility as a "cesspool." Prisoners with serious mental illness in this filthy, noisy, and poorly administered supermax unit universally report that their requests for the most mundane items such as cleaning supplies or lightbulbs are ignored. Many are in the dark much of the time. They are left locked in their cells and entirely to their own devices because officers rarely visit the segregation pods except when they are delivering meals.

Because of this reprehensible neglect and lack of appropriate attention from staff, the prisoners protest in increasingly desperate fashion. Thus, as soon as a visitor like me enters a pod, there is much yelling about urgent needs, including the need to have officers take a very sick prisoner for an emergency medical visit (the other prisoners advocate for their sick neighbor). The longer the officers fail to respond to prisoners' very appropriate needs, the more prisoners will do things like cut themselves with a piece of a broken lightbulb, "flood the range" (cause their toilets and sinks to overflow so that water pours out onto the common area), set fires, and make a lot of noise. Eventually some are even driven to "buck the tray flap," sticking their own arm through the food port when it is opened by an officer who is about to pass them a tray. Sometimes officers hit their protruding arm with a nightstick or flashlight, but often they merely leave the food port open and move on to the next cell without delivering the meal. Thus even when prisoners resort to desperate measures to draw attention to their needs, the officers respond with punishments and deprivations.

Several prisoners reported that officers next made all prisoners who had put an arm through the food slot put their mattress on the filthy floor next to the door of their cell and from then on kneel on the floor at the back of their cell if they wanted to be fed at mealtimes so that officers could throw the container of food through the food port onto the mattress and the prisoner would be unable to reach the open port in time to put an arm through it. If the prisoner refused to put his mattress on the floor and kneel, the officers refused to deliver the meal. Some prisoners actually went hungry rather than accept the humiliation of being fed in this manner.[22] "When the food tray is thrown into my cell the food spills out onto the floor," one of the affected prisoners reported, "and if I refuse to go to the back of my cell, I cannot eat because the officer will refuse to give me my food tray. I have gone without eating approximately 4 or 5 times in a two week period because I would not go to the back of my cell and have my food thrown onto the floor. I refuse to go to the back of my cell because having my food thrown at me makes me feel like an animal." Other prisoners had similar stories and similar reasons for being angry. They complained about how officers kept "messing with the trays" and required them to get on their knees at the back of the cell. "We ain't no dogs," one prisoner exclaimed.

The prisoners with mental illness are being doubly "disappeared." Before they came to prison, they frequently lacked adequate psychiatric or mental health care, recovery opportunities, and housing in their community. Then, after being disappeared from their communities into the prison, they were further disappeared from the prison general population into segregation pods where they would be shut up in darkness and in filth for almost every hour of every day of their life. Here officers have total control over them. It is extremely common for prisoners to be ignored, disrespected, terrorized, and treated like animals, but they essentially have no power and no recourse.

The entire process thus comes down to an endless escalation of harm. Prisoners become very creative as they devise increasingly extreme and even bizarre forms of resistance to what they perceive as unrelenting, unfair, and brutal forms of punishment. But the bizarre drama that unfolds in the solitary confinement units does not lead to rehabilitation, only to ever more emotional damage to the prisoners and to their chances of "going straight" after they are released from prison.

A basic premise in psychology is that positive rewards attain greater constructive behavior change than negative sanctions for unacceptable behaviors. The prison culture of punishment does not, on average, change prisoners for the better. Worse, it makes their rehabilitation and successful preparation for reentry into the community almost impossible.

EVEN THERAPY HAPPENS IN CAGES

Besides making treatment and rehabilitation very difficult, the culture of punishment literally invades the treatment space. A poignant example is the "therapeutic cubicle." Therapeutic cubicles or "programming modules" are small holding cells, approximately the shape of a phone booth, made of steel and Lexan (indestructible plexiglass). Five or six of these cubicles are bolted to the floor in a room where group treatment is conducted. Typically in supermax units each prisoner is brought into the room in turn, in shackles, and placed in a cubicle. Then the therapist or teacher enters and begins the session. Prisoners call these cubicles "cages," and many describe feeling, for obvious reasons, as if they are being treated like something subhuman.[23]

At first, programming cubicles might have seemed a reasonable way of ensuring the safety of a psychiatrist, psychotherapist, or case manager who needs to meet with a mentally ill prisoner deemed a security risk. However, in my entire career, I have seen only perhaps a handful of prisoners who require that kind of restraint. Yet in many maximum security and supermaximum security units mental health staff will visit with a prisoner only if that prisoner is in a programming cubicle.

Programming cubicles are much like supermax isolation itself: they were originally devised only for the "worst of the worst" but came to be used for a

FIGURE 8. Prisoners participating in group therapy in the administrative segregation unit at San Quentin Prison. Photo by Lucy Nicholson, Reuters, 2012.

larger and larger share of the prison population. Most prisoners, even in a supermaximum security prison, are entirely polite and well behaved at their appointments with doctors. If there are prisoners who require ongoing close security precautions, their number is tiny. It simply is not the case that all mental health appointments have to occur with the prisoner in a cubicle.

The routine use of cubicles for every contact with mental health staff has the unfortunate effect of further increasing the distance and alienation between prisoners and staff. In so doing, it inhibits communication between them and makes prison staff less aware of prisoners and their needs. And as with many other measures, we have to ask whether what we do to prisoners makes them more or less likely to feel respected, or to resort anew to drugs and crime after they are released.

PRISONER RESISTANCE AND PRISON REFORM

There are many ways for prisoners to resist. On the most personal level, they can try to maintain their dignity and not let the degrading conditions wear them down. That is not easy to do. Many prisoners cannot do it, and their emotional health suffers. I greatly admire the prisoners who are able to sustain their pride and their self-esteem through years of solitary confinement, and I worry for those who are less capable of it.

Options for dissent are often limited. The culture of punishment requires not only prisoners' compliance with the interminable list of rules but also a more general acquiescence. There is, for example, an implicit prohibition against prisoners speaking truth to power. Prisoners who dare to speak out and resist the absolute control enjoyed by correctional authorities, especially when they organize to do so, risk massive repression. Prisoners have very limited options for expressing dissent of any kind, even when they are trying to make very reasonable demands that their rights be respected. And prison authorities too often try to trivialize their demands for fair treatment by castigating their attempts to express themselves as a form of misbehavior, or worse, as mere mayhem. Yet in some instances organized resistance has led to at least some degree of prison reform.

For example, in 1971, two weeks after George Jackson was killed at San Quentin, over 1,000 of the 2,200 prisoners at Attica Correctional Facility in Attica, New York, took control of the prison and made demands. The state of New York began negotiating with the Attica prisoners and actually agreed to grant over two dozen of their demands, but then Governor Nelson Rockefeller ordered the state police to retake the prison by force. There were many deaths. As Heather Anne Thompson's history of the uprising has shown, the eventual result was a backlash against efforts to make prison conditions more humane. Nevertheless, in the decade that followed, the prisoners' grievances and demands did receive a hearing, and "Attica's immediate impact was to spark some serious reforms of the American criminal justice system."[24]

A full-blown rebellion such as occurred at Attica in 1971 is quite rare. A much more frequent form of protest against unjust prison conditions is the hunger strike. In all cases I know of where a significant number of prisoners joined an organized hunger strike, all less severe options for registering their grievances had been closed off. Prison authorities like to focus exclusively on the fact that hunger strikes violate prison rules and rarely take seriously the demands of the hunger strikers. Between 2011 and 2013 three hunger strikes occurred at Pelican Bay State Prison, initiated by prisoners in the SHU. The demands of the hunger strikers were so reasonable, the strikes so well organized, and the popular support so massive that the prisoners' message could not be ignored.

By engaging in the hunger strikes, the prisoners risked their health and their lives and risked suffering abusive retaliation from officers. Many thousands of prisoners throughout the entire CDCR joined the hunger strikes in solidarity with the prisoners in the SHU at Pelican Bay. They published five very reasonable demands, including an end to abusive practices and group punishments (where all prisoners are punished with more restrictive conditions when staff cannot determine who had perpetrated an illegal act); an end to the debriefing policy (in which prisoners were required to inform on other prisoners if they wanted to be released from solitary confinement, see below); an end to indeterminate and very long-term consignment to solitary confinement; the provision of adequate and nutritious food; and the provision of meaningful rehabilitative programming and quality visitation for prisoners in solitary confinement.[25]

The debriefing policy was one of the most treacherous policies operating in the SHU at Pelican Bay State Prison. In California's prisons until 2015, if a prisoner was identified or "validated" at any time in his prison tenure as a gang member or associate, he would be given an indeterminate sentence to SHU and then would never be transferred out of isolation unless he was willing to tell gang investigators everything he knew about the gangs and give the names of at least three gang members.[26] In other words, he would have to "snitch" to win release from solitary confinement. But the prohibition against snitching is at the core of the unspoken prisoner code, and the prisoner who snitches, especially on gang members, is almost certain to be killed. In fact, sometimes prisoners have been murdered when they were released from SHU simply because other prisoners assumed they must have snitched in order to be released. More importantly, as a matter of honor, most prisoners who had survived a decade or longer in SHU considered themselves "stand-up cons," men who would never snitch on others. They refused to debrief.

The prisoners referred to the debriefing policy as "Snitch, Parole, or Die."[27] The department required them to *snitch* on other prisoners if they wanted to be released from SHU; if their prison sentence ran out they could be *paroled* (but universally prisoners told me that parole was not possible for prisoners in SHU because they were not permitted to participate in the kinds of rehabilitation programs the parole board required as prerequisites to parole); so if they chose not to snitch they would *die* in SHU. The debriefing policy and its effect as an indeterminate sentence to solitary were the main cause of despair in the prisoners I met there, including George Ruiz.

I visited with George Ruiz on two occasions, in 2012 and 2014, in the visiting area of the SHU at Pelican Bay State Prison. The interviews were part of my preparation for expert testimony in *Ashker v. Brown*, the class action lawsuit that grew out of the hunger strikes. I was asked to interview and discuss in my report the ten named plaintiffs. Our visits took place across a Lexan or indestructible plexiglass window. George was brought to the prisoner's side of the window in handcuffs, which were removed so that he could sit on a metal stool and talk to me. The officers left us to have a private conversation. He was a very warm Mexican American man with sad eyes. He seemed like a thoughtful man who chose his words carefully and watched me closely, as if trying to determine whether I would really comprehend the awfulness of his situation. He tried hard to be accurate and responsive to my questions.

Mr. Ruiz was sixty-nine years old at the time of our first interview. He had left school in the eleventh grade and had first entered prison at age thirty-four, for a seven-years-to-life sentence around 1980 (he had to serve seven years, but then he became eligible for parole). The prison had identified him as an associate of the Mexican Mafia (also known as "La Eme") in 1982 or 1984. He had tattoos on his stomach, but none of them actually signified gang association. He had been eligible for parole since 1993 but had been repeatedly told that he would never be paroled as long as he was in solitary confinement. He had applied for parole and had appeared for parole board hearings eight times, but all of his requests were denied. Staff and the parole board told him that he had to debrief if he wanted to leave the SHU, but he said he was against debriefing on principle and would never do it. He firmly believed that he would never be released from SHU and that he would die there. But the greatest source of pain for him was the prospect of never again seeing the family he loved:

> I have two daughters and a son. My daughters find it very hard to visit me because it is so far away. It is very expensive and time-consuming for them to drive for 850 miles from San Diego to Crescent City, as it takes about 14 hours to drive here without stopping. . . . On one of her few visits, my four-year-old granddaughter wanted to hug and kiss me when she was saying goodbye. She started crying because she couldn't touch me through the Plexiglass. My heart was broken right there. I tried to comfort her, but was unsuccessful. My suffering in the SHU is made so much worse because I can't call my relatives and maintain any degree of emotional connection with them. I want to be with them so I can hug them, kiss them and live what little life I have left with them. I want to go home.[28]

The hunger strikes and the *Ashker v. Brown* lawsuit have caused a major shift of policy in the CDCR. A previous class action lawsuit in the early

1990s, *Madrid v. Gomez*, had recognized the damaging effects of solitary confinement on prisoners with serious mental illness and had resulted in a ban on consigning such prisoners to the SHU at Pelican Bay.[29] But that lawsuit, as well as the *Coleman v. Governor of California* litigation that had brought me to the facility in 1992, drew on data related only to prisoners who had been in SHU for two years or less, because that was all the time the SHU had been in operation. Twenty years later, the *Ashker v. Brown* class action lawsuit examined the plight of prisoners who had been in solitary confinement for more than ten years. By then, some had been at the Pelican Bay SHU since it had opened twenty-four years earlier, and some among those prisoners had even been in solitary confinement before being transferred to the SHU at Pelican Bay. For example, Hugo Pinell had been in solitary confinement for approximately forty years, the last twenty-one at the Pelican Bay SHU. Dr. Craig Haney and I were tasked in 2013 and 2014 with answering the question as to what additional harm, if any, solitary confinement of a decade or longer had caused.

In the course of the litigation, the CDCR agreed to make major changes in its policies guiding consignment to SHU. No longer would prisoners who were identified (validated) as gang members or associates (friends of the gang) be automatically given an indeterminate sentence to SHU; instead, only prisoners who were apprehended committing illegal or violent acts would go there. When the lawsuit was eventually settled, the ten named plaintiffs were transferred out of the SHU. Strict limits were set for a sentence to SHU, and other improvements in the policies and conditions were put in place.

The hunger strikes and *Ashker v. Brown* have very large implications. Even with the severe restrictions imposed by the culture of punishment, prisoners stood up for their rights—outside the system by protesting with their refusal to eat and then inside the system as they successfully pursued a class action lawsuit to bring their conditions of confinement up to constitutional standards.

VENGEANCE MAY BE DESTRUCTIVE, BUT IT IS SO COMPELLING

Vengeance drives the punishment function of prison at the expense of the rehabilitation function. Vengeance is a quintessential human sentiment. It is one of our capacities, just as generosity and forgiveness are human capacities.

But certain experiences bring vengeance to the fore, for example unfair treatment at work, gross disrespect, the murder of a loved one, or the very high-profile murder of someone else's child. We have the impulse to kill the murderer in revenge, or in more legal fashion, we may feel driven to seek the worst punishment possible in court. The call for harsher sentences, truth in sentencing, mandatory minimums, three strikes, and the death penalty become louder and more strident each time there is a dreadful rape and murder of a young girl, for example. Immediately, legislatures pass harsher sentencing laws. When the populace feels insecure and endangered, whether because of terrorist attacks or the deterioration of economic conditions for working people, the culture of punishment that prevails in the prisons becomes more harsh and pervasive. This is all very understandable as a personal feeling, and very human. But should such sentiments singularly guide public policy?

In *Discipline and Punish*, Michel Foucault charts the transition in France from the mid-eighteenth century's public spectacles of cruel punishments like drawing and quartering (in which the criminal was torn apart by four horses attached to his limbs) to punishments that were meant to act more on the soul than on the body and were hidden from public view.[30] As he describes this transition, "Punishment, then, will tend to become the most hidden part of the penal process. This has several consequences: it leaves the domain of more or less everyday perception and enters that of abstract consciousness; its effectiveness is seen as resulting from its inevitability, not from its visible intensity; it is the certainty of being punished and not the horrifying spectacle of public punishment that must discourage crime; the exemplary mechanics of punishment changes its mechanisms."[31]

Foucault could have been talking about the contemporary prisoner's plight in solitary confinement. It is secret in the sense that the public knows and wishes to know little about it. Yet the effect of supermax isolation is chilling, the dread of being sent to isolation presumably deterring potential criminals from conducting their crimes—at least that is the theory implicit in the love affair with supermaxes that has permeated departments of corrections since the 1990s. In fact, supermax isolation is not very successful as a preventive measure. But Foucault was not talking about deterrent effects on particular criminals; rather, he was describing the effects of harsh prison conditions on the society at large. It is the ordinary citizen's dread of what awaits in prison, its "inevitability, not its visible intensity," that presumably keeps him or her from breaking the law, and the supermax solitary confinement unit is the ultimate object of dread. Meanwhile, the public ignores the cruelties practiced on those who presumably perpetrated the types of crimes that led to public alarm and tougher sentencing laws. Foucault's work predates the advent of the supermaximum security prison, but he introduced in *Discipline and Punish* the ideas of Jeremy Bentham about the Panopticon, Bentham's futuristic vision of prison architecture involving isolation of prisoners, an architecture where the keepers visually surveil the kept but the prisoners are not able to see anything outside their cell. Like Benjamin Franklin's notion of penitence, Bentham's seemingly humane ideas about panopticism eventually served merely to rationalize the warehousing of prisoners in isolation.

The degree to which a society collectively focuses on vengeance changes with historical events. After 9/11, there was widespread emotional support for President Bush's military "Shock and Awe" campaign against our enemies and anyone else who dared to give comfort to terrorists. But years later, now that the United States has become embroiled in multiple wars in the Middle East, South Asia, and Africa, and as the upshot of our bombing so many putative enemies has been the enlargement of a worldwide army of militant terrorists, a growing number of people have begun to think it is time to step back and reconsider the wisdom of permitting a quest for vengeance to be the guide to foreign policy. The righteous indignation following a horrific terrorist attack like 9/11 is real and needs to be recognized. But its uncensored expression can lead to waterboarding, other forms of torture, and even genocide. After all, genocide is all about vengeance. The perpetrators of genocide often claim they are justified in massacring a tribe or race now because that group murdered their own people years ago. This was true in Nazi Germany in the 1930s and '40s, and in Rwanda and Bosnia during their 1990s atrocities.

We feel compassion for the family of a murdered individual, and we might hope secretly to ourselves for revenge. That private thought that each of us has had is expressed in a broader American mind-set: the mythology of the lawless frontier glorified in westerns, where the quest for revenge is presented as manly, very American, and morally justified. Clint Eastwood's 1992 film *Unforgiven* provides a stunning portrayal of this kind of mind-set. Western tough guys, played by Clint Eastwood and Morgan Freeman, are hired to take revenge on the attacker of a woman in another town, and when they do get their revenge, their actions trigger a series of even more vengeful killings.

That mind-set, if left to prevail in government and global affairs, would lead this country into very dark times, almost inevitably into perpetual war. Why not, instead, think in a level-headed way about how to improve our social arrangements? The criminal justice system actually provides an excellent testing ground for just that kind of thinking. Prison sentences have been progressively lengthened over several decades until now they are so long, for such a broad range of criminal acts, that over two million people are in jail or prison. It has become quite "normal" to think that prison is where they belong. But the United States has far more incarcerated individuals per capita than any other nation, and no other developed country in the world employs solitary confinement on such a massive scale.

When my book *Prison Madness* was published in 1999, one of my media interviews was on a late-night AM radio talk show originating from rural Tennessee. The two male hosts were very conservative and very opinionated. At one point, I was talking about a woman prisoner who had been raped viciously by a correction officer in a Michigan prison, and the more brazen of the two hosts said, "Why should we care what happens to her in prison? She did some awful crime to get there." I responded that actually her crime had been writing a bad check. The radio host went on without a pause to say, "Well that's a crime, she deserved what she got." Finally his co-host interrupted to say he had gone too far, and that prison rape was totally abhorrent no matter what the victim had done. Vengeance often emerges in the form of attempts to forcefully control those to whom the vengeance applies. Prisoners, of course, are a big target for our rush to vengeance.

The legal scholar David Garland has studied the differences in criminological approaches between those of the "age of reform" or welfare state era that began in the second half of the nineteenth century and ended in the early 1970s and those of the "culture of control" that has succeeded the welfare state era and prevails today in criminal justice.[32] According to Garland:

> The criminologies of the welfare state era tended to assume the perfectability of man, to see crime as a sign of an under-achieving socialization process, and to look to the state to assist those who had been deprived of the economic, social and psychological provision necessary for proper social adjustment and law-abiding conduct. Control theories begin from a much darker vision of the human condition. They assume that individuals will be strongly attracted to self-serving, anti-social, and criminal conduct unless inhibited from doing so by robust and effective controls. . . . Where the older criminology demanded more in the way of welfare and assistance, the new one insists upon tightening controls and enforcing discipline.[33]

The supermaximum security prison is the epitome and natural end point of the modern culture of vengeance and control. Another name for the supermaximum security unit is "control unit." And it is no accident that little in the way of education or rehabilitation is available to prisoners in supermaximum isolation units. It is very difficult to create a therapeutic or rehabilitative environment in an age of control, and practically impossible inside a facility designed precisely to keep its inhabitants totally controlled and mostly isolated and idle.

When it comes time to sentence a convicted felon to a prison term, we tend to reason that the more heinous the crime, the more harsh the prison term needs to be. Pursuing that logic, it might seem to make sense to disappear "the worst of the worst" into supermax solitary confinement and erase them from public view, leaving officers to brutalize them however they will with no recourse for the prisoner. But that logic emanates entirely from a motive of vengeance. It would be much more reasonable to shape prison policy according to whether it makes prisoners more or less likely to be damaged to the point where they will return to illicit substances and crime after they are released. If that was our guiding concern, we would discard the culture of punishment in favor of a more therapeutic and rehabilitative prison culture.

THREE

Race Matters a Lot

RACISM IS A PERVASIVE AND DEEPLY entrenched problem in American society, and there are few places where it is more apparent and grotesque than in American prisons. Not only are people of color imprisoned at vastly higher percentages than whites, but they are by and large treated more harshly in the jails, courts, and prisons.[1] Worse, racist behavior by correctional officers is frequently condoned and often encouraged by prison policies and colleagues.

Several years ago I was asked to tour a large prison in a northeastern state to assess the quality of correctional mental health care. The prison, built early in the twentieth century, was very large and dilapidated. It contained many thousands of inmates, and staff told me they found it very difficult to manage so many in such an outdated facility. Parts of the prison were especially dangerous for staff. For example, one area of the recreation yard between two cellblocks was not visible from the high towers on the prison's perimeter where armed guards stood watch over the yards. Hearing from officers how easily prisoners could attack officers in that blind spot made me nervous every time I had to traverse it during my tour. Tensions were high, officers were constantly on the alert lest they be attacked, and prisoners were very aware how quickly officers would resort to force against them simply to prevent attacks.

In that tense environment, racially based discrimination and attacks proliferated. Prisoners told me many stories about how white officers used particular black prisoners as their "punching bags" and sent disproportionately more prisoners of color to the segregation unit. Several prisoners separately told me of an incident they had witnessed that chilled them to the core and increased their terror of racially motivated attacks by officers. The first black corrections officer to work in that particular department of corrections had

68

been hired and had begun work at the maximum security prison a few years earlier. During his orientation, one of the first things the white officers showing him around did was to stop in front of a black man's cell, open the cell door, and proceed to beat the man until he fell on the floor in a puddle of blood. Then the white officers glared at the new black officer. Nothing was said. There was no appropriate reason for the beating, and it was obvious to everyone that the white officers were testing the black rookie, as if to say, "What are you going to do about this? Are you one of us (officers) or are you one of them (the blacks)?" The black officer responded by doing nothing and continued with the training. This story is so abhorrent that, if various versions of it weren't so frequently reported from other places, it would seem difficult to imagine as true. Unfortunately, researchers have shown again and again that such systemic racial violence exists broadly throughout the American prison system—between prisoners, between prisoners and staff, and among the staff themselves.

A documentary film entitled *The 13th* begins with a reading of the amendment that ended slavery in the United States.[2] According to the Thirteenth Amendment, ratified in 1865, "Neither slavery nor involuntary servitude, except as a punishment for crime whereof the party shall have been duly convicted, shall exist within the United States, or any place subject to their jurisdiction." The film's narrators explain how the disproportionate repression brought to bear on young African Americans, including their often illegal disqualification from voting if they have served time in prison and their murder by police on the streets, is not an accident but the product of a corporate agenda that thrives and profits on racism as well as police violence. And the film links that corporate agenda with the popularity of supermax security prison facilities as well as the disproportionate number of prisoners of color who live there.

THE NUMBERS

While only 13 percent of the general population are African American, over 40 percent of prisoners in the United States are African American; while only 16 percent of the general population are Latino, 19 percent of US prisoners are Latino; and while 37 percent of the general population are people of color, 67 percent of prisoners are people of color.[3] As the Sentencing Project, a nonprofit organization working for criminal justice reform, reports, "For black males in their thirties, 1 in every 10 is in prison or jail on any given day.[4] And as of 2016, "Among black males born in 2001, one in three will go to prison at some point during their lifetimes; one in six Latino males will have the same fate. In contrast only 1 out of every 17 white males is expected to go to prison."[5] Similar statistics exist for women prisoners throughout the United States. According to the Center for American Progress's research on female prison populations, 1 in 111 white women, 1 in 45 Latina women, and 1 in 18 black women will go to prison at some point in their lives.[6]

Why are African Americans so overrepresented in the prison population? American institutions have a long history of not only permitting but encouraging a disproportionate targeting of racial minorities. Michelle Alexander, civil rights attorney and law professor, has traced that history in her powerful 2010 study of mass incarceration in America, *The New Jim Crow*, and has explored how discriminatory results are guaranteed at every point in individuals' passage through the justice system. Blacks are substantially more likely than whites to be stopped and frisked on the street, to be arrested, to be convicted, to receive a long prison sentence, to be denied parole, and to be sentenced to death.

There is overwhelming evidence for the overt and systemic use of race in American policing strategies, but the ways that racism works are not always so obvious. For example, teenage boys in white and black communities often consume a frightening amount of illicit substances. But as Michelle Alexander and others have shown, a black teenager in the inner city is more likely than a white middle-class teenager to come to the attention of police and be arrested for drug use because there are more police patrol cars in his neighborhood.[7] Once he is arrested, his parents will be less likely to have the money to post bail for him or to seek help from a psychologist or psychiatrist for treatment to help deal with any emotional problem that might have led him to get arrested in the first place. The court will be more inclined to see him as a flight risk and will be less disposed to place him in a diversion program as an alternative to jailing him. Because of the black teenager's race and economic status, he will be less likely to have access to a good attorney, and his white counterpart's family members will appear more convincing to judges when they claim that their child will never break the law like this again. In other words, the white kid—especially if he or she is middle class—will more often go free, while the black kid—particularly if he is from a poor family—will go to prison. The legal scholar William Stuntz has argued that many such disparities are due to a lack of equal protection in a system where police and prosecutors have too much discretion and where local government rather than the federal government determines the way criminal trials proceed.[8]

In the many small and large determinations that officers of the law must make from the moment they suspect an individual of wrongdoing all the way to a trial or prison term, they can use discretion that is too often swayed by racial bias. A police officer responding to a call that a man in the community is yelling and acting bizarrely belligerent has the discretion of arresting the man for disturbing the peace or taking him to a psychiatric hospital where it can be determined if he is a danger to himself or others and therefore warrants involuntary hospitalization. In many urban areas, officers routinely arrest black men who are creating a commotion whereas they are more likely to take white men in equivalent circumstances to a psychiatric hospital for evaluation. Further, police officers on patrol have the discretion to pull people over and check their identification and auto insurance if they have witnessed an infraction or otherwise have "probable cause" to investigate something, but they can misuse that discretion by systematically and disproportionately pulling over more blacks than whites. Such racial profiling has been challenged in the courts as a violation of the Constitution and the Civil Rights Act, but though patently illegal it still persists. Racial bias can also influence whether officers keep the encounter civil and routine or escalate it in a manner leading to the use of force and the filing of criminal charges. These issues have received considerable public attention recently on account of the Black Lives Matter movement and video evidence of officers' interactions with black citizens that has been uploaded onto social media.

Added to the subjective bias of police in the community and judges in court are the laws and policies that blatantly discriminate against people of color. For example, until Congress passed the Fair Sentencing Act of 2010 and President Obama signed it into law, the possession of crack cocaine was punishable by a sentence up to ten times longer than the sentence for an equivalent amount of powder cocaine. Since crack cocaine is a preferred illicit substance in low-income black communities whereas powder cocaine is preferred in middle class communities, sentencing guidelines prior to the law's passage sent disproportionate numbers of blacks to prison.[9]

The disparities do not stop at the prison gate. On average, white prisoners are more likely to hold spots in desirable rehabilitation and education programs and prison jobs. When I was hired by the Civil Rights Division of the US Department of Justice in 1981 to investigate race relations in the Michigan Department of Corrections, my official report noted that by and large the jobs and industry assignments in these prisons that were highest paying—including carpentry, tool and die, and machine maintenance—were filled to a very great extent by white inmates, while the jobs that were less prestigious, less well paying, and less relevant training for postrelease employment—including cafeteria work, porter, and janitorial positions—were filled disproportionately by black inmates. Whites were being taught at higher skill levels and tended to be in supervisorial positions, while blacks were doing the menial work and tended to be lower in the status hierarchy—that is, if they were working at all. For example, during my tour of the Michigan State Prison in Jackson, I saw a majority black prison population on the recreation yard, but when I walked into a large industrial workshop where prisoners were being trained to work with electric tools on a production line where furniture was manufactured I was shocked to see mostly older white prisoners filling the spots in that program.

In the same investigation of the Michigan facilities, my report noted that a very large majority—greater than in the population as a whole and in some units approaching 100 percent—of prisoners in punitive segregation units were black, while just as great a majority of inmates in protective custody units were white. And the Michigan prison was not an isolated instance: although the federal government does not report statistics on the racial composition of supermaximum security units, plenty of research shows that across the country, people of color make up hugely disproportionate percentages of the population in solitary confinement.[10]

For example, a 2012 study by the American Friends Service Committee found that 51 percent of the prisoners in Arizona's two state supermax prisons for men were Latino compared to 41 percent of the general prison population in Arizona, and 9 percent of the male supermax prisoners were Native American compared to less than 5 percent in the general prison population. African Americans showed little statistical difference between supermax and general prison populations, but the study noted that although African Americans constituted only 4 percent of the total state population of Arizona, they were "found in prison at a rate over three times that of the state population," so that they were still "grossly overrepresented in prison and in supermax at extraordinary rates."[11] The organization concluded with a damning assessment:

> There is an unmistakable pattern in Arizona where prisoners of color are nearly always placed in supermax facilities and other conditions of isolation at significantly higher rates than white prisoners. This is an especially

disturbing trend considering that people of color are already incarcerated at extraordinarily higher rates than white Arizonians. Given that there is no evidence that race can even remotely be tied to prison violence or rule violations, this suggests an inherent bias on the part of the Arizona Department of Corrections and staff who are responsible for the classification of prisoners, and the application of repeated disciplinary actions that can result in placement in isolation.[12]

New York exhibits a similar pattern: according to a 2014 report, while 18 percent of the entire state's population is black, black people make up 50 percent of the New York State prison population and 60 percent of the people in New York's SHUs, and for prisoners under age twenty-one, black youths constitute 66 percent of those in solitary confinement.[13] And though there is no national-level data, various surveys and censuses conducted by the Bureau of Justice Statistics report similar racial disparities for supermax facilities in Arkansas, Connecticut, Colorado, Maryland, Massachusetts, New Jersey, and Rhode Island, as gathered and tabulated in Margo Schlanger's extensive 2013 review.[14]

At the same time, black and Latino prisoners have also been shown to be significantly less likely than whites to receive mental health treatment. This is a crucial disparity because mental health treatment is needed if prisoners with serious mental illness are to cope with life in prison and control potentially disruptive behaviors that might get them placed in solitary confinement.[15]

The origins of the modern American prison are deeply embedded in the history of slavery.[16] Before the Civil War, jails in the South were mostly filled with white prisoners. The slave owner did not need jails to discipline his slaves. But after the Civil War, when black people previously held as slaves were freed, and then especially during Reconstruction, laws—dubbed the Black Codes—were written that made it very easy for white plantation owners and sheriffs to arrest former slaves for vagrancy, panhandling, and other minor charges. Black prisoners were then leased out to the former slave owners, who would put them to work in the fields. But the plight of the black fieldworker would often be worse than slavery. A slave owner might beat and whip a slave, rape slave women, and destroy slave families, but he would not work the slave to death—that would destroy his investment in the slave as chattel. Now, if the plantation owner—who might be leasing for prison labor the same people whom he had previously owned as slaves—worked black prisoners to death or beat them to death, he could go back to the prison that had leased them to him and complain that he had gotten a defective prisoner who had died on him, and the warden would replace the dead man with another prisoner at no additional cost.[17]

Today racism takes other forms, but it is still one of the most—if not *the* most—urgent and critical issues in the criminal justice system. After all, since the civil rights movement, it is no longer acceptable for whites to openly express racist sentiments toward African Americans. But they can subliminally direct the public's fears toward men of color simply by reinforcing an association between them and crime. G. H. W. Bush won the 1988 presidential election only after the Republican Party broadcast attack ads accusing the Democratic candidate, Massachusetts governor Michael Dukakis, of being soft on crime because he had paroled Willie Horton, a black man who went on to commit more awful crimes.

Despite overwhelming evidence to the contrary, we still hear the claim that the disproportionate representation of people of color in prisons is due not to systemic racial bias within the criminal justice system but to some innate quality in the individuals who are being incarcerated. But the broad evidence supporting the role of racial bias makes clear that the latter perspective is what psychologists and sociologists would refer to as an attribution error.

The term *attribution error* was introduced to describe the common tendency for people to attribute their own behavior to external factors (the situation in which they find themselves) but others' behavior to internal factors (disposition or character). Crime is a good example. The social variable with the strongest correlation with the crime rate is the unemployment rate. When more people are out of work and starving, more resort to crime. What then is the cause of crime? Is it social and historical forces, including economic trends or racism, that led to a large number of hungry unemployed individuals? Or is it all about the personal attributes of individuals who perpetrate the crimes? Of course, scholars are more interested in the social determinants, what social psychologists Craig Haney and Philip Zimbardo term "the situation," and mental health clinicians are more interested in what inclinations dwell within the mind of the criminal. Both are relevant perspectives.[18] But when interest in what goes on in the minds of criminals obliterates the search for social determinants of crime, an unfortunate attribution error has occurred that sets up a self-fulfilling prophecy (it is always easy to find psychological test results that correlate with criminal involvement) and results in too little attention being paid to the social causes of crime.

Examples of this kind of situation can be found in more commonplace settings, such as an elementary school. For example, a first-grade class of twenty-two students is relatively orderly and effective in its educational goals. Then the state budget is cut and the number of children in the class is raised to twenty-eight. The classroom becomes more unruly. Several students begin to act out and get in trouble. What has changed? The students who would get in trouble did not have a sudden change of personality traits in the interim. Rather, if one looks at the students in a first-grade class, one can make good guesses about which students would get in trouble were the class size to grow: energetic, enthusiastic students who have trouble sitting still and keeping their voice down under the best of circumstances. When the class size was twenty-two, the teacher would keep an eye on these students, giving them energy-absorbing activities when they started to display signs of boredom in class. But when there are twenty-eight kids in the class, the same teacher has less time to think about what activities might absorb the energy of each child. Then the classroom becomes noisier and more chaotic, and the energetic children are blamed.

What is the cause of the noise and chaos in the classroom? Is it mainly the presence among the children of a few students who become noisy and restless when not occupied with interesting projects? Or is it the growth in the class size that causes the noise level to rise and the teacher's effectiveness to plummet? A popular diagnosis that was invented in response to this situation is attention deficit disorder, and many of the kids who have trouble sitting still in class are prescribed stimulant medications such as Ritalin or Adderal. But in a certain proportion of cases, this is an attribution error—the more energetic students are being blamed for the chaotic classroom milieu. If the class was made smaller (the situation was addressed), the problem would be ameliorated and fewer kids would need medications.

With regard to race and crime, are blacks innately more criminal or more violent than whites? Is it their genes? Their personalities? Or shall we assign more weight to social dynamics that selectively consign young people of color to jail or prison? For hundreds of years in America—and even in broad swaths of the country today—it was a very popular idea to blame crime on the innate characteristics of black men and women. That attribution error has fed into racist views and played an enormous role in shaping the criminal justice system as it operates today.

There is no question that individual factors and social factors are interwoven. We are all social beings, and social factors determine many aspects of the way we think and live our individual lives. But when we find that African Americans make up 13 percent of the total population and over 40 percent of the prison population, it is clear that something in our social arrangements has gone horribly wrong: it is time to start undoing the tragedy that has evolved in our prisons and turn our attention to the social causes of these cruel and stark racial disparities.

RACISM IN SOLITARY

Solitary confinement units are the sites of some of the worst racism in prisons. The "gladiator fights" at California's Corcoran Correctional Facility in the late 1980s and early 1990s are one of the darkest and most dramatic examples of this. Corcoran contains a SHU that houses 1,800 prisoners deemed to be the "worst of the worst." Though in many facilities SHU prisoners go to the recreation area alone, SHU prisoners at Corcoran are placed on the small "yard" with other prisoners. However, instead of seeing this time as a rare moment for the prisoners to have much-needed interaction with other people, a group of officers and their supervisors took it upon themselves to set up "gladiator fights" among the prisoners. They would release into the tiny recreation yard two very tough men who would feel compelled to fight to the death because of being from different racial groups and rival gangs (blacks in the Black Guerilla Family, whites in the Aryan Brotherhood, and Mexican Americans from Nuestra Familia or Norteños and the Mexican Mafia or Sureños). Officers watching from the guard's control booth above would then place bets on the outcome, even calling female officers from other parts of the prison to come and watch. When it became clear which of the prisoners was going to be the victor, the officers would order them to cease and desist, but since the fights were invariably vicious, the prisoners involved might not immediately break it up. If they did not, the officers watching the fights shot the participants with nonlethal riot guns or deadly rifles. Seven men involved in arranged gladiator fights were shot and killed over a two- or three-year period, while over fifty were wounded by gunshots. The officers filed falsified reports on the incidents, claiming they had to shoot to protect lives. An officer from the prison, the rare whistle-blower among officers, eventually went to the FBI to report these arranged gladiator fights and murders. There was an investigation and a trial. But all of the officers were eventually acquitted of any wrongdoing.[19] In one of the civil lawsuits brought by the family of a prisoner shot to death in a gladiator fight, Preston Tate, the jury eventually awarded the family several million dollars.

The gladiator fights were held in strict secrecy with no press coverage until the whistle-blowing officer exposed the abuse. Prison authorities made no effort to take responsibility for crimes being committed inside the walls. As Tim Cornwall, a journalist for the *Independent*, wrote at the time: "The worst abuses were said to occur under the tenure of warden George Smith, who ... was dubbed 'Mushroom George' because 'mushrooms like to be kept in the dark,' one guard said. Mr. Smith kept a picture of John Wayne in his office to project a tough image and turned a blind eye to his subordinates' tactics."[20]

Surveillance videos documented several of the fights; evidently officers passed these around much in the way that the community outside might pass around videos of boxing championships. Robert Navarro, Tom Quinn, and Corey Weinstein from the nonprofit prisoner rights group California Prison Focus were able to gain possession of the videos from materials discovered in court for the civil lawsuits that were brought by families of the dead "gladiators," and with them they created a documentary film entitled *Maximum Security University*.[21] All of the officers involved had submitted identical incident reports saying the shootings had been needed to save lives. But the videos used in the film show that prisoners who had been fighting had definitely stopped fighting and begun walking away from each other before they were shot and killed by officers with rifles in the control booth.

Even where officer incitement of racial conflict is not as explicit as in gladiator fights, the racism of prisoners and racially tinged harassment by officers can intersect, as I reported from my tour of a supermax facility in Indiana as a psychiatric consultant for a 1997 Human Rights Watch inspection:

> Walking through a housing section in the B-East pod, we were startled to find an African-American prisoner in a cell covered with racist graffiti. Among the cell's more prominent markings was the slogan "White Power," which was scrawled on the wall in thick, four-foot-high black letters and interrupted by a large swastika; the phrase 'fuck all niggers' was scratched into the mirror, and an intricate drawing of a hooded Klansman poised over the bed. The prisoner stated that he had been transferred to the cell, which had been defaced by a prior occupant, six days previously in the wake of conflict with a guard.
>
> When questioned as to why a black prisoner was forced to spend over twenty-three hours a day in a cell where he had little to do but contemplate racially offensive symbols and slogans, corrections officers said that the prisoner had been placed there purely out of space considerations.[22]

I noted in my report, however, that given the racially polarized atmosphere evident at the prison, guards should have been trying to alleviate racial tensions, rather than exacerbating them.

Despite the scope of blatant discrimination in American prisons, only a small part of the racism there will ever be prosecuted in the courts simply because it is so difficult to prove in court that the racist acts actually occurred. A little more than a decade ago I investigated a supermax security facility, the Allen B. Polunsky Unit, in West Livingston, Texas, where Texas's Death Row was located, while I was preparing a report for a lawsuit brought by a Death Row prisoner. During my investigation I reviewed statements from prisoners living on Death Row that a group of white officers who called themselves "White Is Right" were harassing prisoners on account of their race, typically by planting contraband in the prisoner's cell or destroying his property in the course of a cell search. Prisoners also told me that the White Is Right officers were harassing a white occupant of Death Row because he refused to turn against prisoners of other races, and because he was known to help prisoners of other races fill out legal forms.[23]

When I uncover testimony like this, the racial discrimination is difficult to prosecute in a court of law. There was no firm proof that the White Is Right officer clique existed, and of course staff had denied it. But several prisoners who had no way to communicate with each other had separately testified to its existence, so there was a certain degree of independent corroboration of the alleged facts. Sometimes this will be enough proof for the court; other times it will not.

Blatant racism is too often the rule in prisons. One group, mainly white officers, have absolute control over another, disproportionately black prisoners, and often nobody is looking. Robert King, one of the Angola Three, who spent twenty-nine years in solitary confinement at Angola State Prison in Louisiana, provides in his autobiography a graphic description of the unbounded racism there.[24] He recalls that in 1971 black prisoners in the South were starting to resonate somewhat with the new confidence of Black Power on the streets. In Angola State Prison, where King had just been transferred, "There was a new psyche among the prisoners: not the subdued and broken spirit I saw in years past, but one of defiance, of people standing up. The mood in the streets had caught up with the men in prisons." The prison was in an uproar because an officer had just been murdered and the authorities did not have any credible suspect for the crime. King had not even been at the prison when the murder occurred, but he and three other black prisoners were sent to the "main prison dungeon" because they had "wanted to play lawyer for another inmate." "In the dungeon, I witnessed even more severe repression. Prisoners who had been scooped up for 'investigation' [into the death of the officer] were made to run the gauntlet past [all white] guards wielding bats and clubs. They were stripped of all clothing, their heads were shaved, and they were kept in bare, empty cells. White prisoners were spared this humiliation. None were beaten, placed into lockdown, or even investigated in the guard's death. The beatings and intimidation of Black prisoners went on for days."[25]

I have uncovered many similar incidents of egregious and blatant racist beatings in my career as a forensic psychiatrist. But many more times, too many to list, the racist discrimination has been more subtle. Quite often it has concerned officers' discretion.

DISCRETION AND RACIAL DISCRIMINATION IN PRISON

Just as discretion on the part of police on the streets and judges in the courts can be—wittingly or not—an instrument of racial discrimination, so can discretion on the part of correction officers in prisons. Indeed, in prisons, where long lists of rules govern just about every aspect of prisoners' behavior and circumstances, officers' discretion prevails at every turn. For example, in many prisons male prisoners are not permitted to hang pictures of naked women on the walls of their cells. When I tour a prison and view cells where such pictures are hanging, and a ranking officer is accompanying me on my tour, I sometimes ask the officer or commander if this kind of poster is permitted. He may tell me no and order the prisoner to take it down, but more often he will say it's against the rules but staff allow it in order to avoid even more fractious relations between officers and prisoners.

We all break rules and even calculate the likelihood of being caught for doing so. Thus I walk across the street in the middle of the block instead of using the crosswalk at the corner, committing the offense of jaywalking. Before deciding to break the law, I look around to see if a police officer is present. Sometimes there is a police officer or squad car, but I jaywalk anyway, and the officer does not cite me. That is the other side of discretion.

Correction officers cannot possibly enforce every single prison rule every hour of every day. I observe prisoners passing a "line" from cell to cell in a lockdown unit, meaning they send messages to other prisoners in cells on their pod by passing a note on a string to their immediate neighbor, who sends it on to the next cell, and onward until the intended recipient pulls the message in from the "line" on the ground along the cell-fronts. While touring prisons I have witnessed this kind of line in operation, and the officers accompanying me on the tour said nothing about it. Just as with the pinup pictures, they were choosing to let the matter go. Of course, sometimes they do yell at the prisoners to get rid of the line, and at other times they write a disciplinary ticket for a prisoner who sends or receives a message in this way.

Several years ago I personally observed the initials KKK tattooed on the wrists of a couple of white officers in the supermax unit of the Wabash Valley Correctional Facility in southern Indiana, just after I had heard independently from two black prisoners that those particular officers regularly singled them out for abuse. My observing the tattoos lent some credibility to the prisoners' complaints. Then, when I found that those particular officers gave black prisoners disciplinary write-ups where the prisoners complained the "tickets" were entirely bogus, I had serious cause for skepticism about the prisoners' alleged misbehaviors.

In a supermax prison, officers frequently need to use their discretion when deciding whether to label a prisoner "Mad" or "Bad." A prisoner screams relentlessly or smears feces on the wall. An officer figures either that the prisoner is acutely psychotic and his bizarre acts are driven by command hallucinations—voices telling him to scream or smear feces—or that the prisoner is causing a commotion or faking mental illness to gain an improved living situation in the mental health unit. On one assumption the officer may call for the intervention of a mental health clinician; on the other, he may send the prisoner to segregation as punishment for unacceptable behavior. We know that prisoners of color are disproportionately consigned to punitive solitary confinement whereas white prisoners disproportionately are sent for mental health treatment or to protective custody. It is not a huge leap to conclude that in a significant number of cases, more in facilities where there is blatant racism, the racial biases of officers result in more write-ups for disciplinary infractions for prisoners of color, and that is why so many end up in solitary confinement. Sadly, there is all too little staff training to effectively help officers with race relations. Exacerbating the problem, white officers frequently come from rural areas that surround the prisons, while black prisoners tend to emanate from inner-city ghettos.

One's race determines almost all aspects of one's experience in prison, and racial tensions are palpable. These tensions do not always arise from white staff's acts of discrimination against black inmates. Often, they are more diffuse. For instance, inmates often tell me about incidents where an officer was more lenient with a white or a black prisoner, the other prisoner jumped to the conclusion it was because of race, the two began to fight, and the officer wrote both of them tickets. In an environment where racial discrimination is so obvious, and where very stressful conditions are the rule, race becomes the issue around which tensions gather and trouble erupts.

In prison, newly arriving prisoners quickly learn to "stick to their own kind." For instance, a long time ago, when I toured the Southern Michigan State Prison in Jackson, Michigan, a facility that at that time housed many thousands of prisoners, there were two serving lines in the large cafeteria: one entirely of white inmates, the other of blacks. The inmates and staff who worked these serving lines were likewise segregated, whites serving whites and blacks serving blacks. The inmates might have been said to choose this arrangement—but there were ways staff could have prevented it, and many inmates might just as well have preferred a more integrated arrangement but, given their circumstances, might have felt they could not step out of line.

The newly arriving prisoner also learns that if he had friends of various races growing up, and he sees some of his friends of other races on the prison yard, he cannot be seen greeting them warmly or spending time with them. Prisoners become very aware, some tell me "hyperaware," of the race of everyone in their vicinity. As one relatively slight white male prisoner told me, "If you're white, you don't want to be caught in the area of the yard where blacks or Mexicans hang out. When trouble breaks out you want to be with your own kind." This is true whether or not the prisoner is gang affiliated. White prisoners in western states, for example, hang out near the Aryan Brotherhood, a notoriously racist gang whose members often have swastikas tattooed on their bodies. Prison yards are typically very segregated, with blacks in one area and whites in another, and in western states including California, Latinos are split between the area where the Norteños gather and that where the Sureños gather. Mexican American prisoners mill around near the gang of their geographic region even if they have nothing to do with gangs. If a melee breaks out, it will be between races or between the

Norteños and Sureños. Membership in the gang is not as important as a shared cultural identity.

A worrisome sidelight to and window into interracial frictions in prison was the plight of Irwin (not his actual name), a Jewish man I interviewed several years ago. He had been released from prison after serving over twenty years in some of the toughest maximum security prisons in the California Department of Corrections and Rehabilitation. During the years Irwin spent "inside," beginning in 1980, conditions were very harsh in California's overcrowded prisons: gymnasiums had to be converted into dormitories housing two hundred prisoners, crowding made for disturbingly loud noise, and there was widespread racial conflict. Irwin was Jewish, and there were prison gangs that stigmatized and assaulted Jews. As soon as he walked onto a large recreation yard in the Reception Unit, a young neo-Nazi came up to him and told him he hated Jews. At one prison, an older facility that housed thousands of prisoners in rows of forty cells stacked four high and sharing a common air space, a prominent gang identified as Nazi, and its members openly expressed their hatred of Jews. There were violent incidents. The white prisoners were controlled by this "skinhead," anti-Semitic gang. When Irwin looked around the large recreation yard, he saw black prisoners grouped on one side of the yard, Latinos on another side, and white prisoners in an area where the neo-Nazi gang enjoyed a certain level of authority. Fearing for his life, he stayed in his cell as much as he could and did not even go to shower for weeks at a time. Instead, he took "bird baths," using the sink in his cell to wash himself. The anti-Semitic gang ordered other prisoners not to talk to him. In the large dining hall, which was also very segregated by race, if he sat down with some white prisoners the neo-Nazi gang members would come over and tell the others they could not sit with him because he was a Jew. He was jumped by other prisoners on multiple occasions and had to fight to protect his honor and his reputation. Other prisoners hassled his cellmate for celling with him and pressured his cellmate to fight him, so the cellmate started challenging him. A vicious fight ensued. The two men fought in their cell, neither would "snitch" to officers about who started the fight, and both were punished with months of solitary confinement for fighting. Racial animosities were high during Irwin's entire tenure in prison, and much of the violence was along racial lines. He felt he was always in grave danger because he was persecuted by the gang who controlled the white prisoners but he could not seek support from African American or Latino prisoners. So he literally had nobody to turn to.

As I mentioned in chapter 1, "lockdowns" are another form of punishment that can be put into use entirely on the basis of race. If a Mexican American prisoner is murdered on the prison yard, and various informants report the perpetrator was Mexican American, then the cellblocks where both Sureños and Norteños are consigned will be "locked down," meaning everyone remains in their cells twenty-four hours per day until the authorities figure out who perpetrated the murder and whether it is safe to end the lockdown. Or a deadly fight involves a black and a white prisoner and the black and the white cellblocks are locked down. These lockdowns can last many months. A few years ago, the mainly Mexican American cellblocks at California's Folsom Prison were locked down for over eight months.

Prison authorities do not deny that the lockdowns are racially based. For example, in 2003 and 2004 at the High Desert State Prison, a maximum security facility in Susanville, California, all black prisoners had been locked down following an unsolved assault on an officer, presumably by a black prisoner. The prisoner plaintiffs in a subsequent class action lawsuit claimed that the lockdown of cell blocks by race violated the Civil Rights Act as well as the Constitution. In a hearing to establish the facts, federal circuit judge Marsha S. Berzon had confronted the attorney for the California Department of Corrections and Rehabilitation. As journalist Danny Walsh recorded the scene, Judge Berzon "repeatedly demanded that Deputy Attorney General John Riches II explain the actions of the prison officials." She noted that the CDCR had taken the position that "we locked down black people because they were black."

"Yes," the deputy attorney general replied. "Because the blacks were the ones [who were] creating the security risk."

"That—I mean—that is just a flatly racist statement," Berzon retorted.

"Of course it is," Riches said. "This was a race-based security decision."

The panel of federal judges ruled that targeting of black prisoners in this way constituted racial discrimination, and they ruled for the prisoner plaintiffs in the case.

What goes on in our prisons is a window into our larger social arrangements. And racism is not the same in all eras. The enslavement of African Americans based on the color of their skin is no longer legal, and Jim Crow laws and racial segregation have been deemed unconstitutional, But racism in America continues to mutate into new forms. As Michelle Alexander argues so forcefully, racial inequities of our criminal justice system are the contemporary version of a society-wide racial caste system.

Public attention is all too rare or too brief when white officers set up gladiator fights between prisoners of color and murder more than a few. And if even these events do not spark public outrage, how much will anyone care about the injustice of relegating so many African American and Latino prisoners to solitary confinement where there is no rehabilitation, while at the same time placing more white prisoners in rehabilitation and mental health treatment programs? It is time for the public to pay much closer attention to the racial drama being played out in horrifying ways in the American criminal justice system, and by extension, in our society at large.

PART TWO

The Human Damage

FOUR

The Decimation of Life Skills

THE DECIMATION OF LIFE SKILLS involves the systematic obliteration of the capacity to love, work, and play.[1] These are the three realms that Freud related to psychological function and disability. When rehabilitation programs do exist within a prison, ideally, though without explicitly mentioning the link, they attempt to address prisoners' functioning in all three of these realms. For example, the ability to sustain quality social relationships (love) is supported by group therapy, classes on anger management or parenting skills, and substance abuse treatment and recovery programs.[2] Programs focused on educational opportunities, job training, and skills development, along with cultural and athletic pursuits, foster prisoners' work skills and nurture a capacity for pleasure in both work and recreation. In stark contrast to these efforts to support prisoners' psychological health, prisoners in solitary confinement receive none of the above. Isolated prisoners are denied social interactions and receive no training aimed at improving their capacity to relate intimately and socially to others. They are barred from all activities related to any kind of work—indeed, any growth in productivity or work skills is stunted as prisoners remain idle for twenty-three hours a day, day in and day out. Solitary confinement, on average, inflicts an emotional flatness and total absence of vitality that not only does not improve but severely impairs prisoners' capacity for normal human functioning.

In this chapter I will look at the decimation of life skills in relatively stable individuals. (Of course, where there is serious mental illness the decimation of life skills becomes even more dire, but I will leave the topic of prisoners with serious mental illness to chapter 5.) I will address first the damaging effects of solitary confinement generally and then, more specifically, the damage wrought in a smaller subgroup of prisoners who spend more than a decade, sometimes several decades, in solitary.

Confinement for more than two months in an isolated unit such as a super-maximum facility is well known to cause severe psychiatric morbidity, disability, suffering, and mortality.[3] For hundreds of years, it has been known that human beings suffer substantial physical and mental deterioration when they remain in solitary for a significant length of time. And reams of psychiatric and psychological research over the last four decades have confirmed over and over the same broad patterns of psychological harm. Indeed, in a 2005 amicus brief submitted to the Supreme Court and following a rigorous review of the extant research literature on supermax confinement, a group of widely recognized experts on solitary confinement concluded: "No study of the effects of solitary or supermax-like confinement that lasted longer than 60 days failed to find evidence of negative psychological effects."[4]

Pioneering research by Hans Toch in the mid-1970s identified, from in-depth interviews with prisoners in New York state facilities, an emerging cluster of symptoms that he called "isolation panic": building physiological and psychic tension that led to panic and rage, loss of control, psychological regression and breakdown, and incidents of self-mutilation.[5] Later, in the early 1990s, Craig Haney, a social psychologist, began documenting the prevalence of severely detrimental effects of isolation on a randomly selected group of prisoners housed in Pelican Bay State Prison, a supermax facility that had opened in 1989. (At the time of his interviews, prisoners had been in isolation for no more than four years.)[6] More than 80 percent of the prisoners Haney evaluated developed or had worsening conditions of overwhelming anxiety and nervousness, regular headaches, severe insomnia, and chronic lethargy and tiredness. Over half complained of having persistent nightmares, heart palpitations, and fear of impending nervous breakdowns. Equally high numbers of prisoners reported an inability to break out of obsessive ruminations, confused thought processes, an oversensitivity to stimuli, irrational anger, and increasing fears of any kind of interaction with other people. And the list goes on: more than half of the prisoners reported violent fantasies, emotional flatness, mood swings, chronic depression, and sensations of overall deterioration, while nearly half reported hallucinations and perceptual distortions and a quarter reported thoughts of suicide.[7]

Similar findings emerged from the research of the psychiatrist Stuart Grassian, who in the 1980s began studying the experience of prisoners in solitary at the maximum security state penitentiary in Walpole, Massachusetts.[8] He described a particular set of symptoms resulting from the deprivation of social, perceptual, and occupational stimulation in solitary confinement and argued that they constituted a major, clinically distinguishable psychiatric syndrome that could have the features of a delirium and among the more vulnerable population could result in an acute agitated psychosis and random violence—often directed towards the staff, or directed inward and resulting in self-harm and suicide. Grassian also demonstrated in numerous cases that the prisoners who end up in solitary confinement are generally not, as claimed, "the worst of the worst"; they are, instead, the sickest, most emotionally labile, impulse-ridden, and psychiatrically vulnerable among the prison population.

Two-thirds of the prisoners Grassian initially studied had become hypersensitive to external stimuli (noises, smells, etc.) and about the same number experienced "massive free floating anxiety." About half of the prisoners suffered from perceptual disturbances that for some included hallucinations and perceptual illusions, and another half complained of cognitive difficulties such as confusional states, difficulty concentrating, and memory lapses. About a third also described thought disturbances such as paranoia, aggressive fantasies, and impulse control problems. One in five had cut themselves in suicide attempts while in isolation. In almost all instances, Grassian noted, the prisoners had not experienced any of these psychiatric reactions before being placed in solitary.

It is important to note that the psychological changes I am discussing, like the ongoing symptoms of posttraumatic stress disorder (PTSD), have biological correlates.[9] There has been much press coverage of American soldiers returning home after losing a leg or witnessing at close hand the death of a buddy in battle, and experiencing severe symptoms including debilitating flashbacks, nightmares, and panic attacks. Prisoners who have witnessed murders behind bars or have been the victim of prison rape evince similar symptoms. With severe trauma, the adrenal gland secretes adrenaline and cortisol. When high levels of adrenaline and cortisol flow through the body often or continuously, physical changes take place in the brain. Receptors on the neurons become less sensitive (in technical terms, they "down-regulate") to avoid being overwhelmed by the stimulation. Certain pathways in the brain are created and strengthened: for example, with persistent anger and anxiety there are changes in the temporal lobe of the brain and the limbic system, the brain sites associated with strong emotional experiences. These changes in brain chemistry, neuron sensitivity, and brain transmission pathways can actually be seen with brain imaging procedures such as positron emission tomography (the PET scan). Thus we know from clinical and laboratory studies, and it is well documented in the clinical literature, that PTSD and other psychiatric disorders are accompanied by very significant physical alterations in the brain.

It is likely that the stresses and privations of long-term solitary confinement cause similar changes, though we have no brain imaging studies on prisoners because resistance to research from correctional authorities as well as a history of abusive and coercive medical experimentation in prisons has led to bans on the use of prisoners in medical research.[10] There are observable changes in the electroencephalograms (EEGs, recorded by an instrument that measures brain waves) of individuals who have been in isolation for any length of time.[11] And animal studies are suggestive: for example, researchers have demonstrated changes in myelination in the frontal cortex of mice that were isolated for two weeks immediately after weaning.[12] (Myelin sheaths surround the axons of cells in the brain, and the frontal cortex is the site of advanced mental functions including cognition and judgment, so alterations of the process of myelination will almost certainly have profound effects on mental functioning. The discovery of these changes in mice suggests that comparable changes occur in humans.) Further, according to the neuroscientist Huda Akil, though we cannot study brain changes from solitary confinement directly, there is ample research on various factors involved in solitary confinement—the lack of physical interaction with the natural world, the lack of social interaction, and the lack of touch and visual stimulation—to show that each of these factors "by itself is sufficient to dramatically change the brain." For example, the brain is "an organ of social function. [It] needs to interact in the world." Without social contact, stress hormones keep building to such a duration and intensity that they can "actually shrink" parts of the brain such as the hippocampus, which governs memory, control of emotion, and spatial orientation.[13]

More research is needed regarding the psychological and physiological effects of solitary confinement. But a problem with research inside correctional facilities is that departments of correction are generally very averse to giving researchers access to prisoners. That is at least in part because the prison system wants to protect itself from outside interference in its operations and to hide from public awareness unacceptable occurrences—such as the use of excessive force by custody staff or the preventable deaths of incarcerated individuals. As a result, the majority of the research that is conducted inside the prisons tends to be only the kind that has the seal of approval from the relevant department of corrections. For example, the Colorado Department of Corrections released a widely criticized report of research on the psychiatric effects of supermax confinement, concluding essentially that long-term isolation in a supermax unit has no more harmful effects than maximum security imprisonment for the same period of time.[14] But numerous sociologists and psychiatrists—including myself—have responded to that report, pointing out that it utilized a grossly flawed methodology, that the researchers did not even conduct examinations of the prisoners in person (or even talk to them), and that the actual data derived during the study, if properly interpreted, should have led to an opposite conclusion from that proposed by the researchers—namely that long-term supermax confinement does indeed cause significant emotional harm and exacerbate mental illness.[15]

It is predictable that prisoners' mental state deteriorates in isolation. Human beings require at least some social interaction and productive activities to establish and sustain a sense of identity and to maintain a grasp on reality. In the absence of social interactions, unrealistic ruminations and beliefs cannot be tested in conversation with others, so they build up inside and are transformed into unfocused and irrational thoughts. Disorganized behaviors emerge. Internal impulses linked with anger, fear, and other strong emotions grow to overwhelming proportions. Sensory deprivation is not total in supermax units: prisoners can hear the intermittent slamming of steel doors as well as yelling (one has to yell in order to be heard by anyone from within one's cell). But such noise does not constitute meaningful human communication. Prisoners in this kind of segregation do what they can to cope. Many pace relentlessly to relieve the emotional tension. Those who can read books and write letters do so. But most report problems with memory and concentration. Cesar Villa, a fifty-five-year-old Latino man who had been in the SHU at Pelican Bay State Prison for fifteen years, writes: "In the SHU you're lucky to form a single thought at all. That's why I keep notes for everything. Notes on colors, names, words that look confusing, emotions, social protocol (should I ever meet another human being, I'd like to be ready)."[16]

Paranoia is a frequently reported symptom of long-term solitary confinement. Even prisoners who are relatively stable in terms of their general mental health report feeling paranoid. They hear ambiguous noises and panic out of fear that they are going to be attacked. Or they have great difficulty trusting anyone. Paranoia is difficult to dispel when one's circumstances render one unable to "reality-test" paranoid ideas. We all become momentarily paranoid in one circumstance or another, though we rarely apply that term to the experiences. For example, I leave a phone message for a friend and do not hear back from him for a week. I assume he is mad at me or does not like me. Then I run into him at the market and he apologizes for not returning my call, explaining that he has been ill and not attending to phone messages all week. I think to myself that I was being paranoid to attribute his lack of response to anger or dislike. Or I enter a room and see two people talking quietly near the far wall, as if sharing secrets. I suddenly think to myself they are saying negative things about me. But as I approach them, they turn to me and say, "Hi Terry" in a friendly tone, and it is clear that they were not discussing me. I think to myself, "I was being paranoid."

Most people have moments when they irrationally fear harm from others, only to find that the motives of the others were actually friendly. "I was being paranoid," we say to ourselves after discovering we were wrong about a negative thought that we had harbored minutes before. But in a prison cell, with no trustworthy person to check with, it is extremely difficult to reality-test paranoid ideas. For example, a prisoner in solitary confinement hears two officers talking loudly and laughing at the far end of the tier, but he cannot decipher what they are saying and assumes it is something negative about him. He gets frightened that they are about to enter his cell and beat him up. There is nobody he can talk to who can help him decide if he is being paranoid, so he experiences a burst of anxiety and files the thought in his memory. A little later, an officer yells at him for no apparent reason and he guesses that this must be further evidence he is disliked and about to be attacked by officers. I come to interview him a little while later and he looks very anxious as he reports that officers on the unit are out to get him, and I can see how the paranoia has been building in him.

Many prisoners who have spent years in solitary also report to me that the anger they feel all the time keeps building in intensity, and they worry that they will lose control of it and get in more trouble. They lose a lot of sleep on account of that anxiety. In fact, if one is in solitary, losing one's temper with an officer will likely lead to a write-up for a disciplinary infraction, and a frequent punishment meted out by hearing officers for talking back to or disrespecting an officer is a longer stint in solitary confinement.

The emotional harm is made even worse by sleep deprivation, which is a frequent occurrence in isolated confinement. There are noises at night as other prisoners, such as those suffering from serious mental illness, cry out. Then, besides the slamming of doors, officers yell out orders on the cellblock or pod. The lights are usually on all night. Prisoners from around the country tell me that for these and other reasons it is very difficult to sleep in supermax units. Loss of sleep intensifies psychiatric symptoms by interfering with the normal diurnal rhythm (the steady alternation of day and night that provides human beings with orientation as to time), and the sleep loss creates fatigue and magnifies cognitive problems, memory deficits, confusion, and sluggishness. It also amplifies anxiety: for many prisoners, the slamming of doors wakes them with the fear that someone will come into their cell and attack them.

TRAPPED FOR OVER A DECADE IN SOLITARY

In 2013 I was asked by attorneys representing prisoners in the *Ashker v. Brown* class action lawsuit to investigate the effects of very long-term solitary confinement (over a decade) upon prisoners who did not exhibit an obvious serious mental illness.[17] George Ruiz, whose story I reported in chapter 2, was among the ten named plaintiffs. The *Ashker v. Brown* class action litigation was unprecedented. The prisoners who were complaining that they were being subjected to cruel and unusual punishment were not "special-needs" prisoners: in other words, they were not suffering from serious mental illness and they were not juveniles. Rather, they were alleged to be gang members or gang affiliated, and that had been the justification for keeping them locked in solitary for decades. The Center for Constitutional Rights and collaborating attorneys took the case for the prisoner plaintiffs.

My interviews with the ten named plaintiffs occurred in a noncontact visiting room in the SHU at Pelican Bay State Prison, a space stripped of all physical reminders of the exterior world. There were no windows, no natural light, and no wall decorations; the temperature was chilly and the entire scene sterile. There was a small cubicle on each side of a thick pane of Lexan (shatter-proof plexiglass) between the visitor and the prisoner, and a phone on both sides of the "glass" that permitted conversation. The prisoner was brought in wearing handcuffs and ankle cuffs, the hardware was removed by the accompanying officer, the prisoner sat on a stool bolted to the floor, and I sat on a chair on the other side of the glass. Conversations began slowly with the legal purpose of my visit and my disclosure that our conversation would not be confidential and that instead I planned to tell the prisoners' stories in my report for the lawsuit. The men all complained of feeling very sad that they'd had no physical contact for many years with any human being other than the officer gruffly accompanying them, not even a handshake, and of course that lack continued through our meeting. The closest thing to physical contact that I could offer was my palm against the Lexan window to meet the palm they offered from the other side as we parted.

All of the prisoners I interviewed for the lawsuit had been in the SHU for over ten years, some since the opening of Pelican Bay in 1989, and many had already been in segregation at another facility for some time prior to their transfer to the SHU at Pelican Bay. What I found over the course of my interviews was more or less what I had discovered in examinations of other prisoners in their situation. The symptoms they reported matched those already on the long list associated with SHU confinement, including anxiety and hyperalertness, startle responses (e.g., jumping when they heard a door open because of fear that someone would "come in on them"), severe chronic insomnia, memory and concentration problems, paranoid ideas, compulsive activities such as pacing or repeatedly cleaning their cells, and severe despair. They also universally complained that they felt especially lonely because they had little or no contact with family and loved ones on account of the distance from their home plus very restrictive visiting policies, and because they were not permitted phone calls.[18]

All of the prisoners complained that their despair was worsened greatly by their recognition that the only ways to get out of SHU were to "snitch, parole, or die."[19] As explained in chapter 2, the California Department of Corrections and Rehabilitation required that alleged members and affiliates of prison gangs be sent to solitary confinement for an indeterminate term, from which they could win release only by "debriefing," or informing on other gang members—a move that not only was prohibited by the prisoners' unwritten honor code but could get the informer killed once he was released.

Parole was the second possible route to release from SHU. If the prisoner in SHU completed his prison sentence, he would be paroled and released from prison altogether. And the third possibility was to die. All the prisoners I interviewed in the SHU told me they were convinced they would die there, since they refused to snitch, and they would never be granted parole while locked in SHU because the parole board would want them to demonstrate good behavior in general population as well as the completion with good marks of rehabilitation programs not available in SHU.

As noted earlier, it is impossible to deprive a prisoner of all social contact, even in solitary. In some units, prisoners can communicate with others on their block by banging or shouting. In some, prisoners are double-celled. But even when prisoners in SHU have some limited opportunities to talk to staff or other prisoners such as a cellmate, they gradually talk less and less. There are several reasons for this. Some prisoners speak of how the constant staff pressure to "debrief" makes it difficult for them to really trust their neighbors. They believe that what they say could be distorted and reported to staff during the debriefing procedure by someone who decided to inform, and they are afraid that if they say the wrong thing to someone they will be revalidated (a renewed determination will be made that they are gang affiliated) or they will suffer some kind of retaliation. Others say they don't talk much because they have nobody of their own race on the pod, and still others because living so close together makes tempers flare and they would rather not have enemies.

The anger characteristic of all prisoners in solitary confinement was intensified among prisoners in very long-term confinement because of the hopelessness they felt about ever being released. As Todd Ashker described it, "I'm locked in a cell, powerless, I have to rely on these people [staff] for everything, and they treat me as less than human. As soon as you realize that this will never end, and that you are stuck being at the mercy of staff who hate you, then you become more depressed, hopeless, and angry." But after a long period of isolated confinement prisoners have learned to keep their anger to themselves, and they make a constant effort to control it by suppressing it. Part of this effort involves keeping quiet about their feelings and not talking very much to others, whether staff or other prisoners. They isolate themselves more and more, even within the context of SHU confinement. The effort is exhausting: as one prisoner put it, "I am so busy suppressing feelings and isolating myself all day, and so much anger builds up in me from the conditions, and then I can't sleep at night." Prisoners' extreme guardedness in speaking makes any conversations that they do have seem trivial, and speaking comes to seem so pointless that they may give up talking altogether. Eventually they become so successful in suppressing their feelings that they do not even know what they are feeling, and as a result they feel numb or dead. Deprived of connection, they experience what the philosopher Lisa Guenther has described as a form of social death:

> Social death is less a matter of being denied the natural rights and freedoms of an individual than of being isolated in one's individuality, confined to one's separate existence and blocked from a meaningful sense of belonging to a community that is greater than oneself. Without a living relation to past

and future generations, who am I? Do I still have a stake in historical time? If the meaning of my life is confined to my biological existence, then it amounts to almost nothing; one swift blow to the head, and it could all be over.[20]

Over and above those symptoms, the men I interviewed reported that they felt more and more that there was no use doing anything because nothing would ever change. So they shut down and became quite unmotivated to do anything (the memory loss and concentration problems contributed to this phenomenon). They grew listless and increasingly lacking in initiative to do anything, even exercise. (Some of the prisoners described this state as depression, some as deadness.) Spending endless hours silent and alone, entirely out of touch with how they felt, they began to feel unreal and nonhuman.

I have conducted over a thousand interviews with prisoners in a variety of correctional settings, and I have never before found a pattern at this level of specificity described so universally by a group of similarly situated individuals. These men were very disabled, but their disability was not readily apparent because, after all, they were living in a cell and meals were brought to them in their cell. Only upon release to the general prison population or the larger society can others see the profound damage that isolation does to prisoners' capacity for connection and general life functioning, as I will explore in chapter 8.

The physician and prison reform activist Corey Weinstein has frankly described how "organizations doing relief work with the homeless report psychiatrically disabled parolees from the SHUs living on the streets in a confused and disorganized state. Prisoners released from long-term SHU confinement describe problems with socialization and impulse control. Prisoners who fit this general description will be less able to get along and seek employment than they were when they went into prison, they will become a burden on families and communities already suffering from lack of resources, jobs, and social services."[21] Consequently, as research has repeatedly shown, long-term solitary confinement makes postrelease adjustment difficult to impossible and drives up recidivism rates.[22]

When required in court to identify the causes of the decimation of life skills, I explain that it has multiple causes, including the experience of being incarcerated and the constant threat of assault in prison, but that the most significant cause by far is long stints in solitary confinement. Attorneys for the state jump in at this point and ask, "What percentages of the cause would you assign to incarceration itself, to specific traumas, and to solitary confinement?" I cannot assign a precise proportion of the harm to each factor because it varies in individual cases. But I can say, to a reasonable degree of medical certainty, that time in solitary is a major part of the cause. The longer one spends idle in a cell by oneself, the more one's skills for living in the community disappear, the more impaired one's capacity to love, work, and play. It is predictable that prisoners' capacity to function deteriorates in isolation even if they do not suffer from a diagnosable mental illness. Since 93 percent of prisoners will eventually reenter the community, it is important that we consider the long-term consequences of their spending significant stints in solitary confinement. By now large numbers of ex-prisoners who spent long periods in solitary confinement have returned to the community, and too many feel they are not fully alive. Sociologist Todd Clear has studied how high incarceration rates damage entire communities in terms of broken families, weaker economies, distorted politics, and increased crime.[23] High rates of *solitary* incarceration damage communities and families even more.

I am very concerned about the ex-prisoner in the community who is house-bound to a greater extent than he would like, feels anxious when he leaves the house, feels disconnected from his body, eats nervously to excess and gains weight, uses alcohol or illicit substances to deaden the physical and psychic pain, lives alone or with family but with minimal contact with people outside the small number he lives with, does not date or, if in an intimate relationship, has trouble sharing feelings and inner experiences, has low energy, has no particular initiative to do anything, and feels sad or depressed much of the time. I have consistently found that ex-prisoners who spent a significant time in solitary confinement have more serious problems of this kind than do ex-prisoners who never spent much time in solitary. The decimation of life skills is a very real phenomenon that causes immense pain, suffering and disability, even when there is no official serious mental illness to diagnose.

WHEN DOES IT BECOME TORTURE?

There has been robust international debate about how to define torture, as was instanced by advocacy in George W. Bush's administration for "torture lite" measures such as stress positions, waterboarding, and sleep deprivation that are not visibly gruesome or mutilating. By the definition of the United Nations Torture Convention of 1984, however, torture is "any act by which severe pain or suffering, whether physical or mental, is intentionally inflicted on a person for such purposes as obtaining from him or a third person information or a confession, punishing him for an act he or a third person has committed or is suspected of having committed, or intimidating or coercing him or a third person, or for any reason based on discrimination of any kind, when such pain or suffering is inflicted by or at the instigation of or with the consent or acquiescence of a public official or other person acting in an official capacity."[24] Similarly, Article 2 of the Inter-American Convention to Prevent and Punish Torture states:

> For the purposes of this Convention, torture shall be understood to be any act intentionally performed whereby physical or mental pain or suffering is inflicted on a person for purposes of criminal investigation, as a means of intimidation, as personal punishment, as a preventive measure, as a penalty, or for any other purpose. Torture shall also be understood to be the use of methods upon a person intended to obliterate the personality of the victim or to diminish his physical or mental capacities, even if they do not cause physical pain or mental anguish. The concept of torture shall not include physical or mental pain or suffering that is inherent in or solely the consequence of lawful measures, provided that they do not include the performance of the acts or use of the methods referred to in this article.[25]

Following revelations about the abuses carried out by the US military at Abu Ghraib, I was interviewed by journalists a number of times about possible parallels between the shocking abuses at Abu Ghraib and at Guantanamo and the everyday realities of American prisons.[26] Of course there are parallels: the stripping naked, the threats of great bodily harm, the purposeful humiliations, the central aim of terrorizing captives and breaking their will to withhold information or to resist any command from their captors. An example of the phenomenon is contained in my declaration as a psychiatric expert witness about unconstitutional conditions in supermaximum Unit 32, on Death Row at Mississippi State Penitentiary in Parchman.[27] I included this description of the special punishment to which Mr. Willie Russell, the lead plaintiff, had been subjected for two years:

> Willie Russell describes his experience being housed in Cell 225 for two years, one of four "punishment" cells on Death Row with plexiglass doors (covering the standard door). I have seen this kind of double door in super-maximum security units in other states. Once one is locked inside such a cell, the temperature and humidity begin to rise within minutes because the plexiglass (or Lexan, an indestructible form of plastic) retains the body heat and humidity

within the cell. The temperature rises rapidly, and life in the cell becomes unbearable. In the summer heat at Parchman, this one aspect of the punishment cells would make them entirely unacceptable by any standard of human decency or of health and mental health minimum standards. But in addition to this cruel and entirely excessive and punitive measure that clearly serves no legitimate penological objective, Mr. Russell reports that his cell is always filthy, the rain pours in through the walls onto his bed, the toilet floods the cell with backflow from other prisoners' toilets, there are bugs everywhere, the cell is filled with mosquitoes at night, he cannot sleep at night because the lights are on 24 hours per day, he is not permitted to have a fan, he is not permitted television or radio and there are no activities, and he is even more isolated than other prisoners on Death Row because the Lexan shield on his door makes it impossible for him to talk to anyone. For two years, he was permitted no mattress, no pillow and no sheets, and had only a blanket and the concrete for a bed. This kind of punitive deprivation and degradation is barbaric, and shocking to human sensibilities. It is the kind of cruel and unusual punishment that is well known to cause intense anxiety and rage, psychiatric breakdown, and in a large proportion of cases, suicide.

The plaintiff class prevailed in the Willie Russell class action, and conditions are much improved at Parchman today. This work is ongoing. But clearly the treatment of Mr. Russell constituted torture. Those who have spent a long time in a solitary confinement unit, much like those who have been tortured during war, suffer lasting damage and never make a complete recovery. In the big picture, the decimation of life skills, destroying a prisoner's ability to cope in the free world, is the worst thing solitary confinement does. In that process are all the elements of torture even without hoods, waterboarding, or electric wires. The clause in both the United Nations convention and the Inter-American Convention to Prevent and Punish Torture that "the concept of torture shall not include physical or mental pain or suffering that is inherent in or solely the consequence of lawful measures" is ambiguous. But the Inter-American Convention clarifies that ambiguity by adding: "provided that they do not include the performance of the acts or use of the methods referred to in this article." Presumably the exclusion clause for "lawful measures" is inserted to make an exception for the death penalty, presumably so that governments that advocate the death penalty and other lawful forms of "pain or suffering" will sign the convention.

In 2011 the UN's Human Rights Council on Torture and Other Cruel, Inhuman, or Degrading Treatment or Punishment concluded that any period of solitary confinement in excess of fifteen days is a human rights violation and that "the social isolation and sensory deprivation that is imposed by some States does, in some circumstances, amount to cruel, inhuman and degrading treatment and even torture."[28] On this point I am very much in agreement.

Dr. Almerindo Ojeda, human rights advocate and founding director of the University of California Davis Center for the Study of Human Rights in the Americas, distinguishes between an "extensional definition" of psychological torture, based simply on a set of practices, and an "intentional definition," which would declare these practices to be psychological torture only if certain criteria for the intentions of the perpetrators were met.[29] He says an extensional definition should be adequate: the perpetrators' intentions should not be required to meet specific conditions for psychological torture to be in evidence. The practices Dr. Ojeda lists in the extensional definition include isolation; deprivation of food, water, and sleep; spatial disorientation through confinement in small places with nonfunctional windows; temporal disorientation due to denial of natural light (and I would add a lack of clocks and watches); sensory deprivation or overstimulation; and induced desperation through indefinite detention or random placement.

Just about every practice that Dr. Ojeda lists is present in the supermaximum security units I have toured, though the entire list is not necessarily in evidence in each facility. For example, in supermaximum confinement units many prisoners experience induced desperation. They fear that they will never be released because the severe isolation stokes their anger about what they consider unfair and excessive punishment, and they are very aware of the fact that their anger will lead them to get into arguments with officers that will result in additional disciplinary write-ups or "tickets," and therefore additional time in isolation.

All of the men I interviewed at the SHU at Pelican Bay in 2012 and again in 2013 exhibited almost all of the characteristics that are described in the literature about survivors of torture, as described for settings other than prison isolation units. For example, the psychologist Rona Fields, who has researched torture in Northern Ireland and Portugal, provides a list of psychological consequences of torture including anxiety, fear, depression, irritability, introversion, difficulties in concentration, chronic fatigue, lethargy, restlessness, communication difficulties, especially in the expression of emotion, memory and concentration loss, loss of a sense of identity, insomnia, nightmares, hallucinations, visual disturbances, headaches, and suicidal crises.[30] This list is very similar to what I have observed in the occupants of supermax isolation cells.

Professional organizations in the United States, including the American Psychiatric Association, the American Public Health Association, and the American Academy of Child and Adolescent Psychiatry, have issued strong warnings about the human damage caused by prolonged isolation, especially for prisoners with mental illness and youth.[31] One US court, in the Walker case described in chapter 2, has gone so far as to call it torture:

> Our Constitution forbids correctional practices which permit prisons in the name of behavior modification to disregard the innate dignity of human beings, especially in the context where those persons suffer from serious mental illness. We cannot sanction correctional practices that ignore and exacerbate the plight of mentally ill inmates like Walker, especially when that inmate is forced to rely on the prison for his care and protection. The plain meaning of the dignity clause commands that the intrinsic worth and the basic humanity of persons may not be violated. Moreover, if the particular conditions of confinement cause serious mental illness to be greatly exacerbated or if it deprives inmates of their sanity, then prison officials have deprived inmates of the basic necessity for human existence and have crossed into the realm of psychological torture.[32]

International bodies have also strongly condemned the practice, as documented in the UN's Istanbul Statement and its Mandela Rules.[33] The massive amount of research supporting these conclusions just continues to grow.

FIVE

Adding Madness to the Mix

AN ALARMINGLY LARGE PROPORTION of prisoners consigned to super-maximum security isolation in recent decades suffer from serious mental illness. Two Canadian criminologists, Sheilagh Hudgins and Gilles Côté, reported in 1991 that 29 percent of prisoners in a large SHU suffered from severe mental disorders, notably schizophrenia, and a 2003 report on solitary confinement in New York State found that "fully one-quarter of the 5,000 prisoners in New York's SHUs suffered from serious mental illness."[1] Human Rights Watch has surveyed the depressing plight of the many prisoners with serious mental illness in solitary confinement.[2] I have reported my own findings from litigation-related investigations.[3] Meanwhile, it has been known for decades that while suicide is approximately twice as prevalent in prison as it is in the community, fully half of all successful suicides that occur in a correctional system involve the 3 to 8 percent of prisoners who are in some form of isolated confinement at any given time.[4]

It is by now clear that for prisoners prone to serious mental illness, time served in isolation exacerbates their mental illness and too often results in suicide. This is the main reason that federal courts have ruled that prisoners with serious mental illness must not be subjected to long-term isolation.[5] Federal judge Felton Henderson, ruling in *Madrid v. Gomez* regarding the SHU at Pelican Bay State Prison, wrote: "Many if not most, inmates in the SHU experience some degree of psychological trauma in reaction to their extreme social isolation and the severely restricted environmental stimulation in SHU."[6] Further, he asserted, "The conditions in the SHU may press the outer bounds of what most humans can psychologically tolerate."[7]

In court I argue that the harsh conditions of solitary confinement that cause severe psychiatric symptoms in previously healthy prisoners inevitably have a devastating effect on prisoners prone to mental illness. In far too many cases the effects include psychosis, mania, compulsive acts of self-abuse or suicide, and often some combination of the three.[8]

PSYCHOSIS

During my tours of supermax isolative confinement units in fifteen states, I have encountered the most severely decompensated and psychiatrically disabled individuals that I have seen anywhere else in my forty-year career as a psychiatrist (including state, county, and private psychiatric hospitals).

Many of the things we do to people in our prisons cause or exacerbate mental illness. Some of the ways madness is provoked and acted out in our prisons today are reminiscent of the asylums of the 1940s and 1950s, as portrayed by Olivia de Havilland in the 1948 film *Snake Pit*. In the asylum era, when individuals suffering from serious mental illness were confined in large public psychiatric hospitals, institutional dynamics came under the spotlight. Erving Goffman, Thomas Scheff, and other "sociologists of deviance" hypothesized that institutional dynamics played a big part in driving patients to regress into impotent and bizarre aggressive behaviors and in sidetracking clinicians into self-fulfilling biases in their diagnosing.[9]

Consider this hypothetical example of their theory: A young man who is different from other children—dresses eccentrically, is not proficient in social situations, and is likely to say things others view as "strange"—is brought to the asylum by family members who consider him "crazy." He protests loudly that he is not crazy and that in fact his parents who want him locked up are actually the crazy ones. The psychiatrist interprets his increasingly loud protests as signs of the very mental illness being ascribed to him. The young man is involuntarily admitted to the asylum. As he realizes he is being deprived of his freedom, his protests become louder and more desperate. The staff take his emotional protests as further evidence confirming the diagnosis of psychosis; he is placed on a locked ward and deprived of most familiar means of expressing himself. At some point he does something irrational such as throwing a chair through a window in order to express his outrage over being deprived of his freedom; the staff are even more convinced of his "madness" and lock him in an isolation room with no clothes and no pens or writing materials. Being even more incensed and more desperate to express himself, he smears feces on the wall of the isolation room and proceeds to write messages with his finger in the smears on the wall. Of course, Goffman and Scheff were very concerned about the self-fulfilling prophecy in the patient's escalation and the staff's diagnostic process, and they warned poignantly that incremental denial of freedom to individuals within "total institutions" (this term from sociology includes both asylums and prisons), whether they actually suffer from a bona fide mental illness or not, leads them inexorably into increasingly irrational and desperate attempts to maintain their dignity and express themselves.

In crowded correctional facilities, where rehabilitation programs are sparse and prisoners are relatively idle, the worst traumas and abuses are reserved for prisoners suffering from mental illness. It is not difficult to figure out the reasons for this unfortunate dynamic. For example, the slang term for prison rapist is *booty bandit*. Consider the booty bandit's options in selecting potential victims. He wants to choose his victim well: raping the wrong person, like a gang member, or even a prisoner with friends, might lead to lethal retaliation. But if he selects a prisoner with significant mental illness, a loner who is not likely to have friends who would retaliate, he is more likely to get away with the rape and avoid retaliation. For this and other reasons, prisoners with serious mental illness, especially if they are not provided a relatively safe and therapeutic treatment program, are routinely victimized by other prisoners.[10] In women's prisons, rape and sexual assaults are more often perpetrated by male staff, but women who have experienced earlier traumas and those suffering from mental illness are likewise singled out for victimization.[11] And of course the repeated traumas they are forced to endure in prison make prisoners' mental disorders and their prognoses far more dire. Then, whether to penalize them for fighting to avoid rape, or to protect them after they have reported a custodial sexual assault, they are relegated to solitary confinement.

To understand how isolation exacerbates psychosis, one need merely look at the symptoms that emerge in emotionally stable prisoners (like those described in the preceding chapter) and then consider how the same symptoms would affect someone suffering from serious mental illness or prone to a psychotic breakdown or suicidal crisis. The same stressors that lead relatively stable prisoners to feel angry and paranoid are very likely to push an individual prone to psychosis over the brink, with the result being an acute psychotic episode. Psychologists theorize that the ego (the reality-testing and administrative agency of the mind) of an individual prone to psychosis is relatively brittle and fragile, so that when the ego disintegrates under stress the individual becomes psychotic. According to that theory, mounting anger can precipitate a psychotic episode by overwhelming the fragile ego's capacity to cope, and as the anger mounts the individual's thoughts speed up and become ever more fragmented and irrational until a point of no return is reached when the individual becomes frankly psychotic.

I met Andrew (not his real name), a twenty-eight-year-old African American man in the supermaximum security unit of a large prison. The prisoners consigned there spent nearly twenty-four hours per day in a cell with fluorescent lights and no window to the outside. Andrew was clearly very angry as he entered the prisoner's side of the visiting booth where I was waiting to speak with him. The officers accompanying him removed his handcuffs and locked him into the booth, and we spoke on phones through a Lexan window. It took me some time to grasp what he was trying to tell me. His sentences were very abrupt and incomplete, and many lacked a subject or a predicate. He seemed unfocused in his speech, though I could detect fragments of explanations or reasons he felt so angry. He admitted that he was feeling paranoid, but he told me that he really could not be sure the guards were not poisoning him. The cold food in the solitary confinement unit tasted awful, several times he had found bugs in the meat, and he often felt sick to his stomach after eating a meal alone in his cell. He glared at me as he asked, "How can I be sure they're not trying to poison me?" After I explained to him that I was an expert witness in a class action lawsuit examining just the kind of issues he was talking about, he calmed down, becoming less angry and perhaps a little more coherent. He proceeded to tell me that he had had no emotional problems before being locked in solitary some months earlier. But immediately after they put him in his cell and closed the cell door his anger began to mount. He felt that the "ticket" (disciplinary write-up) that had led to his being punished with solitary confinement was entirely "bunk," but he was not permitted a fair hearing before being punished with administrative segregation. Then, the more angry he became about that, the more he found that his thinking became irrational. When an officer came by to deliver his food tray, he would get into an argument with him, and then the officer would give him an additional disciplinary write-up. Each time he received a ticket, he lost privileges and amenities. He lost the right to buy items from the commissary, he lost his time on the recreation yard, he lost the right to go to the library in the supermax unit, he lost the phone call he would have been permitted once per month. And each time officers gave him what he considered an unfair ticket, his anger mounted and his thoughts became more confused.

It was as if the anger and the irrational thoughts were spiraling together out of control while his ego was falling apart. There are other theories in psychology about the etiology of psychosis, but this general theory helps explain why individuals who are prone to paranoid psychosis so readily decompensate or break down in solitary confinement. In the prisoner prone to psychotic decompensation (this might be someone who has experienced psychotic breakdowns in the past, or someone like Andrew who has not yet suffered a first psychotic episode), the anger drives increasingly irrational thoughts, and eventually the person having the psychotic episode tries to organize his thoughts by constructing a delusional story about what is going on. The increasingly strained understandings devolve into paranoia. This is only one of many threads that intertwine in the evolution of psychosis in solitary confinement.

MANIA

Mania is a disorder of mood, in contrast with schizophrenia, a disorder of thought. Often there is no clear demarcation line between the thought disorder and the mood disorder and we speak of schizoaffective disorder or bipolar disorder with psychosis. Inappropriate or uncontrollable moods are the pathognomonic (singular and distinct diagnostic) sign of bipolar disorder, where mania resides at one end of a spectrum of moods and depression at the other end. Although additional studies are needed to provide the full range of statistics, I would confidently estimate that prisoners experiencing manic episodes have a very difficult time in prison. There is broad evidence to suggest that in a significant number of cases where disciplinary write-ups were issued for fighting or being too loud, the prisoner charged with the rule violation was actually in the throes of a manic mood swing when he got into trouble. While schizophrenia tends to have an unmistakable presentation, replete with hallucinations and delusions, mania can easily go unnoticed. And I do find many prisoners in solitary confinement whom I assess to be experiencing a manic mood swing. Imagine what it is like for someone who needs to stay active, move around, and utter uncensored thoughts to be locked into a prison cell nearly twenty-four hours per day. He or she would certainly tend to go crazy. Because the mood swing is not as obvious as hallucinations or bizarre behavior, prisoners who experience manic mood swings are typically considered "Bad" rather than "Mad," and they are overrepresented in solitary confinement units, just the places where they should never be sent.

While the statistics regarding suicide for prisoners in SHU are horrific, there is also an epidemic of nonsuicidal self-harm, such as "cutting" or swallowing sharp-edged objects, in prison isolation units. For example, in Texas solitary confinement units, while suicide is five times more likely than in the community, self-harm is a full eight times more likely than it is in the community outside prison.[12]

Psychiatrists can often tell the cutting is not suicidal because someone who is depressed and truly suicidal will say, after cutting him or herself, that she is so worthless she has failed even in the act of self-destruction, whereas someone who cuts himself for other reasons will say something like "I felt better after I saw the blood (or felt the pain), it reassured me that I am still alive." Staff tend to think prisoners committing nonsuicidal self-harm are manipulating to get out of isolation, but the tragic truth is that the acts are compelled to a great extent, not voluntary, and that they are a symptomatic response to the very high anxiety induced by the harsh conditions of solitary confinement. In other words, there may be some manipulation involved, and of course prisoners in solitary will do what they can to win their release, but still the prisoner who feels he has no other option short of cutting himself is very troubled and requires mental health treatment. And the first step in an effective mental health treatment intervention would be to remove the anxious, self-harming prisoner from isolation and then to explore the possibility that he or she is severely depressed or anxious or plagued by traumatic memories.

There is something of a "catch-22" involved in the aftermath of self-harm incidents in supermax isolation. In many cases, the cutting is driven by the anxiety that isolation and idleness create, so removing the individual from isolation—for example, by taking him to the doctor in the infirmary to have the lacerations sutured—probably will result in a momentary reduction in the anxiety and need to cut. The doctor will likely see a calmer prisoner and tend to agree with officers that the self-harm was a manipulation to get out of solitary. But then, after the doctor orders that the man be sent back to his isolation cell, the anxiety mounts once again and there are further incidents of cutting.

I am frequently asked whether prisoners with serious mental illness are selectively consigned to SHU, or whether the harsh isolative conditions trigger the psychotic, manic, or self-harming or suicidal response. The answer, of course, is both. Prisoners with serious mental illness often present a management problem. They disobey rules—for example, a rule against walking across a certain patch of grass or a rule against talking while waiting in line, or they talk back to officers or get into fights. And staff do disproportionately send them to segregation, in many cases because staff do not know what else to do with them. But even if they were not evidencing acute psychosis or a suicidal crisis before they were transferred to SHU, the harsh conditions have an especially toxic effect on these vulnerable prisoners.

Between the 1970s and the second decade of the new millennium, while the prison population was growing exponentially, the proportion of prisoners suffering from serious mental illness was also expanding. Today, according to a recent study, there are ten times as many individuals suffering from serious mental illness in our jails and prisons as there are in our psychiatric hospitals.[13] I have spent my entire career explaining how the things that are done to people in prison make their mental illness much worse. Crowding in prisons, victimization, a lack of meaningful rehabilitation programs, and long stints in solitary confinement all exacerbate whatever mental illness is already apparent, and in very many cases the crowding, forced isolation, and idleness cause psychiatric breakdowns and disability even in prisoners who had no previous history of mental illness. Two case examples might be instructive.

Bill

The case of Bill (not his real name), a fifty-seven-year-old African American man who has been in prison in the Midwest since the early 1990s, illustrates how drastically an individual's mental state can deteriorate with harsh prison conditions and with prison authorities' narrowly punitive and symptom-suppressing approaches to the behaviors that predictably result from that deterioration. Bill was not psychotic or bipolar when he entered prison in his late twenties, according to intake assessments. But by 1996 he was so manic and psychotic that the medical staff treated him with an antipsychotic medi-

cation, and he has been on enforced medication orders (equivalent to medi-
cation-over-objection) ever since, and at very high doses. His clinical chart
indicates that he is being given an involuntary intramuscular injection containing 275 mg of Haldol Decanoate (an oil-immersed antipsychotic medication; the oil makes its effect last longer) every four weeks. That dose of Haldol
can have serious side effects, but he has been prescribed even higher doses in
the past. When Bill becomes manic, he becomes psychotic. He also becomes
paranoid and assaultive. On several occasions he has assaulted officers, and of
course he has been punished with more time in solitary confinement. He has
been alone in a cell in segregation for most of the two decades he has been
behind bars.

Bill is someone who should never be left alone in a cell nearly twenty-four
hours per day. He seems to assault officers only when he is in the throes of an
acute manic and psychotic episode. I cannot tell from chart notes whether
mental health staff believe that Bill's assaults are ordered by command hallucinations (imagined voices telling him to assault the officer), or driven by
his paranoia, or driven by the strong feeling that the officers are treating him
unfairly. In any case, the symptoms of his mental illness increase his physical
energy level. Agitation, mania, rapid speech, impulsive action, hyperactivity,
rage, and other high-energy states are recorded in the mental health notes
over many years. Mounting anger is one of the most frequent symptoms
reported by relatively stable prisoners in solitary confinement, but in a prisoner with serious mental illness where rage is a symptom in any setting, solitary confinement obviously exacerbates the psychiatric condition and the
risks that he poses to himself and to others. With a person like Bill, whose
psychosis worsens when he is manic and angry, placing him in an isolative
environment literally supercharges his psychosis and rage, while—in the
cruel irony typical of solitary confinement—it is his psychosis and uncon-
trolled rage that are the problem behaviors for which he is being retained in
isolation. He literally bounces off the walls, even with the extraordinary
doses of psychotropic medications. And there has been a pattern of progressively increasing dosages of enforced antipsychotic medication while he has
been in solitary confinement. Antipsychotic medications are sedating, and it
is likely that the mental health staff kept increasing the medication dosage to
suppress his agitated, irrational, and assaultive behavior. But medications
alone do not constitute adequate psychiatric treatment, and the isolation
clearly makes his condition and prognosis worse. Indeed, I can say to a reasonable degree of medical certainty that his psychotic and manic condition

has been exacerbated severely by the very long time he has spent in solitary confinement. Yet he is never admitted to a psychiatric inpatient unit, where he needs to be when he is acutely psychotic and manic.

Mental health staff visit Bill in SHU, mainly at cell-front during weekly rounds. Bill refuses to cooperate with the visits, so they last only a few minutes, and with no confidentiality or privacy during a "cell-front interview," probably little clinical information is gleaned except that he appears irrational and manic and is badly soiling his cell. Of course security is an issue, and he can be dangerous. But mental health units, both inpatient and intermediate care units, have to include adequate security staff and precautions.

Even on the very high dosage of enforced medication, he was recently reported to be smearing feces in his cell and talking irrationally. His declining mental state over many years is evidence that isolation, even with very high dosages of involuntary antipsychotic medication, has a toxic effect on him. But the staff consider him very dangerous and keep him in the circumstances that worsen his psychiatric condition, with sedating doses of medication being the only treatment intervention. High doses of Haldol over many years cause very serious side effects and can cause death. This is entirely unacceptable treatment and violates all standards of mental health care as well as human decency. But the real tragedy is that Bill's social skills and capacity to function have been decimated by the years he has spent in solitary confinement.

Gene

Several years ago, during a tour of a supermax prison, I met one of the most severely disturbed individuals I have encountered in the entire course of my career. Because of confidentiality, I cannot use his full name or the name of the prison, and I will refer to him here as Gene.

I interviewed Gene in an office on a pod of the state's supermax facility. This engaging middle-aged African American man in dull tan prison garb exhibited a silly smile almost constantly during our interviews, frequently when smiling was quite inappropriate. He told me that he had many siblings, his father had been abusive, and his mother had been murdered when he was nineteen. He had been in several psychiatric hospitals before coming to prison and he had taken strong antipsychotic medications, which caused muscle clenching (a side effect of antipsychotic medications is extra-pyramidal syndrome or EPS, which includes muscle clenching) but did lessen his emotional symptoms. When I asked Gene how he spent his days, he reported that he paced all day and did not talk to anyone. He rarely went to recreation (the prison logs indicated that he was in recreation barely one or two hours per week). He admitted to cutting himself repeatedly, using pieces of metal he would break off his metal bedpost or the heater vent in his cell. On multiple occasions he intentionally set his cell on fire and smeared feces over his body and on the wall of his cell. He admitted with some embarrassment that he was always doing these bizarre things in response to voices in his head commanding him to do so. Over the course of our conversation, Gene repeatedly insisted that we return to the topic of the poisoning he believed was going on through his food and pills. He described "extreme" bodily reactions to the poisoning, including very bad abdominal pain and pain in his heart. He claimed that the warden and the nurses were the ones trying to poison him, but when I asked why they would do that he said he could not explain it. He said that he would cut himself after seeing spirits outside the window or hearing voices telling him to cut himself.

Gene explained to me the act of smearing feces: "I was under so much pressure, staff talk bad to me, write tickets, they talk mean to me, some guys cut off their penis, so I smeared feces." He displayed the scars on his legs where he had cut himself and said, "I knew I had to do more to protest the poisoning and torture." He believed the poison also made him do things that he did not want to do and that got him in trouble. In response to a question whether he was afraid, he responded: "Yeah, I don't have fear, on certain things I go too far, people are scared to talk to me because they've heard all this stuff." He contrasted the pod where I found him, a special behavioral treatment unit, where "[the prisoners] don't scream, they don't cut, they don't kick on doors," with the high-security unit he had been on until he was transferred, where "they do cut, scream, and kick on doors." When I asked him why he had set fire to his cell a while back, he first seemed surprised that I asked; then he replied, "I'm hyper," and proceeded to go off on a tangent about his childhood. I asked him if he was angry and he said "Sometimes." "Sometimes I'm just having fun," he added. "Sometimes I want to die, when I see fire I feel like someone is there."

When Gene wanted to talk to someone, he banged loudly on his cell door. Eventually mental health staff would come by, talk to him through the food port of his cell door, and ask what was his problem. He laughed heartily as he told me he repeatedly told them, "Nothing." He told me that it was freezing cold in his cell and that when he was moved into it he saw feces and blood on the cell walls. He did not voluntarily go to see the prison psychiatrist. When I asked him why not, he said, "I found out they lie."

Gene had been in prison nearly twenty years when I interviewed him. For just about his entire prison term he had been in isolated confinement. He had been in the state's supermax facility for many years, but before that he had been in segregation cells in other prisons. He repeatedly ran into disciplinary problems and had a large number of disciplinary tickets or write-ups. He had been shot with immobilizing gas and "extracted" from his cell many times.

Despite what seemed to me to be a very clear case of paranoid schizophrenia—a textbook case in just about all regards—the correctional psychiatrist and psychologist at the supermax prison adamantly insisted he was "merely malingering." As a result, Gene was receiving no psychiatric medications.

MALINGERING AND OTHER MANIPULATIONS

Malingering, the feigning or exaggerating of symptoms in order to gain something (secondary gain), is an important issue in forensic psychiatry.[14] Is the prisoner faking hallucinations in order to be diagnosed mentally ill and qualified for more comfortable and safer housing and programs? Here, there are two main types of error to watch out for. We can diagnose mental illness where it does not exist (a "type 1 error"), or we can fail to diagnose it where it does exist (a "type 2 error"). We make a type 1 error when we erroneously qualify individuals for mental health treatment who do not really need it. The malingerers are in this group. But we make a type 2 error when, overrelying on the concept of malingering, we fail to qualify individuals for mental health treatment that they legitimately need. No mental health assessment system is perfect. But if we weigh the risks, the greater risk of harm lies with the type 2 error.

Malingering certainly occurs in prison. There is a strong desire to escape from culpability or win placement in a more tolerable setting. The clinician must be aware of this possibility so that scarce mental health resources will not be squandered on prisoners who are not suffering from any significant psychiatric disorder. On the other hand, clinicians' attributions of "malingering" too often mask the presence of serious mental illness. The unfortunate result is failure to diagnose, which can lead to unfair punishment of prisoners whose rule-breaking behaviors are actually driven by their mental illness. Of course, the ultimate tragedy is when excessive concern about malingering leads mental health staff to miss what would otherwise be clear signs of an impending suicide.

Several years ago I examined a prisoner—whom I will refer to here as Ted—who had a history of serious mental illness prior to arrest, replete with multiple psychiatric hospitalizations and prescriptions of antipsychotic and mood-stabilizing medications that reportedly improved his mental state. The court that sentenced him had first ruled that he was incompetent to stand trial, and only after his condition improved with hospital treatment was he convicted and sent to prison. He received no psychiatric treatment while in the prison general population and quickly got into trouble. He broke rules: for example, he failed to keep his cell clean as required by officers, he failed to return to his cell in time for scheduled "counts" (specific times of day when prisoners are required to stand at their cell doors to be counted), and he talked back to officers giving him orders, as people with mental illness are prone to do (whether because they do not fully grasp the rules, or cannot control their rule-breaking behaviors, or cannot control their temper, or are vulnerable and get "suckered" by other prisoners). In any case, this broken individual wound up in segregation as punishment for several rule violations and fighting. In segregation, he decompensated (had a psychotic breakdown), experienced a reoccurrence of auditory hallucinations, and displayed extremely regressed behavior. He was sent to a crisis unit in a different prison where the less stressful conditions, including less hostile interactions with staff, permitted him to settle down, and soon his symptoms subsided. Only then did the psychiatrist see him. Probably wondering why the psychologist at the sending institution was wasting his time by transferring this nonpsychotic and currently nonsuicidal prisoner, he diagnosed "no diagnosis" and "malingering" in one column of his note on the chart, and "antisocial personality disorder" in the second column. When the prisoner arrived back in the segregation unit at the sending institution, he was accused of "fooling" everyone into thinking he had been suffering from a bona fide psychiatric crisis. He was given a disciplinary write-up for being deceitful with staff.

People with serious mental illness, on average, are no different than the general population in their willingness to stretch the truth or manipulate others in order to protect themselves from negative consequences or attain something that seems unattainable by other means. Approximately the same proportion of both groups is willing to lie. Yet even these individuals may still be mentally ill. A person could be exaggerating symptoms or attempting to manipulate staff, yet at the same time be suffering from a serious mental illness or be authentically suicidal.

This was clearly the case with Gene. He would bang on his cell door and say he needed psychiatric help; then, when mental health staff arrived and asked what was wrong, he would say, "Nothing" and laugh. The possibility that deceitfulness or malingering can coexist with serious mental illness is too often lost on custody and mental health staff who have decided at some point that a particular individual is Bad, not Mad, and is "merely malingering" to escape the consequences of his badness.

Clinical research shows that the longer an individual's acute psychotic episode is left untreated—that is, the longer the individual is left to hallucinate and evolve entirely delusional ideas and a very pathological thought process—the worse his or her prognosis.[15] We do not know yet whether the worsening prognosis is due to a developing habit to act and think in psychotic fashion, or whether it is due to changes in brain chemistry, or some combination of the two. But in any case, when delusions become "fixed" or permanent (like Gene's delusion about poisoning), the individual's mental illness becomes more severe, more resistant to treatment, and more disabling. Community mental health clinicians try in every way they can to remove the stresses that propel an individual into psychosis. We provide a sheltered and therapeutic environment, we provide intensive treatment including but not limited to medications, and we try to protect the individual from repeated traumas—whether they be social, familial, or environmental—all in the hope of improving his or her condition and prognosis.[16] Conversely, and tragically, if the individual is left in a situation that is extremely stressful and traumatic, for example solitary confinement, then the psychosis worsens and the prognosis becomes more grave. (This is the underlying reason why courts have ordered that prisoners who suffer from serious mental illness must not undergo supermaximum security confinement.)

If a prisoner undergoes a psychotic breakdown and is immediately transferred to a correctional psychiatric hospital or crisis unit and is supplied the psychotropic medications and treatment that are appropriate for his acute condition, he is likely to recover and have a relatively good prognosis. If the same prisoner is left to hallucinate in his cell or suffer from harsh prison conditions such as those in the supermax isolation units where Gene and Bill were confined, then his condition is likely to deteriorate further until he reaches the point where he is laughing inappropriately, smearing feces, and experiencing bizarre and fixed delusions that do not yield to treatment. Sadly, this is the plight shared by individuals like Gene and Bill and many others suffering from serious mental illness. They need to be removed from the toxic environment of a supermaximum prison and placed in a treatment setting where they can be given the medications and the comprehensive mental health treatment that their mental illness requires.

One of the largest problems with the use of solitary confinement and its consequent damage to prisoners' mental health is how this affects their potential release into the community. Unfortunately, life in long-term solitary confinement—coupled with a lack of adequate mental health resources and rehabilitation programs—almost inevitably leaves a prisoner's mental health damaged to such an extent that the courts and prisons eventually turn to finding ways to avoid releasing these individuals into the community for fear of the trouble they might cause—even though their prison sentences are completed. This tragic situation arises from problems with the culture of punishment and the broad use of isolation, as well as the unfortunate ways that mental illness is assessed and treated.

As I described above, when prisoners with serious mental illness are condemned to long stints in isolated confinement with little or no mental health treatment their mental condition deteriorates and becomes more chronic and resistant to treatment. But something else that is also seriously problematic occurs: the evidence showing that the prisoners have been improperly assessed and treated often disappears. If the individual in an acute psychotic episode can be provided a safe and healing environment free from physical or sexual violence, and be given adequate mental health treatment, he or she stands a good chance of going into remission, suffering a minimum of disability, and having a fairly positive prognosis—that is, his or her mental health will be seen as the core problem, and effective treatment will be given to ameliorate it.[17] But if that individual is instead sent to prison, is erroneously determined by the mental health staff not to be suffering from a serious mental illness, and is then raped on the yard, gets into fights as he tries to ward off further sexual assaults, and is punished by being consigned to a long tenure in solitary confinement with no mental health treatment, his deteriorating behavioral responses will be viewed as a discipline problem. That response will obscure the fact that the individual's deterioration was caused by harsh conditions of confinement plus a failed treatment for serious mental illness.

In this way prisons perpetuate a self-serving attribution error as they continue to punish prisoners for behaviors that the prisons' own harsh conditions and inadequate treatment have brought on.

Prisons rely on two ways to block the release of chronically disturbed prisoners at the end of their sentence. First, they can charge a prisoner with a crime committed *during his or her incarceration* in what is called an "outside case." Then, if the prisoner is convicted, the additional sentence effectively extends the length of his or her prison sentence. Second, they can avoid releasing prisoners deemed too much of a risk back into the community by proceeding with a "civil commitment," a second period of forced confinement—after their sentence is already completed—within a psychiatric hospital.

First I will describe how an "outside case" works. Not too long ago, officers would handle disciplinary problems inside prison by meting out punishments, including a relatively brief time in "the hole." To get into segregation, a prisoner had to break rules inside prison. In the average case (there are variations from state to state and in the federal system), when a prisoner was being punished with a determinate sentence in segregation and his prison term ran out (i.e., he reached his determinate release date), he would be released from segregation and from prison. In some states, if an offender was released with time remaining on his punitive segregation term, the next time he entered prison he would be returned to segregation to serve out that segregation term.

But with the advent of supermaximum security isolation, officers more often charge prisoners who "throw" (body waste) at an officer, or who cause damage to an officer even in the process of being "extracted" from a cell, with a crime that will be prosecuted in court. In one case, during a cell extraction, an officer sprained a finger while wrestling with the prisoner he and four other officers were taking down, and he charged the prisoner with assault on an officer. When the corrections officer files a charge against the prisoner, very often a prisoner already in isolation, the local district attorney prosecutes the new felony case, and a judge in the local court sits over the new felony trial. If the prisoner is convicted, for example, of assault on an officer for spitting, then many more years can be added to his sentence, which is all the more likely because he is a repeat offender.

This is a relatively new development. More corrections staff are charging prisoners with outside cases based on violations and assaults that occur inside the prisons. As a result, prisoners in isolation are seeing their prison terms lengthened on account of actions they take inside isolation units, often driven by mental illness that was exacerbated by the isolation. In some cases, the prisoner is correct in assuming that he will never get out of prison. This all-too-common scenario is an example of the downward spiral that prisoners endure within the current system, and it is what I mean when I say that the evidence of prisoners having been improperly treated is actually disappearing. The failure of the treatment is turned into a disciplinary problem—obscuring the failure of the system—and the prisoners are ultimately penalized for the kinds of behavioral responses that scientific and sociological research has repeatedly shown to be the direct result of the psychological and emotional trauma of incarceration in long-term solitary confinement.

A second way prison authorities avoid releasing very disturbed prisoners straight out of isolation into the community is to seek what is called postrelease civil commitment to a psychiatric hospital, a procedure that is being instituted by new laws in many states. But these laws—like the "outside cases"—are largely just another example of how prisons punish prisoners for a situation that stressful conditions and inadequate mental health treatment and rehabilitation brought about.

I can present an illustrative case. A few years ago, a distraught mother consulted me about her son, a California prisoner who was about to serve out his term but was slated for civil commitment under California's mentally disordered offender (MDO) law. This law permits a correctional psychiatrist, with the agreement of a psychiatrist at the state mental hospital, to order a prisoner with serious mental illness who has completed his prison sentence to be transferred involuntarily to the state mental hospital (in other words, to be civilly committed) because he is deemed a danger if released to the community. Many other states have equivalent statutes for postincarceration civil commitment.

It turned out that her son, in his late twenties, had served three years in prison and during that time had developed a psychotic disorder. He was pre-scribed antipsychotic medications but often refused to take them. His inappropriate behaviors, including exposing himself to female staff, landed him in punitive segregation, where his psychiatric condition deteriorated further. The criteria for civil commitment under California's MDO statute included (a) the prisoner has a "severe mental disorder"; (b) the mental disorder was a cause or aggravating factor in the commission of a serious offense; (c) the conviction was for a violent offense and the prison term was determinate; (d) the prisoner has been in treatment for the disorder for ninety days or more; and (e) psychologists or psychiatrists of the California Department of

Corrections and Rehabilitation and the Department of Mental Health certify that, because of the severe mental disorder, the prisoner poses a substantial danger of physical harm if released.

I have serious qualms about postincarceration civil commitment in general,[18] but this man's immediate case did not provide a reasonable venue for testing my theory about the validity of the law. Courts have not been receptive to the argument that postincarceration civil commitments constitute double jeopardy—that is, the prisoner has already served the sentence but is now to be twice punished with another term in custody on a locked hospital ward, this second time on account of mental illness. The courts' reasoning is that while civil commitment entails involuntary confinement, it is not punishment. Double jeopardy, then, is limited to "twice being punished" for the same conduct and not, shall we say, twice being confined.[19]

There is, however, another level to the basic issue of fairness. Since more than 93 percent of prisoners eventually leave prison, the critical issue in corrections should be how well their prison experience prepares them to succeed at "going straight" once they are released. This is where the logic of tougher sentences falls apart and the need for better treatment and rehabilitation programs becomes obvious.

In the case of this woman's son, I reviewed the man's clinical situation and told his mother that I did not advise challenging the MDO law and trying to have him released. Even though his prison sentence had run out, I told her that his condition was likely a response to suffering the kinds of ill effects that individuals with serious mental illness suffer in isolated confinement, and that if she argued vociferously for his release and he then exposed himself while out in the community he would be charged with a new felony offense. It would be better that he comply with the civil commitment proceeding for the time being, that she and the family visit him often and try to influence him to adhere to treatment in the state hospital where he would be sent, and that they work toward his speedy release once he took part in social rehabilitation programming and attained remission.

At this point, a few years later, this individual is functioning relatively well in the community and staying out of trouble. However, this is hardly evidence of a successfully structured rehabilitation program. Why structure an incarceration system in such a way that it actively damages the mental health of the prisoners, so that you then need to put those prisoners into additional confinement afterwards to try to allow them to psychologically recover from the traumas inflicted on them during their incarceration?

We know from extensive research that prisoners suffering from serious mental illness fare very poorly when subjected to harsh conditions such as overcrowding and long stints in punitive segregation. They tend to suffer more serious psychiatric breakdowns, or they tend to become suicidal. We know that individuals suffering from serious mental illness who do not receive adequate mental health treatment tend to deteriorate and have a much poorer prognosis than if they were adequately treated. We know that because of budget constraints and staff shortages, mental health care in prison is often deficient in many regards, in spite of conscientious efforts by many correctional clinicians to provide quality care. And we know that a significant subpopulation of prisoners who suffer from serious mental illness are considered "Bad" and not "Mad" because of clinicians' excessive concerns about malingering. Thus many prisoners with serious mental illness do not receive adequate mental health care, suffer terribly from the effects of prison crowding, find their way into long-term segregation, and continue to exhibit severe psychopathology as they reach the end of their prison term. Despite the courts' current opinion on this issue, it is difficult for many psychiatrists and legal scholars—not to mention the prisoners and their families—to understand how it is a fair solution to simply de facto punish the prisoner by subjecting him or her to additional forced confinement in a state mental hospital, rather than fix the problems in the prisons that are so dramatically exacerbating these individuals' mental conditions.

There is no question that a subpopulation of prisoners in segregation remain disturbed/disruptive at the end of their sentences and pose a difficult challenge to custody and mental health staff, and that these prisoners are prone to get into further trouble in prison or in the community when they are released from isolation. But this challenge only shows up the failure of prisons' foolhardy strategy of relying so much on isolation in the first place. When departments of correction use isolation as a solution to behavior problems and assaults within prisons, they only make the problem worse because the harsh conditions of isolation and idleness predictably make prisoners more chronically disturbed and disruptive.

When prisons and district attorneys prosecute more outside cases and try to secure postrelease civil commitments, their goal, whether they say it explicitly or not, is to hide evidence of the damage done to prisoners from the excessive use of isolation inside the prisons. If prisoners who are broken by long stints in isolation and seem to pose a high risk of future turmoil remain locked up—for a longer prison term or for a stint in a locked psychiatric hospital—then the danger of postisolation or postrelease disruptive behavior and aggression will appear to have been averted. But while this strategy in a sense hides the evidence of human breakdown in isolation units, it certainly does not provide a fair, humane, or effective way to "correct" the errant path of disturbed offenders.

SIX

Women Do Not Do Well in Solitary

WOMEN ARE ESPECIALLY VULNERABLE to solitary confinement in the prisons where they are doing time. For some women, the experience of solitary confinement can reenact past traumas, including sexual and physical abuse as children and domestic violence as adults. For others, the threat of being transferred to solitary is a powerful tool for enforcing their submission and can prevent them from reporting abuses like being sexually assaulted by a staff member. For all women, social connection is very important, and being deprived of it a huge and damaging hardship.

WOMEN PRISONERS AND TRAUMA

I interviewed a prisoner, Tanya (not her real name), a thirty-two-year-old African American woman, just after she was transferred out of the SHU in a large women's prison in New York. She had been in prison for several years and was expecting to be released to the community three or four months after our interview. As a girl, she had been locked in a dark closet for extended periods as punishment for even small transgressions by an abusive mother. She suffered flashbacks, panic, strong startle reactions, and other post-traumatic symptoms, all much worse when she was in SHU. She was taking no medications, but in the past she had been prescribed antidepressant and mood-stabilizing psychotropic medications. She eventually refused the medications because they were given in too high a dose, causing side effects, and she was receiving no counseling.

When Tanya walked into the lieutenant's office on the pod, the room I was using to conduct interviews, she moved slowly, seemed hesitant, and looked very frightened. The room was small, perhaps ten feet by ten feet, the lieutenant's desk was cluttered with papers, and I had to rearrange the furniture to create a space where we could sit opposite each other to talk, without having the desk between us. I spent a long time explaining the lawsuit I was planning to testify in, *Disability Advocates, Inc. v. New York State Office of Mental Health*, and the rules for confidentiality as applied to our interview. I did that much explaining not simply because the details about the case and confidentiality were important but also because I wanted to give her a little time to get a sense of me and decide if I could be trusted and if she was safe enough with me to relax her guard.

Because of rule violations, she had been consigned to SHU and had spent two years there before being returned to general population a week prior to our meeting. The SHU had an "extreme effect" on her, and she described to me how she "flipped out"—including frequent anxiety attacks and paranoia. She felt closed in and felt she suffered from the harsh way SHU inflicts emotional pain. She associated being in SHU with being in the closet as a girl and had many "reliving" experiences while in SHU, the sense that she was being locked in a closet again. Her mother would beat her before locking her in the closet, and the two occasions when officers did a "takedown" she felt she was reliving that traumatic experience. She had been taken from her mother at age eleven and placed in three different foster homes before going to live with her grandmother. In SHU she cried a lot and was overwhelmed by very painful memories. She described wanting to tell staff about the closet, but as in many SHUs the staff did not really engage prisoners in conversation. In SHU, Tanya experienced flashbacks to abuse by her mother, had nightmares, and had phobias about rats and dogs biting her. She told me that officers used searches to harass prisoners and that they did it more to her because they knew she couldn't control her temper. She was hoping she would be able to stay out of trouble for the short time left in her prison term so she could leave without doing more time in SHU.

Women prisoners are in double jeopardy for post-traumatic stress disorder (PTSD). On average, women's preincarceration backgrounds include much trauma, and then when they go to prison new traumas await them, including strip searches (often by male officers), beatings, robberies, sexual assaults, and time spent in segregation. As Tanya's story illustrates, harsh prison conditions and new traumas that occur behind bars are more difficult for women to cope with when they have past histories of multiple traumas.[1] In other words, there is a very real danger of "retraumatization."[2]

Research beginning in the 1990s uncovered a shockingly high rate of trauma that children in the inner city experience themselves or witness, including domestic violence and drive-by shootings. In particular, women prisoners who spend time behind bars have a very high rate of past sexual victimization. On average, their lifetime prevalence rate for sexual victimization is two to three times higher than that of the general population.[3] And though personal backgrounds of extensive trauma show up in the lives of both male and female prisoners, women report prior trauma more often than men. One Bureau of Justice Statistics survey showed that female inmates (43 percent) were at least three times more likely than male inmates (12 percent) to report having sustained physical or sexual abuse in their past.[4] Other studies have given higher rates: in a sample of 150 women prisoners in New York, 59 percent had been sexually abused and 70 percent physically abused as children.[5] And the Federal Bureau of Justice Statistics reported in 1999 that "nearly 6 in 10 women in State prisons had experienced physical or sexual abuse in the past," often by an intimate (one-third of those reporting abuse) or a family member (one-quarter).[6] But all these figures are likely to be gross underestimates of the pervasiveness of abuse in the backgrounds of women prisoners. After all, it often takes some time and a significant amount of trust-building contact to elicit accurate reporting of abuse histories. The criminologist Barbara Owen, in her three-year study on the lives of women in a large California prison, found that 80 percent of the women prisoners had been sexually and/or physically abused prior to incarceration.[7]

As the criminologist and African American studies scholar Beth Richie has noted, for low-income women of color especially, the services of institutions supposedly designed to protect and support them when they are abused may be lacking or may even compound the harm, particularly if they fight back physically against their abuser. Not only do poor black women tend to live in communities where they are not protected by government agencies, but because they are less likely than their white counterparts "to subscribe to traditional gender roles, to marry, to depend on men for economic support and live with their children's biological father, or to present as innocent victims and report abuse to law enforcement officers" they are less likely to be viewed as "real victims" of abuse. "Black women who report male violence to state officials are more likely to encounter uninformed service providers, unsympathetic community members, and rigid representatives of the state who blame them for their experiences and ignore the structural pre-conditions that surround them and their families."[8]

It is also suggestive that a large proportion of prisoners, between 60 and 80 percent, have a history of substance abuse and that a larger proportion of female than male offenders have reported a history of drug use.[9] Many addiction specialists theorize that abused individuals who use drugs are trying to self-medicate in an ineffectual attempt to control post-traumatic symptoms.[10]

Corrections staff give too little thought to ways past traumas affect current problematic behaviors that come to their attention. Past traumas too often return in the form of reenactments, such as strip searches or a sexually abusive officer reminding a woman of a stepfather who raped her. Women, on average, are less prone to violence within jail and prison, present a lower escape risk, and do not require as high security as do their male counterparts,[11] but they are generally assigned the same security classifications and subjected to the same disciplinary procedures as male prisoners, and this can create hardships for them.[12] Women have different needs for modesty and privacy, and quite often their needs are ignored as they are forced into prison routines.[13]

In solitary confinement in particular there are myriad opportunities to be reminded of past traumas. Violent takedowns or "cell extractions" reenact earlier physical abuse. Further, since prisoners in SHU or Observation are watched at all times, typically by male guards, even when showering or using the toilet, and may have their clothes taken away as a punishment, female prisoners' exposure is a violation that may trigger memories of past violations. Women in punitive segregation units must request each change of tampon or sanitary napkin from an officer, and when the officer is male this can be very embarrassing. There is no comparable male experience. And in SHU the number and intensity of strip searches and body cavity searches increase. These searches can be very traumatic. I have testified in lawsuits where I have heard described how women prisoners must bend over and spread their buttocks and their labia during strip searches, often when male officers are in the room. One woman prisoner at the Western Massachusetts Regional Women's Correctional Center (WCC) in Chicopee described her experience:

> When women are moved to the Segregation Unit for mental health or disciplinary reasons, they are strip searched. With four or more officers present, the inmate must: take off all her clothes, lift her breasts and, if large, her stomach, turn around, bend over, spread her buttocks with her hands and cough, and stand up and face the wall. If the woman is menstruating, she

must remove her tampon or pad and hand it to a guard. An officer with a video camera stands a few feet away and records the entire strip search. This officer is almost always male.[14]

Because so many women prisoners have prior histories of massive and repeated trauma, such experiences predictably have horrendous results in terms of serious emotional problems and dysfunction.

TRAUMA AND MENTAL ILLNESS

Just as in SHUs for men, mental illness is rampant in SHUs for women. For women, as for men, solitary confinement makes mental illness worse, and women, like men, kill themselves in SHU at a much higher rate than in a general-population prison.[15] But there are gender differences. As the American Civil Liberties Union reported in 2014, "A staggering proportion of incarcerated women suffer from mental health problems. Among prisoners in federal facilities, almost fifty percent more women than men have been diagnosed with mental health conditions. And much higher numbers of women in state prisons and local jails are reported to suffer from mental health problems than similarly situated men."[16] The need for connection remains singularly important for women prisoners. Isolation denies women connection with others and can cause serious depression.

The story of a woman I interviewed, Anita, shows how for women suffering from mental illness the traumatic experiences of prison can combine with painful memories and the isolation of SHU to produce severe deterioration in their mental state—a deterioration that the prison mental health systems typically do not adequately address. Anita had been in top-lock for two months at a large women's prison in New York. Top-lock is a form of solitary confinement where the prisoner is locked in her cell on a general-population unit twenty-four hours per day. She was thirty-two years old when I met her and had been in prison for three years serving a sentence of five to fifteen years for manslaughter. She had been in psychiatric hospitals twice for suicide attempts prior to her incarceration. She told me she remembered a stepfather beating her mother on several occasions when she was young but that the flashbacks that plagued her during her time in prison were about the suicide of a male friend when she was sixteen. Several months before I met her, she had witnessed another prisoner setting herself on fire. She had difficulty falling asleep and would wake in the middle of the night, seeing images that seemed real for a moment (until she realized she had been dreaming) of the burning woman screaming. She told me how when she looked at me she saw the face of the woman prisoner who set herself on fire and burned to death. She had been having severe memory problems ever since she was relegated to SHU, and by the time she and I talked she could not even remember the crime that had landed her in prison.

Anita had been receiving mental health treatment in prison and she had been diagnosed with PTSD, but she told me that she rarely talked to an actual therapist.

"It's mostly pills," she said.

There was a note on her clinical chart that the PTSD symptoms had diminished, but when I spoke to her the nightmares were still ongoing, and she was still seeing images of the burning woman upon waking. Another note in her chart documented ongoing flashbacks, nightmares, anxiety, and other symptoms typically related to PTSD.

Stories of women prisoners with mental illness and their involvement with solitary follow a familiar pattern of escalating symptomatology; desperate rule-breaking actions; escalating punishments; still worse symptoms and more desperate actions, including suicide attempts; transfer to Observation, and often further traumatization there, until the prisoner denies having further suicidal ideation; and transfer back to SHU. The experience of Candie Hailey in the criminal justice system illustrates how the use of solitary confinement for prisoners with mental illness can cause symptoms to spiral out of control.[17] Hailey, at age twenty-eight, had been charged with assaulting a baby during a fight with the baby's mother on a New York street. Eventually she would be acquitted by a jury at trial, but before the trial occurred she spent three years at Rikers Island, over two of those years in solitary confinement.

Like so many others in this situation, Candie began to harm herself: "She regularly hurt herself by banging her head against her cell wall or cutting at her wrists with broken light fixtures. And at least eight times during her time in solitary, she was hospitalized for suicide attempts that included swallowing a hair remover product."[18] The response was to send her to an observation cell. After a period of time in its even more extreme austerity, she was returned to her isolation cell. The cycling between observation cell and isolation cell was repeated ten times before attorneys at the Urban Justice Center were able to intervene with the court and have her moved to a new intensive, high-security treatment unit at Rikers, the Clinical Alternative to Punitive

Segregation (CAPS) unit. There, with intensive mental health treatment designed to help prisoners who had trouble following rules at Rikers, she remained relatively stable until she was finally released from Rikers.[19] Later she described her experience: "I've been through hell and back. My soul died but my body is alive."[20]

Consider as well the case of Maria, a twenty-four-year-old Latina woman who had been in prison for five years and was to go to the parole board a few months after our visit. She suffered from schizophrenia and took antipsychotic medications. She had also experienced quite a few traumas during her life, including sexual abuse by a stepfather. Thus she was both seriously mentally ill and a trauma survivor, a common double affliction in women prisoners.[21]

Maria was in general population in a New York prison for women when I interviewed her, but she had been in SHU for eight months during the previous year. She had attempted to kill herself three times while in prison, each time by overdose while in SHU. She had been placed in an observation cell many times at different prisons, in each case when she became suicidal after placement in SHU. After a few days in Observation she would be transferred back to SHU. In other words, she repeatedly cycled between an isolation cell and an observation cell and back to isolation. She told me that nobody talked to her when she was held in Observation; the staff merely came around on rounds each morning for a few minutes to ask if she still felt suicidal, and a nurse delivered her psychotropic medications to her in her cell. "Finally I would just get fed up with being naked and having no privacy in Observation and would tell them I was not feeling suicidal any more." Then she would be transferred back to an isolation cell in the SHU.

In SHU, Maria was not permitted to talk to anyone or she would get a disciplinary ticket. She explained to me how if she was not at her door, fully dressed, right at the specific times when officers performed "counts" and delivered food trays, she would miss her meals or her time in recreation or her shower. (Of course, when a prisoner suffers from serious mental illness and is taking psychiatric medications it can be quite difficult for her to pay attention and be at the door at the appointed times.) As was the case with every other woman prisoner I have met in solitary confinement settings, the social isolation was a source of enormous distress. Maria told me that being forced to dwell alone with nobody to talk to for months on end caused her to feel very depressed, and that was the real reason she made suicide attempts. Besides attempting to overdose on pills that she would hoard after "cheeking" them when the nurse came to her cell, she would bang her head against the wall or try cutting herself with metal strips she broke off from the legs of her bed. She received approximately twenty-five disciplinary tickets while in SHU, many of them for "destroying state property" (presumably the bedposts).

Maria confided that she found the repeated strip searches conducted in the SHU to be extremely humiliating. While policy called for strip searches to be conducted by women officers, often there were not enough women officers on duty and male officers would conduct the searches—for example, when she had to leave or return to SHU for a medical appointment or a visit. Then, in the observation cell, she would be left naked with nothing but a paper gown to cover herself. Observation cells were just that: the front panel of the cell would be constructed of transparent Lexan, so she would be in view of staff passing by or sitting at a nearby desk. But there were usually male staff in the vicinity, and she always felt exposed and humiliated. And she would have to use the toilet within view of male officers through the Lexan window of her cell.

We tend to associate PTSD with panic attacks, flashbacks, and nightmares. And such symptoms often occur in individuals who are relatively stable emotionally. But if an individual suffering from schizophrenia is traumatized—raped, for example—often her reactions are not going to be limited to flashbacks and nightmares. She may hear a stern hallucinated voice in her head telling her this is what she deserves, and it may be the voice of the stepfather who raped her when she was a child. Psychiatrists, hearing that the voices are more insistent, explain her clinical situation as a flare-up or an acute exacerbation of the schizophrenia. But actually, no matter what the diagnosis, the woman's exacerbated symptoms are a reaction to the recent trauma, which is often reminiscent of past trauma. Too often clinicians lose sight of the trauma because they are singularly focused on the signs and symptoms of schizophrenia. In any case, someone like Maria, who suffers from schizophrenia as well as the aftereffects of multiple traumas, should never be in solitary confinement. And certainly when she becomes seriously suicidal and needs to be transferred to an observation cell, she must not be returned to solitary confinement.

SEXUAL ABUSE AND SOLITARY CONFINEMENT

Emma, a thirty-year-old African American woman who was in prison for six years, was regularly abused by guards during her time in solitary confinement and Observation. She came from an unstable, low-income family: her mother was a drug addict, she was raped at age five, when she was placed in foster care she was sexually abused by her foster dad, and she was physically abused by various people all through childhood. She was also abused as an adult before going to prison, including getting a beating from a drug dealer.

When she entered prison she talked to officers about past sexual abuse, but then they "came on to" her. One officer persuaded her to have sex with him, and when she became hysterical a few hours later she was sent to Observation, where she was given a smock and no clothes. Then that officer visited her in Observation. She tried to cover herself, but he wanted her to masturbate in front of him. She said she did it because it was the only way she could get food. "I wasn't the only one doing it," she explained. "He gave sandwiches [to everybody]. That went on for a while. Then there was touching." I asked if she had consented, and she said she believed she had to work to get food. (Legally, there is no consent to sexual contact with staff: it is illegal regardless of whether it is voluntary or involuntary.) He didn't force her, but he manipulated her by keeping things from her and then giving them to her only if she performed sexual acts. When she was transferred from Observation back to SHU, the same officer repeatedly visited her and sexually abused her. She kept pushing the emergency button and saying she would hurt herself because he was there, but staff failed to respond. Then she began cutting herself when he was around. "There were no cameras," she said. "He could do anything to me in segregation."

In segregation she became panicky and volatile. "I went off a lot, throwing trays, getting angry at officers, I paced the floor, I felt like the walls were closing in on me, and then I screamed, 'Let me out of here, I can't breathe!'" It was particularly frightening to her that male officers could look at her at any time through the window in her door. "You couldn't cover it, got an infraction for covering the window. Women officers would let me cover the window for a minute, but males would demand I uncover it and would take the paper I used to cover the window."

She spent a lot of time cycling between segregation and Observation, repeatedly going to Observation because she would cut herself to get away from the abusive officer. Eventually she reported him. When I asked if there was retaliation, she said that after she reported, she received only two squares of toilet paper per day. Then officers started coming into her cell and taking things, like family pictures. The loss of her pictures was very painful: "When you come to prison you forget who you are and become just a prisoner, but your pictures remind you of family." She believed that other staff members, if they knew the officer whom she had reported, would provoke her on purpose to do things that would have her sent to the Observation cell. Also, they would let the officer who had sexually abused her come onto the unit.

When I interviewed her, four years after her release from prison, in preparation for my testimony in a class action lawsuit about the sexual abuse of women prisoners by staff, Emma was still unstable and traumatized. She was trying to study for her GED and go to college, but she could not concentrate. Instead, she obsessed about memories of prison sexual assaults. She reported a tendency to "go somewhere else." For example, while she was sitting in class or doing her homework, a word would trigger memories of an experience in prison and devastate her emotionally. Emma's experiences of sexual abuse in prison and its lasting effects, as well as the retaliation she encountered for reporting sexual abuse, are shared by many other women prisoners.

Sexual abuse occurs frequently in women's prisons and specifically in SHUs. It takes many forms: not just coerced sexual acts but the lecherous looks or comments of the officer accompanying a woman in handcuffs to a distant section of the prison or watching her in the shower; the lewd propositions—"Nice tits" or "I'd like some of that ass, right there"; the pat-down or strip-searches that take a little too long, especially lingering over the breasts and in the crotch.[22] And perhaps even more debilitating than sexual assault itself is living with the constant threat that such assault could happen at any time.

While preparing for expert testimony about sexual abuse in women's facilities, I spoke with many women prisoners who were survivors of prison sexual abuse. In many of them, I discovered all the signs and symptoms of post-traumatic stress disorder (PTSD) with lasting disability.[23] But I was even more struck by their lasting depression, their lethargy, their lack of initiative, their sense of drastically diminished personal possibilities, and their sense of shame and diminished self-esteem.[24] An underlying theme throughout my work is that prison rape does not occur without a culture of misogyny that supports it, even encourages it.[25] I do not mean to imply that all prison staff are misogynists or that all male staff assault women prisoners. A much more frequent violation of women prisoners, practiced almost universally by staff in women's facilities, is complicity by silence as colleagues carry out the abuse. As discussed earlier, correctional officers (and police) adhere to a "Blue Code,"[26] an unofficial code of silence that prohibits their informing on each other. Some staff have been whistle-blowers, reporting sexual abuse of women prisoners and even testifying at trial about it, but they are very rare exceptions. In almost every instance of sexual abuse that I have uncovered in preparation for expert testimony in civil lawsuits brought by women survivors of prison sexual abuse, other officers knew about the abuse and in many cases even provided alibis for the perpetrators.

In many prisons it is common practice for a woman prisoner who has reported sexual abuse by a staff member to be transferred to solitary "for her own good" while the investigation goes forward, presumably for her protection. But because women prisoners dread solitary so much, and because they fear retaliation for reporting, many women opt not to report custodial sexual abuse. Or they wait for a long time before reporting abuse. I am often asked as I testify at trial why, if the women I am testifying about were so traumatized by staff's sexual assaults, they waited six months or a year to report the assaults. I explain as I have here that the risk of retaliation is so great, and the dread of solitary confinement so intense, that women survivors of prison sexual abuse have to think long and hard about whether they want to report the abuse at all. In other words, the presence of a solitary confinement unit in the prison casts a shadow over the entire facility. Officers intent on perpetrating custodial sexual abuse know this and count on their victims not reporting the abuse.

The most pronounced display of the inherent homophobia and misogyny in prison culture involves transgender or trans individuals. Prison staff usually house (preoperative) trans women in male prisons, where they run a high risk of being sexually assaulted.[27] In one high-profile case, a trans woman prisoner was repeatedly raped after she had been forced to share a cell with a "tougher" male prisoner.[28] The plaintiff alleged that the California Department of Corrections and Rehabilitation had been deliberately indifferent because they knew or should have known that placing a female-identified prisoner in a cell with a male prisoner would result in sexual abuse and rape. A CDCR research report conducted in compliance with the Prison Rape Elimination Act had determined that "sexual assault is 13 times more prevalent among transgender inmates, with 59% reporting being sexually assaulted while in a California correctional facility."[29]

In an effort to avoid this kind of trouble, corrections officials frequently place trans women prisoners in solitary confinement in men's prisons. Supposedly they are not being punished and their housing in solitary is merely an administrative matter. But they *are* being punished: they are alone in a cell nearly twenty-four hours per day and do not have access to jobs or programs. In a prison culture where misogyny and homophobia prevail, separation is indicated for individuals who will predictably be victimized, including vulnerable youths and some gay and transgender adults. But as noted in chapter 1, there is a difference between separation, which still allows these individuals the freedoms and amenities permitted by their classification level, and isolation, which unjustly deprives them of those freedoms and amenities.

The Prison Rape Elimination Act (PREA) that was signed into law in 2003 mandated the establishment of a Prison Rape Elimination Commission that met for several years and proposed standards for compliance with PREA. On May 16, 2012, Attorney General Holder signed the National Standards to Prevent, Detect, and Respond to Prison Rape.[30] It was a great day for advocates of safety for women and other vulnerable populations in prison. The standards require "zero tolerance" in jails and prisons for sexual abuse. I testified twice before the Prison Rape Elimination Commission. The hearings were conducted on a very high level, with participation by correctional administrators, human rights advocates, and experts in the field. One of the issues discussed at length during the hearings was whether women who report custodial sexual abuse should be consigned to solitary confinement pending the outcome of the department's investigation into the alleged abuse. The commission heard testimony about women prisoners who are very reluctant to report sexual abuse because they fear it will come down to "my word against his," and because meanwhile they will be consigned to dreaded solitary confinement. The PREA standards that Holder signed address this problem, but with a certain degree of ambiguity. They require that "inmates at high risk for sexual victimization shall not be placed in involuntary segregated housing unless an assessment of all available alternatives has been made, and a determination has been made that there is no available alternative."[31] A report by Solitary Watch found that as of 2013 PREA "ha[d] not stopped the widespread practice of utilizing solitary to punish those who speak out." Between that and other retaliatory practices, such as moving prisoners who have reported sexual abuse to other facilities, physically attacking them, or labeling them as having had a prior relationship with an officer, women "have powerful motivations to keep . . . quiet." The dread of solitary in particular "bull[ies] who-knows-how-many into silence."[32]

Consider a twenty-eight-year-old Mexican American woman prisoner who was raped by a male officer and waited six months to report the violation. She described to me how she was terrified the entire six months, could not sleep, and had paranoid ideas about the officer coming and killing her. She eventually decided to report him. Now she is in a SHU, an automatic placement for women who report on officers in that state. She is in a cell, alone. She cannot have visitors. She cannot talk to other women prisoners or to an advocate. And she is facing an interrogation by an investigator about her allegations against a male staff member. How able is she to think clearly about her options and how to handle the situation while her anxiety and paranoia are exacerbated by the isolation?

SOLITARY CONFINEMENT AND SUBORDINATION

In women's facilities, gendered domination subjects women to abuse and involves the infantilizing and demeaning of women to make them subservient.[33] The most likely abusers are male staff, but all too often a woman officer joins the men in demeaning women prisoners to prove that she is "one of the guys" by not displaying "weak" feminine proclivities such as empathizing with, empowering, or caring for her female wards. Of course, there are exceptions, and many women prisoners have told me that the only way they survived imprisonment was with the support and encouragement of women staff members. But more often women prisoners tell me how women staff members treat them as horribly as the male staff, and just like male staff, infantilize them, demand their subservience, and too often sexually assault them. Both male and female staff frequently address prisoners, grown women, as "girls." Prisoners learn to passively follow orders, see themselves as undeserving of agency and power, and remain silent when they are mistreated or abused. If they protest or demand their rights, they get bogus disciplinary write-ups and time in "the hole" or solitary. There are also much more subtle forms of retaliation against a woman who does not "know her place." A frequent reprisal is a bogus "ticket" (a disciplinary write-up). Approximately 80 percent of women prisoners have children, and their problems with self-esteem and, too often, depression, have much to do with their failures as mothers.[34] In many prisons, when a woman receives a ticket, a part of the punishment is denial of visits. She will likely be sentenced to a term in solitary confinement, but the even worse punishment, from her perspective, will be that she cannot see her children. The alternative is to accept the subservient role, to silently tolerate the subtle and not-so-subtle forms of harassment and abuse, and thereby to protect her visits with her children.

The story of Yraida Guanipa shows how SHU is effectively used to intimidate and punish those who speak up. When Guanipa was a prisoner at the federal prison in Miami, she repeatedly and unsuccessfully tried to get medical help for heavy uterine bleeding, then went on strike, refusing to do kitchen duty until the condition was addressed. She was put in SHU for refusing a direct order. Transferred to the Federal Correctional Camp in Coleman, Florida, she repeatedly requested programs that would enable mothers to spend more time with children and went on hunger strike when authorities did not respond. Hunger strikers were supposed to go to medical, but they transferred her to another facility in Tallahassee and put her in another SHU. She said of solitary: "It was the worst inside the worst. . . . You don't hear anything, you don't see anything. I was afraid I was going to lose my mind. . . . If you tell a doctor you're feeling suicidal, they put you in a worse situation—in the hole without your clothes on, so you don't say anything." Once she got out, she says, "I was so scared after that that I vowed never to do another hunger strike again."[35]

It has been quite a shock for someone like myself, who supported the Second Wave women's movement and participated in the profeminist, antiracist men's movement of the 1980s and onward, who applauded and grew personally with the advances women have made in society at large, to tour jails and prisons and meet women who are being subjected to reprehensible abuse as if the gains women made over the past century had never occurred. After being trained in subservience in prison, women have great difficulty getting back to the task that was interrupted by their arrest: becoming empowered and designing a quality life.

How can the horrific scenarios that occur on a regular basis in our jails and prisons possibly decrease the likelihood that prisoners will return to substance abuse and crime when they are eventually released? If prison is so traumatic that prisoners who have a history of prior traumas are retraumatized, they will be far less capable after leaving prison of functioning well in the community. In other words, trauma is an important part of the mechanism for the failure of a department of corrections to correct.

Women who have been traumatized—whether they have been imprisoned for a crime or not—need a safe place to heal, with staff who care about them, understand their pain, and offer them hope.[36] They require trauma-informed services.[37] The culture of punishment makes this kind of safety and understanding nearly impossible to achieve. If staff are to help traumatized women readjust to a healthy, crime- and substance-abuse free lifestyle after they are released from prison, there must be a rehabilitative attitude throughout the corrections system.

SEVEN

Youth in Isolation

THE JUVENILE JUSTICE SYSTEM was created around the turn of the twentieth century on the premise that young offenders are different from their adult counterparts: their immaturity makes them differently culpable for criminal acts, they require positive educational and social experiences if they are to grow into productive adults, they have greater potential for rehabilitation than do adults, they are more vulnerable in institutional settings, and they can easily become as adults very different from who they were as juveniles. In other words, juveniles have not had a long time to become habituated to criminal ways; they are more malleable and therefore more amenable to educational and rehabilitative programming; if teachers, counselors, and parole agents are successful at redirecting a significant number of them into law-abiding pursuits, they are more likely than adult lawbreakers to turn their lives around. And, if the project of juvenile justice succeeds, there will be fewer damaged souls and habitual adult criminals.

Sadly, we are today witnessing the dismantling of the juvenile justice system. De facto budget cuts in juvenile justice, by the standard of the amount of public monies spent per capita on each juvenile in custody, have resulted in deficiencies in educational and rehabilitation programs in juvenile facilities and, by extension, more abusive practices such as beatings and excessive solitary confinement.[1] A growing proportion of children and adolescents are tried as adults and sent to adult prisons, where they are victimized and all too often find their way into long-term solitary confinement. According to the US Bureau of Justice Statistics, there were 1,790 youth under age eighteen in adult state prisons in 2011.[2] I will present a tragic case that illustrates the harm of this trend.

THE HORRORS AWAITING YOUTH IN
ADULT DETENTION

Ryan entered the large maximum security prison in the Midwest at age seventeen, before he had anything but peach fuzz on his cheeks. He was tried as an adult and sentenced to five years in a maximum security prison. White, five foot six inches tall and slight, he was what's known as a "fish," "meat," or "bait" in a maximum security prison. As soon as he got off the bus, prisoners lining the path to the reception office started their catcalls: "Nice ass!" "Come bunk with me and I'll show you a good time!" "Hey, wanna suck my dick?" The catcalls were coming from older, much larger men, and they persisted the entire time he was walking across the yard under guard. He had heard from other youth at the county jail where he'd been awaiting trial that prisoners would fight over who got to claim him as sexual prey.[3] And he was told by other kids that his options were, basically, "Fight or fuck!"

A slightly older cellmate at the jail, who had already done some prison time, summed up for Ryan what young prisoners like him are forced to confront: "You can ask for protection, they call it 'lockin' up,' but if you do that you're branded a sissy from then on, and either someone will rape you in the protection unit or eventually you'll get out of protection and they'll attack you on the yard. You can go out on the yard and take your chances, but being small with no stubble on your face you'll have to do a lot of fighting. You can hook up with a gang, and they'll take care of you, nobody will bother you because they'd be afraid of the gang's retaliation, but then you're in a gang and the cops [correction officers] will probably put you in segregation. Or—this is what I did on my last bit [prison term]—you can punch someone really hard and get into a fight. The cops will break it up and throw you in the hole for fighting. You'll be in seg [solitary confinement] for a while, and that's a rough go, but at least you'll be safe and you won't have snitched, asked for protection, gone into a gang, or gotten raped."

Ryan had been raped before, by a stepfather when he was seven. There had been a lot of violence in the home where he grew up. His mom was a crank (methamphetamine) addict, his father had deserted the family when he was a few months old and he never saw him again, and there had been a series of "stepfathers," the men in his mother's life, several of whom beat him as well as his mother. Only one raped him. He had never had any counseling for the early repeated traumas. He was always agitated and couldn't concentrate or sit still at school. He got in a lot of fights: as he explained them to me, he was small and the other boys bullied him, but he decided early to stand up for himself and make them think twice about attacking him. He thinks he started using street drugs by the ninth grade to help him calm down, maybe to suppress pain from all the violence at home. He progressed from marijuana to crank and heroin. He dropped out of school in the ninth grade. Then he got caught stealing to support his habit, and that was the crime that sent him to prison at seventeen.

At the reception center of the adult prison he was stripped naked, was made to stand in a large, cold, high-ceilinged room with a lot of other incoming prisoners, and was examined gruffly by a doctor in front of all the other guys. "He grabbed my balls and had me cough, it was totally humiliating." He was issued prison garb and grilled by a classification officer who asked if he was gay or in a gang. He remembers being shown to the cell where he would be sleeping, and then he was sent out onto the prison yard. He walked around feeling terrified, not knowing who was going to jump him, but he knew he had to stay away from the places where prisoners of other races were gathered, he had to stay near the white guys, and he had to act as tough as he could given his age and size. He was mulling over his options and had not yet settled upon a survival strategy when a much larger, older man grabbed him, pulled him into a storage bin, and raped him brutally. His rapist told him that if he told anyone about the rape he would kill him and that he planned to find him the next day and rape him again.

When I met with Ryan, several months later, he was in solitary confinement in the supermaximum security area of the prison. He told me that he had never had "mental problems" before coming to prison, but when I met him he was distraught, suicidal, and exhibiting clear signs of psychosis. He reported that after the rape he didn't know what to do. He nervously approached a guard and asked what he was supposed to do in his situation. The officer said Ryan had to tell him who had raped him and then the officer would "take care of" the matter. Ryan was terrified and could not think straight, but he knew that the last thing he was going to do was to "snitch." He had been told that snitching would get him killed. So he did not tell the officer what had happened, saying instead, "Forget it," and went back out on the yard. He went up to another white prisoner who was only a little larger than him and hit him as hard as he could. Their fight was vicious, he sustained cuts and bruises on the face and ribs, and when the officers broke up the fight they took him to the infirmary. The nurse asked him what happened, but he responded with generalities and did not report the rape or his fear of going back on the yard. The officer wrote him a ticket, a disciplinary infraction, and he was transferred to the segregation unit.

Almost immediately after being confined in a cell by himself with nothing to do and no contact with family, Ryan began "falling apart." He felt despair, believing that he would not be able to survive the five years he had to spend in prison. He did not know who to talk to. He started to believe that the people on his segregation tier—the officer who brought him his food trays and the tier-tender, a prisoner whose job it was to keep the tier clean—were secretly plotting to enter his cell and force him to have sex. He could not sleep at night. He did not want to talk to the mental health counselor who came to the front of his cell to ask after him because he was terrified that if he told the counselor about the rape he would be forced to confront the perpetrator and that would lead to retaliation. So he remained in his cell, did not talk to anyone, became increasingly terrified, and began having what he termed "strange thoughts." He told me he was seriously contemplating suicide but wanted me to swear not to tell anyone.

Why is a seventeen-year-old kid who's barely out of puberty in an adult prison fighting for his honor and his life and winding up in solitary confinement, where he suffers psychiatric breakdown and becomes suicidal? Unfortunately, this tragic scenario is becoming commonplace. Where once juveniles were tried before a special court that was relatively sensitive to the experiences and needs of juveniles, more and more juveniles are being "tried as adults" and, if convicted, sent to adult prisons. In some states a judge has to rule in each individual case that the juvenile's crime was so serious he or she does not deserve special consideration as a child and that the crime warrants his trial as an adult. In other states a fixed age is designated, usually sixteen (New York) or seventeen (Michigan), at which a young defendant is automatically tried as an adult and sent to an adult prison. This recent trend constitutes a tragic reversal of over one hundred years of juvenile justice.[4]

Ryan's story illustrates many of the issues in juvenile justice today. He was massively and repeatedly traumatized as a kid. He used illicit substances to cope with the pain. He dropped out of school. He was arrested for a drug-related crime. He was tried as an adult. He was sent to a men's prison. He was sexually assaulted and raped. He did not receive adequate mental health treatment. He acted out and was sent to solitary confinement. He has participated in no educational or rehabilitation programming. And his future looks very bleak. The accumulated traumas, the hiatus in his education and work experience, and the despair that is growing as he sits in a solitary cell all bode very poorly for his future.

SAM, A CASE WITH A BETTER OUTCOME

Sam, a twenty-five-year-old African American cabinetmaker, did five years in a youth prison on the East Coast. The youth prison had been built early in the twentieth century, when the notion of intensive educational and rehabilitative programming for juveniles was in vogue. There were thousands of youth in the facility, and there were many classes and vocational training opportunities. Though Sam was average sized at five foot ten inches tall and not especially muscled, you could feel his quiet strength as he explained that as soon as he entered the youth prison he had decided to sign up for every program he was entitled to and to work very hard acquiring skills so that when he was eventually released from prison—he had three years to serve—he would be prepared to enter the workforce and succeed in the community.

He had been involved in some drug dealing, arrested, and sentenced to three years in prison. He was released after two and a half because his behavior in prison was exceptional. He had actually signed up for every class he could take, he was very careful to avoid fights, and he took part in training programs aimed at helping young wards succeed after they are released. When I met him, he seemed very earnest and sincere. He was quick to express remorse for his prior misdeeds: "I was a stupid kid, too interested in getting high and sex with girls, too uninterested in school. I made a lot of money selling drugs. I felt invulnerable, like I'd never get caught. But like everyone in the drug business, I was eventually arrested and sent to prison. I had street in me, I knew how to take care of myself on a prison yard, so much so that I actually never had a fight in prison. I knew how to act so other guys would stay away from me, they knew if they messed with me they'd get hurt."

Sam had always figured that there was a chance he would be arrested. He had silently resolved that, if he were to be arrested, he would change course and stop dealing drugs. He would make use of his time behind bars to better himself, and when he got out he would go straight. And that is exactly what he did. In prison, he remembers meeting a vocational training instructor, Hal, who was warm, encouraging, and smart. Hal taught woodshop. Sam signed up. He learned to use tools, then moved on to cabinetmaking. That was Hal's specialty. Hal had done time in prison, and in prison he had learned woodworking. He told Sam that he had a lot of potential, that he (Hal) liked the way Sam worked with his hands. And Sam developed his skills with wood in the shop. Meanwhile, Sam not only earned his GED but took several college courses that were available by mail at the prison. When he was released early for good behavior, he moved back into his parents' house and went looking for work doing carpentry and cabinetmaking. He found a job with an old cabinetmaker who also had a criminal record and wanted to help a kindred spirit get ahead. When I met him, Sam had held his job for two years and had received two raises. Meanwhile, he moved into his own apartment and was living with his girlfriend.

I do not want to idealize juvenile detention facilities. They often fall short of the ideal, there are widespread abuses, there are staff who sexually assault the youths, and there is far too much solitary confinement. In fact, I advocate a massive reduction of the prison population, including juvenile justice facilities, to be accomplished with radical change in sentencing laws and robust efforts at diversion. Nevertheless, Sam's trajectory through the juvenile justice system provides a striking contrast to the horror of Ryan's experience in an adult prison.

Adolescence in contemporary American society is a time for the rapid acquisition of the education and work skills that will permit a productive adult life and the social skills that will make for quality family and community life. The psychoanalyst Erik Erikson, in his classic study *Childhood and Society,* describes late adolescence as a critical stage of identity formation and explains why, when there are traumas and blocked opportunities at this critical juncture, the result is likely to be impaired identity formation or "identity-diffusion."[5] The effects of solitary confinement in this context can be extremely debilitating. Among other hardships, the juvenile offender who was tried as an adult has to cope with the terrible victimization of youth in adult prisons, then with being cut off from his parents and loved ones at this critical stage of identity formation, and then with extreme isolation and idleness in solitary. Most individuals bolster a positive identity by evolving intellectual capacities and work skills during adolescence, but these prosocial capabilities are cut off when youths are consigned to solitary confinement. Not surprisingly, the decimation of life skills caused by prison and solitary confinement hits adolescents the hardest.

Young people who are being held in detention facilities are extremely likely to be suffering from a mental illness.[6] The psychiatrist Linda Teplin has provided much of the data we have about the number of jail prisoners suffering from mental illness. She found that over 90 percent of youths in detention suffer from some combination of mental illness and substance abuse: in other words, they are "dually diagnosed."[7] Either they brought these conditions with them into the youth prison or the experiences and conditions of their incarceration brought on and exacerbated a first emotional breakdown. In any case, mental illness is very prevalent in youth detention facilities. Prior trauma is a very important consideration. The psychiatrist Hans Steiner, who has studied trauma histories and the prevalence of post-traumatic stress disorder in incarcerated juveniles as well as in young refugees, determined in 1997 that fully 33 percent of juveniles in the California Youth Authority suffered from post-traumatic stress disorder, and that shocking figure leaves out many other youths who were traumatized previously but do not have enough current signs and symptoms to qualify for that diagnosis.[8]

Placing an individual in solitary confinement when it is known that individual is at extraordinarily high risk of psychiatric breakdown or suicide is a clear example of deliberate indifference. The tragic case of Kalief Browder has had immense impact upon the public debate. President Obama, in a January 26, 2016, talk on criminal justice, cited Kalief's story as a cautionary tale about solitary confinement. Kalief committed suicide after spending two years in solitary at Rikers Island. He had been arrested at sixteen, had spent three years at Rikers Island, two in solitary, and then had been released with no trial and no actual charges. A week after Kalief's death the New York State Assembly passed a bill banning solitary confinement for juveniles and for individuals with serious mental illness or a developmental disability.[9]

Quite a few young people in our juvenile detention facilities and prisons were prone to mental breakdown when they entered prison: in fact, their prodromal symptoms (symptoms that appear long before an actual psychotic breakdown) may well have driven the actions they were eventually convicted of. It is fair to estimate that, selectively, individuals who are arrested for a crime and sent to a juvenile lockup are far more likely than the average person to suffer from a serious mental illness or be prone to mental breakdown. This means that a significant number of youth and young adults in juvenile detention and prison facilities are prone to suffer a serious psychiatric breakdown or commit suicide.[10] It is deliberate negligence to subject those individuals to extended solitary confinement, which would clearly exacerbate the mental disorder. Youth are seriously damaged by solitary confinement. Of course there are exceptions, youth who spend years in solitary confinement and then emerge and go on to college and a relatively high-quality life. That kind of result, however, occurs only against great odds.

Youth report all the troubling symptoms that adults experience in solitary. But many of these symptoms are more serious in adolescents than they are in adult prisoners. I have already discussed the despair and the reasons it is correlated with a high suicide rate in solitary settings. But young people also have more energy than adults—far too much to be able to just sit in a "box." If a restless teenager out in the world is confined to his bedroom as punishment, he often has a great deal of trouble suppressing his anger and acting appropriately. Now consider what it would be like for one of these young people bursting with energy and enraged by trauma to be placed in solitary confinement, and you can see why he or she is extremely likely to accumulate disciplinary write-ups for arguing with or swearing at guards. Adolescents in particular have trouble containing their youthful vigor, so they literally bounce off the walls in a solitary cell.

THE RISK OF SUICIDE

There is an extraordinarily high risk of suicide among juveniles in detention.[11] Mental health clinicians assess the risk of suicide by considering what are called risk factors. Youth in prison, on average, already have a large number of demographic risk factors for suicide before they even show up for a psychological assessment. They are likely to have had much prior trauma, they are at high risk of being attacked in prison, they tend to be relatively impulsive, the prevalence of suicide among adolescents is quite high, and so forth. Therefore the juvenile in detention is clearly at very high risk of suicide. Placing adolescents in solitary confinement, which is well known to raise the rate of suicide significantly, is a cruel example of willful indifference on the part of prison authorities.

Ten years after I testified in *Walker v. Montana* (see chapter 2), I was asked to return to Montana to examine and testify in court about Raistlin Katka, a young man who had been tried as an adult and sent to Montana State Prison at age fifteen.[12] He had been consigned to the same supermax unit as

Edward Walker and, like Walker, had misbehaved there and was put on a Behavior Management Plan (BMP). I met Raistlin in a visiting booth in the supermax isolation unit, called Max, at Montana State Prison. We had to speak across a Lexan window, and I strained to hear his quiet voice. He had curly auburn hair, a boyish grin, and a teardrop tattoo just under and to the side of his right eye, and he was obviously quite intelligent and articulate.

Raistlin's history was very sad. He had been massively abused and neglected as a child. His father was the abuser, his mother made passive by her drug use. She neglected him while his father beat him relentlessly with belts and hangers. His father abused him in other ways as well—for example, locking him in his room for days or a week at a time as punishment for a bad report from school or a report from a neighbor that he had ridden his bicycle in the wrong place. When he was locked in his room he was permitted to come out only to attend school and then had to return to his room until it was time to go to school the next day. He had to eat meals alone in his room while his father and half siblings (from his father's prior marriage) ate at the table. His half brothers beat him at least once with a baseball bat, and his father knew about it and did nothing to stop them. The beatings at his father's hands were accompanied by his father yelling degrading epithets at him and otherwise emotionally abusing him.

When Raistlin was twelve his abuse came to the attention of Child Protective Services, and he was taken from his parents and sent to foster care. Because of the traumas of his childhood and his emotional difficulties he dropped out of high school, but he made an effort to read everything he could get his hands on and exhibited impressive general knowledge. He had been expelled from a number of group homes for disobeying orders and fighting. Though he was involved in relatively little criminal activity as a teen, if he felt he had been wronged he would fight—caregivers called him a "fighty kid"—and he was eventually prosecuted for slugging the director of a foster care group home where he was residing. Initially he was put on probation, but he violated the terms of probation, and that was a felony. He was tried as an adult and, at age fifteen, was sent to adult prison.

Soon after he arrived at Montana State Prison, an older man grabbed his testicles. Having been warned by other boys that he had to show how tough he was if he wanted to avoid being someone's sex slave, he hit him as hard as he could. When officers asked him what happened and how the fight started, he was silent. He had been warned by other boys in jail never to "snitch." He was sent to the supermax isolation unit for fighting. In supermax he soon became very depressed and disoriented, lost control of his anger, talked back to officers, and disobeyed orders. The result was further disciplinary write-ups, a much longer stint in supermax isolation, and the institution of BMPs.

In most states, and Montana is no exception, when adolescents are incarcerated they are entitled to educational opportunities, at least through the high school (or GED) level of education. But if the youth is confined in an adult prison and lands, for whatever reason, in punitive segregation, he is denied any further educational opportunities because he is in maximum security or on a BMP. He is denied the "privilege" of education. When I testified in court about Raistlin's situation, I insisted that this denial of educational opportunities was not acceptable, according to all standards of decency and laws requiring that minors be provided an opportunity to gain an education, and that Raistlin was being denied an education at a critical stage of development, which would have deleterious effects on his chances of becoming a loving and productive adult in the community.

Raistlin was very energetic in court. He sat at the table in the front of the courtroom reserved for attorneys and parties to the lawsuit. While testimony proceeded, he kept leaning over and whispering to his attorney, Andree Larose. During a break I asked her what they were whispering about, and she said Raistlin was assisting her more than the other way around: he would tell her when a witness was leaving out part of the story or had testified about something that was not true. I was very impressed how well he understood the courtroom process and the legal strategy for his case.

In prison, while on a BMP, Raistlin became severely depressed and made repeated suicide attempts, on a couple of occasions attempting to bite through the veins of his arm. Each time he tried to take his own life he was put in an observation cell in another unit within the prison for a few days and then was sent back to his isolation cell. In fact, most completed suicides that occur among the population in solitary confinement take place in an isolation cell after the prisoner has been returned from Observation.

Raistlin told me that he really does not know what he was thinking, but every time he was placed in solitary he "went crazy" and could not control his self-destructive impulses. On several occasions, the mental health staff opined that his suicide attempts were "manipulations," his aim being to have himself removed from supermax isolation.

I remember testifying in court about Raistlin and reporting how much despair he felt and how very high the suicide risk was. The correctional psychiatrist and a psychiatric expert witness hired by the defense in Raistlin's case felt otherwise. They testified that Raistlin was not that seriously depressed: he was just manipulating to get out of solitary confinement. Besides, the prison had a full range of mental health services available and could handle any suicidal crisis that might arise. The Judge told me in an almost apologetic tone that he was in a difficult position: I was arguing quite convincingly that Raistlin was at high risk of suicide and needed to be transferred out of the prison and into the state psychiatric hospital for his own safety, but two other psychiatrists were saying he was merely manipulating and that if he did become suicidal the prison's mental health clinicians could provide the appropriate treatment. The judge opted to leave Raistlin in the prison supermax unit with the proviso that the prison's psychiatrist would keep a close eye on him. That was on Thursday.

I returned home to Oakland, and Raistlin was placed on "suicide watch" inside the supermax unit. On Saturday, correction officers locked him alone into the shower, where he found a razor blade and proceeded to cut his neck and arms so deeply that he passed out and practically exsanguinated. He needed to be rushed to the emergency room of a local hospital and then to the intensive care unit, where he had to be transfused with four pints of blood and revived. That Monday, the attorneys reappeared in court, and I was hooked in by speaker phone from Oakland. When the judge heard what had happened over the weekend he became furious. He had been lied to. Raistlin had actually been at very high risk of suicide the previous Thursday, and the prison mental health staff were obviously incapable of keeping him safe. The judge seemed shocked that even after Raistlin had been put on suicide watch he would be left alone in a shower and permitted access to a razor blade. The judge took the extraordinary step of ordering a civil commitment so that Raistlin could be removed from the custody of the Montana Department of Corrections and admitted to the state psychiatric hospital on an involuntary basis to receive urgent treatment. Thus, because of the legal intervention by his attorney, Andree Larose, and the American Civil Liberties Union, Raistlin was finally transferred to a psychiatric hospital where his suicide could be prevented and he could receive needed treatment.[13]

BUDGET CUTS FOR THE JUVENILE JUSTICE SYSTEM

The juvenile justice system has not always placed juveniles in cages and housed them in solitary confinement. In the mid-twentieth century and as late as the 1970s it included a collection of robust educational and rehabilitative programs aimed at bumping errant juveniles out of the criminal justice system altogether.

Richard McGee, the visionary director of programs for the California Department of Corrections from the 1940s through the 1970s, set up the California Youth Authority (CYA) to foster education and job training. Under McGee's command, staff had to be advocates for educating the youths.[14] There was rigorous schooling in the CYA, and every youth was required to have a job. There were vocational training programs, camps where the wards of the CYA worked in forestry or farming or fought fires, and there were very creative work-release and parole programs designed to incrementally increase the youths' freedoms and job responsibilities as they progressed from institutional confinement to work outside the institution, then parole in the community, and then independence. McGee retired in the midseventies because he saw trends evolving that he could not support, including massive crowding and relative budget cuts for the programs he had established.[15]

By 1999, a class action lawsuit, *Farrell v. Harper*, had to be brought against the California Department of Corrections and the CYA by the Prison Law Office and Disability Rights Groups. The complaint in *Farrell* included allegations that youth in detention were denied the educational and rehabilitative opportunities that were required by extant laws. In addition, because of crowded facilities and budget shortfalls, youth detention facilities had become out-of-control and very violent places. Staff were using excessive force, especially on the large proportion of the youth suffering from serious mental illness. Many of the youths were subjected to cell extractions and beatings. Too many were placed in small single-occupant cages when they were released to the yard, an experience that was humiliating to them. And a large proportion of the youths either were on long-term lockdown status because the facilities were out of control or were consigned to segregation as punishment for their actions. Sexual predation and abuse were rampant. Medical and mental health care was grossly deficient, and there was widespread dysfunction. In 2003, a consent decree was signed in *Farrell v. Harper* requiring the California Department of Corrections and the CYA (subsequently renamed the Division of Juvenile Justice) to provide wards with adequate and effective care, treatment, and rehabilitation services, including better education, improved medical and mental health care, and centrally, greatly reduced use of force and isolation.

In the state of New York, juveniles are automatically tried as adults at age sixteen. Many are incarcerated at Rikers Island and then, if convicted, are sent to adult prisons. The US Department of Justice declared in 2015 that juveniles at Rikers Island were being abused, were not adequately protected from harm, and were placed far too often and for far too long in punitive segregation.[16] With ever louder calls to improve conditions at Rikers, the New York City Correction Department finally decided to eliminate solitary confinement for sixteen- and seventeen-year-old inmates by the end of the year 2015.[17]

THE SUPREME COURT AND THE LOGIC OF JUVENILE JUSTICE

While the US Supreme Court has not yet ruled on the constitutionality of solitary confinement for juveniles, it has issued a number of rulings about the sentencing of juveniles. The Court ruled in 2005, in *Roper v. Simmons*, that a juvenile defendant cannot receive the death penalty for his crimes. In 2010, in *Graham v. Florida*, the Court ruled that sentencing a juvenile to lifetime imprisonment without parole was unconstitutional for nonmurder crimes. In 2012, in *Miller v. Alabama*, the Supreme Court decided that across-the-board mandatory life sentences without parole for juveniles were unconstitutional. And in 2016, in *Montgomery v. Louisiana*, the Supreme Court held that its previous ruling in *Miller v. Alabama* should be applied retroactively, a decision that potentially affects up to 2,300 cases nationwide. In other words, juveniles as a class have joined the company of prisoners with mental illness and pregnant women as "special populations" who must be protected from some of the worst traumas and abuses that exist in the criminal justice system.

The reasoning of the court merits close attention. In *Miller v. Alabama*, Justice Kagan, writing for the majority, held that sentencing should include consideration of a child's chronological age and such hallmark features of youth as "immaturity, impetuosity and failure to appreciate risks and consequences." Sentencing should also take into account the family and home environment, from which youth cannot usually extricate themselves, even if the home is brutal or dysfunctional, as well as youth's role in the crime and potential to become rehabilitated. The Court was clear that discretionary life without parole sentences should be rare: Justice Kagan wrote, "Given all that we have said in *Roper, Graham,* and this decision about children's dimin- ished culpability, and heightened capacity for change, we think appropriate occasions for sentencing juveniles to this harshest possible penalty will be uncommon."[18] The ruling affects hundreds of individuals whose age and other mitigating factors were not taken into account at sentencing.

In all of these rulings, the Supreme Court relied upon expert opinions, often in the form of an *amicus curiae* (friend of the court) brief. An *amicus curiae* brief in *Miller v. Alabama* by the American Psychological Association, the American Psychiatric Association, and the National Association of Social Workers argues that because juveniles are psychologically different from adults they deserve a certain deference in sentencing.[19] The brief, citing recent research in developmental psychology and neuroscience, argues that juveniles are "less capable of considering alternative courses of action and avoiding unduly risky behaviors," are less oriented to the future and the con- sequences of their "often-impulsive actions," are more susceptible to negative influences including peer pressure, "lack the freedom and autonomy that adults possess to escape such pressures" and are less capable than adults of mature judgment and decision making. Also, because they are still in the process of forming coherent identities, their crimes reflect the "qualities of youth" more than any "entrenched bad character": "Research into adolescent development continues to confirm the law's intuition that 'incorrigibility is inconsistent with youth.'" The writers of the brief summarize neuroscience research that "suggests a possible physiological basis for these recognized developmental characteristics of adolescence" and concludes that "adolescent brains are not yet fully mature in regions and systems related to higher-order executive functions such as impulse control, planning ahead, and risk avoid- ance. That anatomical and functional immaturity is consonant with juve- niles' demonstrated psychosocial (that is, social and emotional) immaturity." The brief concludes: "In short, research continues to confirm and expand upon the fundamental insight underlying this Court's previous decisions: Juveniles' profound differences from adults undermine the possible penologi- cal justifications for punishing a juvenile offender with a sentence that 'guar- antees he will die in prison without any meaningful opportunity to obtain release.'" And of course, in all the cases I mentioned about juvenile sentenc- ing, the Supreme Court has agreed with the opinions of the mental health professional organizations.

The Supreme Court's logic in all of these cases is the same as the reasoning of advocates for a separate juvenile justice system prominently focused on education and rehabilitation, a system that prohibits solitary confinement. Solitary confinement is antithetical to the aims of juvenile justice and the logic provided by the Supreme Court in rulings on juvenile detention. When juveniles are consigned to solitary, in a juvenile facility or an adult prison, no real education or rehabilitation takes place. Their learning experience and their acquisition of social and work skills are interrupted, and the longer they are denied social connection and meaningful activities the harder it becomes for them to catch up with their peers. Isolation poorly prepares one for rewarding intimate relationships with a partner, with children, and with peers. Since the adolescent brain is in a phase of rapid growth, all of the forms of damage I outlined in chapters 4 and 5 are multiplied for youth in isolation. By consigning so many juveniles to isolative confinement, whether in juvenile or adult facilities, we are condemning them to failure at love, work, and play when they grow up, and we are increasing the already significant risk of their developing serious mental illness or committing suicide, as well as the entrapment of a large proportion of them in lives of substance abuse and crime.

EIGHT

_____

The SHU Postrelease Syndrome

A SYNDROME IS "A SYMPTOM COMPLEX" or "a set of symptoms occur-ring together."[1] What led me to first articulate the syndrome I am about to describe was a phone call I received in 1999 from a mother in another state who was concerned about a son just released from prison after completing an eight-year sentence. He had spent the last four of the eight years in some form of isolative confinement. His mother told me on the phone that she was very worried about the fact that, since coming home, he had spent all of his time alone in his room, not even coming out to eat meals with the family. "We are all so worried about him, what's wrong with him?" This family lived quite far from my office, and a visit would not be practical for multiple reasons, so I decided to advise the mother on the phone. I could not know with very much confidence what was "wrong with" the young man (since I had had no oppor-tunity to sit with him), but I had witnessed a very strong impulse to isolate in patients with severe depression, others with psychosis, and still others, like war veterans, suffering from PTSD. I realized I had seen a very similar clinical presentation in ex-prisoners who had spent long stints in SHU. Indeed, a sig-nificant number of the symptoms are reported nearly universally by prisoners and ex-prisoners who have spent prolonged periods in solitary confinement.

I told the mother that she should not worry too much what was "wrong with" her son but rather should take a few fairly simple steps to make his life more tolerable for him. I recommended she tell him that what he was going through was understandable, given his long time in isolation. I recommended that she not pressure him to come out of his room, for dinner or any other reason, and that in fact she try bringing his meal to his room, with the state-ment, "It's okay if you don't feel like joining the family for dinner. I brought you your dinner—when you feel up to it, maybe you can come and join us at the table." She followed my recommendations, and within four days the young man began leaving his room to join the family at the dinner table. But then he would not leave the family home to go anywhere. Over time, he adjusted somewhat to being out of isolation and out of prison, but he would continue to get very anxious whenever he had to be in a social group where he did not already know everyone.

A significant proportion of prisoners in long-term solitary confinement are released from isolation straight into the community. This is called "maxing out of the SHU." The sentence to time in SHU is meted out by a disciplinary hearing officer for rule violations or gang activity that occurs within the prison while the prisoner is serving time. When the prisoner finishes serving his time and is ready for release, the consignment to isolation becomes moot and he must be released from prison. For those who have the resources and the resilience, the transition back into the community, though it may be difficult, is ultimately successful. A period behind bars and in solitary confinement turns out to be, in the long run, an unfortunate misstep on their life path. I laud these individuals' resilience and drive. But for many, the transition is far more problematic. Sometimes there are dreadful repercussions: in a few high-profile incidents, an ex-prisoner released directly from SHU into the community has carried out a violent crime. For example, in 2012 Tom Clements, then the executive director of the Colorado Department of Corrections, was murdered by a man who had been in solitary confinement for many years and was then released from prison, straight out of solitary, when his sentence ran out. Tragically, Clements had been advocating the downsizing of solitary confinement in the Colorado DOC.[2] But outbreaks of violence involving prisoners released from solitary confinement (and indeed ex-prisoners in general) are actually very rare. More typically, if they get in trouble with the law, it is because, on their release, they quickly resort to illicit substances. And whether or not they do this, a very high number of them withdraw into isolation. They end up spending all their time alone or with family, unable to enjoy social interactions and unable to work. These individuals suffer from what I term the SHU postrelease syndrome.

ELEMENTS OF THE SHU POSTRELEASE SYNDROME

The SHU postrelease syndrome appears more often than not in individuals who were in SHU a very long time, after which they were either transferred to a general-population prison or released directly from SHU to go home when their term ran out. Often-reported symptoms include

- A tendency to retreat into a circumscribed, small space, often a bedroom or a cell
- A tendency to greatly limit the number of people one interacts with, usually to close family members and a few friends
- Anxiety in unfamiliar places and with unfamiliar people
- Hyperawareness of one's surroundings—for example, a need to sit facing the door to a room or with one's back to a wall
- Heightened suspicion of everyone who comes close, especially strangers
- Difficulty expressing feelings
- Difficulty trusting others, even one's spouse or first-degree relatives
- Problems with concentration and memory, beginning in the period of SHU confinement and continuing after release, making it difficult to accomplish tasks and to work
- Personality changes, particularly from being relatively outgoing and friendly and having a sense of humor to being more serious, guarded, and inward
- In some, but certainly not all, cases, a tendency to resort to alcohol and illicit substances to lessen emotional pain and make feelings of confusion and anxiety more bearable

A significant number of these symptoms emerge whether the prisoner has been released to the community or simply transferred to a general-population or "step-down" prison setting. Thus, for example, one former SHU prisoner who had been released to the community reported that he was staying in his room for most of his waking hours, while a prisoner who had been released from SHU to the general prison population to serve out the remainder of his sentence reported that he stayed in his cell for most of his waking hours, to the extent that the prison regimen permitted him that choice. In both situations it is as if the individuals released from SHU are trying to reestablish the conditions they experienced there. They have become so habituated to being isolated in a small space that exposure to any larger, more populated area seems overwhelming and frightening. They are re-creating the small world of the SHU in the bigger world of the community or general population prison because, sadly, the small cell environment is what they are used to and where they feel safe.

Judith Vazquez, a Puerto Rican American woman living in New York and then New Jersey, had to spend three years in solitary confinement at a jail while being tried for murder. When she was released from solitary and transferred to a general-population prison, the experience proved traumatic: "Although I overcame my claustrophobia in my jail cell, I developed another phobia—agoraphobia. When the day came for me to be transferred to the state prison, EMCF, the officers had to fight with me, and drag me out. I did not want to leave my cell. I had become used to this life of solitude. I feared being around people. I wanted to be in my cell all alone with my plant. I felt so dehumanized. Sorry . . . again I had to stop writing because my tears were coming down."[3]

This reaction is not unique to Vazquez. When the Colorado DOC, in an effort to reduce solitary confinement, attempted to transfer a large number of prisoners out of solitary confinement to general population, some prisoners refused to leave their cells.[4] They had become habituated to being alone in a cell and did not want to change. The Colorado DOC had to offer them incentives to get them to agree to leave their cells and join congregate activities in the general population, a step-down program, or a residential treatment facility.

When I was interviewing prisoners at Pelican Bay regarding the Ashker suit, one told me that after a long time in SHU just the experience of face-to-face contact can be terrifying. In SHU, 99 percent of one's verbal contact with other prisoners involves disembodied voices (i.e., prisoners cannot see each other from their cells). So when prisoners do meet face to face, for example when one of them is in transit to the "yard" and passes in front of another's cell, they get very anxious because the experience of face-to-face contact has become so unfamiliar.

There is no universal duration for the SHU postrelease syndrome. Some ex-prisoners tell me that they continued to isolate themselves only for the first few months out of SHU, but for others it seems to become a chronic and lasting pattern. Nor is there a clear pattern for the minimum length of time in isolation required to initiate the syndrome. Some prisoners develop severe reactions to SHU almost immediately; others tell me that they remained fairly stable emotionally the first few months they spent in SHU but that any longer duration caused significant emotional problems. Not all individuals consigned to SHU develop serious symptoms, and not all ex-inhabitants of SHU report the syndrome I am describing. It is a little like posttraumatic stress disorder (PTSD) in that regard: not all individuals who endure an equivalent trauma experience the signs and symptoms of PTSD. But significant portions of the SHU postrelease syndrome are reported to me by the vast majority of prisoners and ex-prisoners I meet who have been released from solitary confinement after a long stint.

THREE CASES OF POSTRELEASE LIFE IN THE COMMUNITY

Brian Nelson was convicted of murder and armed robbery at age seventeen. He managed to survive in the Illinois prisons until he went into solitary confinement in an Illinois supermax prison, Tamms Correctional Facility. I visited Tamms and examined him there in preparation for testimony in *Westefer v. Snyder*. At the time, Tamms Supermax was the highest-security prison operated by the Illinois Department of Corrections. The facility consisted of eight self-contained cell blocks, called pods, each containing six wings of ten cells. There was also J pod, a unit designated for behavior modification with disturbed prisoners. Each cell at Tamms had a narrow window placed high on the wall from which it was impossible for inmates to see anything unless they stood on their bed. The cell door was made of steel with small holes that made it difficult to see through. The inmates' view through the steel cell door was of a plain concrete wall. A few hours of exercise each week were permitted in a concrete "yard," about fifteen by thirty feet, located at the end of each pod. The yard was completely empty, with no recreation equipment. The walls were solid concrete. Visits took place across a Lexan window. Communication between the prisoner and the visitor was through a microphone that distorted voices and cut off all conversation if more than one person tried to talk at once. All such conversations were monitored by the guards. Both the visitor and the inmate had to sit on steel stools attached to the floor. The inmate's legs would be chained to a bolt in the floor. Tamms was closed in 2013 in response to an effective organizing effort by prisoners' families, community activists, and state legislators.

Brian Nelson had no official diagnosis of mental illness when he arrived at Tamms. Then he spent the last twelve years of his twenty-eight-year sentence in isolation at Tamms before being released from prison in 2010. When I met with him in 2004 he was clearly suffering from severe depression that made him listless and hopeless. In 2015, the Marshall Project, a nonprofit news organization covering the US criminal justice system, quoted him as saying: "I never had mental health issues before. I never saw a psychiatrist. I never took psychotropic medication. . . . I understand getting beat up. I don't understand what them walls did to my head."[5] The report continues about Mr. Nelson:

Talking about his time in solitary still triggers flashbacks: of pacing like "an animal in the zoo" until large blood blisters erupted on the soles of his feet; of jumping off his bed in an attempt to break his neck on the cement shelf in his cell. (The shelf broke.) . . . Nelson is now the prisoners' rights coordinator for the Uptown People's Law Center, a legal nonprofit in Chicago, where he corresponds with Illinois inmates and investigates their complaints. At first he worked in an office he and his colleagues called "the cell": a small, windowless room that held only his desk, chair, and a bookshelf of dusty legal volumes. "He was very comfortable there, so we didn't push him to move," said his boss, Alan Mills, executive director of the UPLC. Nelson has since relocated into a slightly larger office with a window, but it is upstairs and separate from the law firm's busy storefront. "As long as I'm alone, I'm okay," Nelson said. Five years after getting out, he still refuses to take public transit. During lunch at a crowded diner, he has to step outside several times to calm down. "I am afraid of people. Sometimes I think I don't belong out here." The 20 or so other men Nelson knows from supermax have had an even harder time adjusting. "All of us have a basement, somewhere we can hide," he said. "They come out at night," when there aren't as many people around. Very few have jobs. Most live off their families or receive disability benefits.

· · ·

Francisco, an energetic and articulate Latino in his fifties, had been in supermax solitary confinement for over a dozen years and then had been released from prison and was back in the community living with his wife for nine months when I interviewed him. He told me that in prison

I got less social over the years. It just started happening. Nobody talks to you. There's not much to talk about. I'd ask, "How are you doing." I saw myself changing, I didn't really want to talk. My social skills deteriorated. Slowly, with my wife's help, I am trying to talk. But mostly I don't say much. You stop talking because you've already heard everyone's stories. I didn't have anything to say. As the years go by, you are disintegrating. You don't even know what's happening. You might say "Good morning," or you might not. There's nothing more to say. I kept saying "Good morning," but some people stopped talking altogether. I was also afraid anything I said could be used against me in committee. . . . They'd say that's proof I was in a gang. . . . In SHU, when I got agitated, angry, I would exercise hard to keep from expressing anger and getting in trouble, so I would exercise to exhaustion. Gradually I lost touch with all feelings. You feel dead, you are dead to society, to the mainline. If you don't keep your mind occupied, you lose it. You see guys going crazy. So you clamp down on your feelings, don't talk much, and then you lose touch with what you're feeling.

Francisco proceeded to explain what it was like to be released into the community:

They left me off in downtown. I got out with no money and started walking. I waited for a ride, needed a pay phone to call my wife. I kept trying to get on my feet, get my mind back to normal. My mind is still not normal because in the SHU I started thinking I'd never get out, especially when I was denied at six-year reviews. When I [first] went to the street, it was really weird. I felt all caved in. I always wanted to be in my room and sit. I did not want to go out of the house. I would stay in my room four or five hours. I had TV and music in my room. I didn't like going to the store—too many people. I wasn't used to being with people. I'm always hyperaware, I won't let anyone touch me. It's not easy. It's like coming out of the insane asylum. Now it's been nine months, I still spend a lot of time in my room, that's where I'm most comfortable. I can go to the minimarket, but I can't go to the supermarket. Sometimes my wife talks me into going to a park or karaoke bar. When I got out, a lot of people came for interviews. I drank beer to relax. It's really difficult to go to new places.

. . .

Clyde, a middle-aged African American man, was first released from the Pelican Bay SHU into general population several years ago and later was released from prison to return to the community. He describes what it was like for him to be transferred from SHU to a general-population prison:

I spent nine years in [Pelican Bay SHU], 1992 to 2000. During that time, I was "validated," but not "active." Then I got transferred to general population at Tehachapi. It was traumatic. When I got out of SHU, it was like I was brought back to civilization. I found myself caught up in a desperate reconnection with grass on the yard, and I was still hearing voices from SHU and the slamming of SHU doors, and I could appreciate seeing a bird. [He cries as he recalls the moment.] I didn't know how to act. I celled with one other guy; I went everywhere with him. I was trying very hard to figure out how to function normally. The SHU environment created a military-type exterior: you had to be military to survive Pelican Bay SHU. Then I had to work on changing that exterior. I worked on not being paranoid [he reports he was paranoid in SHU, where he always felt under military attack]. I exercised like a soldier. In SHU, I had exercised compulsively to survive the SHU coldness. I tried to create life where it all felt totally dead. Then, when I got out, I continued the exercise to keep my feelings in check. I did this with no CDCR program in place to help us adjust. Like they said, "You have to recover from that isolation on your own." No therapy, no briefing. I probably could have gotten therapy if I'd asked for it, but I did not understand the trauma of SHU and why the need for therapy. All of my reactions were like someone who had been under attack. I didn't trust anyone. When I was released from [Pelican Bay SHU] to Tehachapi general population, I immediately got involved in securing whatever substance I could. Pruno, pills, marijuana. I isolated myself at Tehachapi, would not go near a crowd. I even created a space on the big yard that approximated the space in a SHU yard. I didn't do any programs, because I was isolating myself. I didn't know why I felt I had to do that.

Eventually Clyde was released from prison, and he now resides in the community. He provided me with an account of what happened after he was released from prison:

When I got out of prison, I did everything I could to escape into euphoria. I isolated myself, I surrendered myself to drug abuse. I had several relapses. I was in and out of drug treatment. Now I've been clean and sober for three years, seven months. I've experienced a lot of hallucinations and delusions. The voices and delusions only happened after I left SHU. In SHU I had been hearing [only] echoing sounds. The first time they became voices and paranoia was after I left SHU in 2000. The hallucinations and delusions are always there. I still hear the kind of yelling and screaming that I was exposed to in the SHU. It seems like there is always someone having a mental breakdown. In Tehachapi [he was in and out of SHU at Tehachapi for short periods], I was always hearing screams of mentally ill in the SHU, and the door slamming. That door-closing sound is something that might not have bothered me in SHU, but then when I was in general population and heard a loud noise I would jump. Then when I was released, I brought that same behavior to the streets. It interferes with every aspect of my life. Still today, if a car backfires, I jump, I'm getting prepared for combat. My heart races. I have flashbacks, always to SHU. I lay in bed now, alone in a room, wanting to urinate, it reminds me of laying in SHU watching TV from bed. I often feel like I am actually back there.

The SHU postrelease syndrome did not abate for Clyde when he left prison. He reports continuing SHU-induced symptoms in the community:

I can't function in a relationship. I can't function in them because I always find a need for compatibility equivalent to having a cellie. A cellie would leave me alone in the isolation I'd become accustomed with. In SHU, I was totally detached from my feelings, I knew of the harsh environment but refused to be sensitive, refused to cry. But since I've been out here, all of those feelings are released. I cry almost abnormally [he cries as he talks]. I came out of the SHU numb. In general population [where he was for a while before being released from prison] I didn't allow myself to feel, but after I got out of prison I slowly reclaimed my feelings. I had several relationships, but I couldn't break down the hard exterior from SHU.

TWO CASES OF SHU POSTRELEASE SYNDROME IN PRISON

The next case report is a man, I will call him Roberto, who was released from the Pelican Bay SHU after longer than ten years but remained in prison in a general-population setting. He was very slow to mix with other prisoners when he was released from SHU. He told me that in SHU a prisoner was locked into the shower and thus not subject to attack but that in a general-population prison multiple prisoners go to the shower at once and the door is unlocked, so there is a certain danger of assault. He worried that he might be paranoid, thinking that whenever he went to the group shower in the general population he was in danger of attack. Roberto could not determine whether his fear of attack was paranoid or reality based. In my opinion his fear was a combination of the two: there was a certain danger of attack in a maximum security group shower area, but he also was inclined to "ideas of reference" (a technical term for paranoid thinking) caused by the many years he had spent in the SHU.

Roberto was very anxious for some months after his transfer from SHU to the general-population unit. He continued to look around all the time to be certain he was not about to be assaulted. He felt that he was obsessing about his safety a lot, in ways he never had before his long stint in SHU. In SHU, he explained, if your cell door opened when it was not supposed to be open, you always had to be ready to defend yourself: it likely meant that another prisoner had arranged to have your door "popped" and was about to enter and assault you. He knew that this was irrational most of the time, but he was always hyperaware of doors opening and closing in the general-population prison. When a door opened, he had a flash of panic. He also became very anxious whenever another prisoner came toward him, in a way that he explained he had never felt in the general prison population prior to going to SHU. He felt he had become quite paranoid in SHU, and his hyperawareness of others in his vicinity seemed to him a remnant of that paranoia, though he reported it had diminished many months after he was transferred out of SHU. He told me, "I was like a hermit at Pelican Bay. Here I am adjusting to being with other prisoners, and by now I do come out of my cell." He also said that for months after his release from SHU he had carved out a very small space in the dayroom or yard in the general-population prison and had limited his activities to that place. Except for the hours when he worked in his prison job as a clerk, he would try to stay in his cell or to be in that particular space only with other prisoners he knew.

· · ·

Antonio, a Latino man with a wife and children in the community, was transferred to a maximum security general-population prison after spending twenty-three years in the Pelican Bay SHU. In SHU, he reported, he had become progressively more isolative and emotionally numb: "You had to, to survive in there." He stated that he had experienced distressing symptoms for several months after his return to general population, including a very strong startle reaction, paranoia, anxiety (especially when someone approached or touched him, or when he had to leave his familiar small area and move out to another section of the yard or the prison), irritability, angry outbursts that he struggled hard to suppress, problems trusting people, problems sharing his feelings with others, severe sleep problems, social isolation, and emotional numbing. All of those symptoms had eased quite a bit several months after he was released from SHU, although he was still experiencing them to a lesser degree. He reported he had had significant hypertension while he was in SHU but that his blood pressure had gone down after his transfer to general population. He felt that being in the general-population prison was much better than SHU, and he believed he had adjusted well to being in general population, primarily because he had a job and could be with other prisoners who had shared his experience in SHU. He also had a girlfriend, and once he returned to general population they had contact visits. But he felt that he was unable to share much of his feelings and inner experience with her because of all those years of isolation and emotional numbing while he had been in the SHU. At the time of our meeting he was working very hard on opening up more with her. He thought that the general-population prison where he had been transferred was a small, familiar place and that the real test of his ability to adjust to current conditions and maintain a normal comfort level would come when he eventually left prison altogether and reentered the much larger and more stimulating world of the community. He was nervous about that eventuality.

A WIDESPREAD PHENOMENON

If prisoners do not die in SHU (and there are tragically many suicides and deaths from treatable medical ailments in solitary confinement units) they will eventually be released from long-term solitary confinement. Many report that although in SHU they suffered many of the symptoms typical of prisoners there, their worst pain and suffering occurred after they were released. In preparation for my expert testimony in *Ashker v. Brown*, I interviewed twenty-four prisoners who had been in the SHU at Pelican Bay State Prison for over ten years. Five of them had been released to the community; nine had been released to "step-down units" or general-population prison settings. All of the fourteen ex-prisoners and prisoners who had been transferred to less restrictive prison settings reported that they continued to keep to themselves in a cell or an area of the dayroom, avoid crowds, be suspicious of anyone entering their vicinity, have strong startle reactions, have sleep problems, and have trouble expressing themselves and their feelings, even to intimates such as a wife or girlfriend.

As for prisoners who go directly from SHU to the community, they also tend to isolate themselves and to lead a constricted life. Some self-medicate with illicit substances, and some experience irrational temper outbursts. The Marshall Project reports:

> Every year, prisons across the country send thousands of people directly from solitary confinement back into their communities. An investigation by The Marshall Project and National Public Radio (NPR) found that 24 states released more than 10,000 people from solitary last year. . . . These individuals go from complete isolation one day to complete freedom the next, yet they are in many ways the least equipped to make the transition home. Inside prison, those in solitary—many of whom suffer from mental illnesses that were either triggered or exacerbated in segregation—often cannot participate in the classes or services offered to other inmates approaching their release

date. And in several states once those inmates in solitary are freed, they are more likely to be released without the help of a probation or parole officer. Those who make the jarring leap from solitary to the streets can easily end up jobless, homeless—or back in prison.[6]

IS IT PTSD?

The SHU postrelease syndrome and post-traumatic stress disorder (PTSD) share many characteristic symptoms and problems. Some of the men I interviewed for the *Ashker v. Brown* litigation do qualify for a diagnosis of PTSD (indeed, one ex-prisoner receives Social Security total disability for PTSD). But many others, though they have suffered multiple traumas, have post-traumatic symptoms that are not sufficiently intense and disabling to qualify them for a diagnosis of PTSD. For this reason, I am not proposing the SHU postrelease syndrome as a variant of PTSD.

The triggering event for the SHU postrelease syndrome, a long stint in almost total isolation and idleness followed by release home or to another prison setting, would arguably qualify as a trauma according to the fifth edition of the *Diagnostic and Statistical Manual of Mental Disorders (DSM-V)*.[7] If I were trying to have this syndrome considered by the relevant committee to be included in a future edition of the *DSM*, I would need to specify the symptoms more clearly, group them, and then require that a certain number of symptoms from each group be present for the diagnosis to be aptly applied. SHU postrelease syndrome gives a name to a significant group of ex-prisoners' experiences, and my hope is that by being able to name the phenomenon and know that others share their pain, they will be better able to talk about their experience with family, ministers, or psychotherapists. In other words, my hope is that having a name for the syndrome will help those who suffer from it to get help and end their isolation.

In PTSD we see a person who has been traumatized and then has strong emotional reactions to the trauma but works hard at suppressing the resulting feelings and agitation. He or she self-isolates, dreading social interactions, and tends to suppress feelings. Then unwanted and dysfunctional feelings break through the individual's attempts to suppress all feelings and erupt in irrational, rageful acts or inappropriate outbursts. The reclusive Vietnam or Iraq veteran who one day comes out of the house where he has been secluding himself and goes on a violent rampage is the tragic exemplar of this pattern.

I do not find that the *Ashker v. Brown* plaintiffs all suffer from PTSD, or that all the horrors of SHU confinement are satisfactorily described as a trauma.

But there are similarities between the plight, for example, of the returning Afghanistan veteran and that of the prisoner released to return to the community after spending an inordinately long period in SHU. In a recent article about delayed suicides among veterans of the Second Battalion of the Seventh Marine Regiment, a battalion that was party to an extraordinary number of deaths in the mountains of Afghanistan, Dr. Roy H. Greenberg, a psychiatrist and health consultant, describes what researchers call "extreme situations." Intense military battles abroad and long-term SHU confinement would both qualify. He writes, "PTSD symptoms frequently worsen when a veteran feels rawly plunged into civilian life. Reading between the lines, one gets the sense that some of the traumatized vets . . . suffered existential disorientation, as if there had been a tectonic shift in the expectable world. This was accompanied by an aching aloneness—even the desire to go back to the dreadfully familiar killing fields of Afghanistan."[8] The ex-prisoner who holes up in his bedroom as if re-creating the environment of the SHU may be experiencing the same desire to go back to what is expectable.

DISTINGUISHING UNIQUE EFFECTS OF SHU FROM OTHER PRISON EFFECTS: IS IT POSSIBLE?

In naming a new syndrome or pathological entity of any kind, clinicians have the responsibility to differentiate the proposed syndrome from other known medical or mental health conditions. Often that is no easy task. For example, two of the symptoms of the SHU postrelease syndrome are difficulty expressing feelings and difficulty trusting others, even one's spouse or first-degree relatives. But these could be symptoms of the prison experience itself, even if there is no solitary confinement. And past trauma can lead one to be very slow to trust and to share one's feelings with others.

In the life stories of the prisoners whom I report on in court, four general themes tend to stand out: (1) preincarceration childhood traumas such as physical and sexual abuse; (2) "prisonization," or the internalization of the norms of prison culture (see below); (3) the idiosyncratic traumas that occur during a prison term, including witnessing or being the victim of physical or sexual assaults, seeing prisoners murdered nearby, being beaten by officers, and so forth; and finally, (4) the harm of long-term solitary confinement.

I have already discussed the high prevalence of trauma in the lives of prisoners. Prisonization, as the social psychologist and prison expert Craig Haney has described it, "involves the incorporation of the norms of prison life into one's habits of thinking, feeling and acting. . . . The longer persons are incarcerated, the more significant is the nature of their institutional transformation."[9] For example, according to John Irwin, who served many years in prison and then became a sociologist of the prison experience, prisonization robs prisoners of the capacity and will to initiate actions on their own: they are always waiting to find out how they are supposed to do something or where they are supposed to stand.[10]

Further, prisonization constricts inmates' sense of who they can be and what is possible for them. When prisoners tell me, "You don't want to get your head into prison, and you don't want to get prison into your head," they are talking about sustaining a sense of being part of the larger community to which they will eventually return. If they can do this, they will be motivated to take advantage of every opportunity in prison to learn skills and maintain relationships that will foster a successful life after they are released. But once they start to think of themselves as "just prisoners," they blend into prison culture by joining in fights and criminal activities there, and their prospects for success after release dwindle significantly.

Prisonization can also lead to postrelease intimacy problems. It too often leads to difficulty trusting others and a reluctance to abandon the "tough guy" exterior long enough to be spontaneous and forthcoming with loved ones.[11] If a prisoner can keep up his connections in the community while serving time, and if he can see himself returning to that community when he leaves prison, then he can begin to seek classes, a slot in a training program, and a job in the prison, all preparatory to being released. Part of a rehabilitative attitude is a firm commitment to helping prisoners keep their heads out of the prison.

As a general rule, the more prisonization, the more difficulty one will have adjusting to postrelease life in the community. Again, visiting plays an important role. Prisoners who are able to maintain quality relationships with loved ones while doing their time are much more likely to leave prison emotionally stable and to succeed back in the community. This makes sense: loved ones keep the prisoner connected with what is going on in the outside world, keep the prisoner's mind on a future in society, help him retain the capacity to love and empathize with others, and make him think twice about getting into the kind of trouble in prison that could delay his release. But many prisoners have relatively few visitors during their years behind bars.

When I testify on these four likely sources of harm, I am asked during cross-examination whether I can distinguish between the harm done by early preincarceration traumas, the prison experience itself, accumulated idiosyncratic traumas, and the harm done specifically by the isolation and idleness of SHU. I respond that all of these things are additive and tend to exacerbate each other. It would be extremely unusual to find a prisoner in SHU who had not already experienced the effects of early traumas, prisonization, and traumas in prison. In fact, these can usefully be viewed as precursors to the SHU postrelease syndrome. It is less important to prove that solitary confinement singularly causes the damage than to understand how long-term solitary confinement exacerbates and magnifies damage already wreaked by the combination of multiple traumas and prisonization. In effect, I am ascribing to the "eggshell skull" legal theory. If one person hits another on the head and the victim dies, and defense lawyers for the hitter argue that the man who died had a skull like an eggshell, subject to easy fracture, the court will determine that the eggshell-like skull of the victim is a preexisting condition and provides no mitigation for the crime of breaking the man's skull. Similarly, the prisoner in SHU has been harmed by prior traumas and the experience of prisonization, but that does not make the harm of solitary confinement more acceptable.

Often it is impossible to separate the four general themes that are intertwined in the prisoner's life. Consider the example of a young man with a history of childhood abuse who is raped on the prison yard, gets into a fight about it, and goes to solitary confinement. Were his subsequent symptoms and dysfunction caused more by prison itself, by the rape, or by time spent in solitary? All of these factors will play a part in his difficult straits.

In some, though not all cases, however, there are ways to distinguish which affronts have caused which symptoms. This involves clinical acumen, including asking the right questions. If a prisoner was raped by another prisoner, then fought back and was put in segregation for a long time for fighting (since according to the unwritten prisoner code one has to fight and one must never snitch), spent several years in SHU, was returned to a general-population prison, and currently is experiencing flashbacks and nightmares, the clinician can ask, "When did these troublesome symptoms begin?" If the prisoner reports convincingly that they began only some months after he was sent to segregation, the clinician can then ask, "What is the content of the flashbacks and the nightmares?" And if the prisoner reports that he sees the walls closing in on him and about to crush him, or wakes feeling as if he is back in a segregation cell, then the clinician can ask if he ever had the experience of walls closing in on him before he spent time in segregation. If the prisoner answers in the negative, the clinician can reasonably conclude that the symptoms were largely caused by the time spent in solitary confinement. Prison, the rape, and the fight served as precursors, to be sure. But like the "eggshell skull," the prior prison experience and prior traumas were background predisposing factors, and the specific symptoms of flashbacks and nightmares were caused largely by the ordeal of solitary confinement.

A REHABILITATIVE ATTITUDE

Part of my investigation for the *Ruiz v. Brown* litigation was a trip in 2014 to the Substance Abuse and Treatment Facility (SATF) immediately adjacent to Corcoran Prison in California's Central Valley. There I interviewed eight prisoners who had been released from the SHU at Pelican Bay State Prison and had been transferred at approximately the same time to the SATF.[12] Several told me that when they had arrived a ranking officer had greeted them and told them he knew they had spent a long time in segregation, and that it could mess with your head, so that when they got transferred out there could be psychological problems. This was "normal," he said, and they shouldn't worry about it: it was pretty usual for guys getting out of SHU to have transient emotional problems and was a little like PTSD. They should be patient with themselves and each other. He told them he would come back to their pod every day he could and meet with them as a group to talk about how things were going, and he recommended that they meet together with him as frequently as possible for a while until they felt better adjusted. He wanted the prisoners to do well, and he told them that. The prisoners I interviewed told me that this officer's instructions and support had helped them through the worst of their postrelease emotional problems. I don't think that ranking officer was a trained clinical psychologist, but he had what I term a rehabilitative attitude.

The officer's intuitive rehabilitative approach can serve as a model for a therapeutic intervention that can help prisoners damaged by their time in SHU to heal and reintegrate. If these individuals remain in prison, their reintegration into the general prison population will serve as a rehearsal for their eventual reintegration into their community when they go home. And if they "max out of SHU," or leave prison straight out of solitary confinement, their caseworker or parent in the community needs to have a working knowledge of the SHU postrelease syndrome and needs to offer some of what the ranking officer at SATF offered the eight ex-SHU residents when they arrived at his prison.

TO LOVE, WORK, AND PLAY AGAIN

In the story that began this chapter, I told the mother to hand over to her son control of his whereabouts. I will not further discuss therapeutic interventions for the SHU postrelease syndrome here except to say that was an intervention I borrowed from our clinical understanding of trauma and the treatment of its aftereffects. Traumas happen to a person: the person has no agency during the traumatic event, which is accidental or is forced upon the sufferer. Consequently, treatment for anyone suffering the aftereffects of trauma must begin by fostering greater agency in the trauma survivor. Permitting her son to decide when he feels safe enough to leave his room and join the family for a meal is the beginning of a process where, one hopes, her son will regain a sense of his own agency and begin to heal.

Today, much long-overdue attention is being directed to helping ex-prisoners succeed after they are released. The SHU postrelease syndrome is an important part of that picture. Here I am merely describing the syndrome. We need to carefully consider what interventions might help affected individuals, after their release from SHU, to regain their functional capacities to "love, work, and play" again. We need to help prisoners and ex-prisoners reenvision a future for themselves.

PART THREE

The Alternative to Solitary

NINE

A Rehabilitative Attitude

A STORY IS CIRCULATING THAT may be apocryphal, but I have tried to gather testimony that it happened, and ranking members of the Washington Department of Corrections I have queried about it say they have no reason to disbelieve it. Here is the story: Several years ago, a large number of cell extractions were occurring in a SHU under the jurisdiction of the Washington Department of Corrections. Since the unit was small compared to the ones at Pelican Bay or Corcoran in California, the central office of the Washington DOC started wondering whether discipline there was not being handled satisfactorily, and they assigned a new unit manager to turn things around. On his first day on the job, the new manager asked the officers to go along with him in an experiment to improve officer-prisoner relations by showing the prisoners more respect—for example, addressing them as Mr. Smith or Mr. Jones instead of using first names, and refraining from raising their voices or swearing at prisoners. Then the new manager talked to all of the prisoners individually, asking them to go along with this experiment as well by calling correction officers "Officer Smith" or "Sergeant Jones" and refraining from swearing at them. Both sides agreed, and in the weeks and months that followed, the number of cell extractions plummeted.

The new unit manager demonstrated what I call a rehabilitative attitude. He paid both the officers and the prisoners the respect of making a personal visit to meet each of them. He proposed mutual respect between officers and prisoners, and he gave both officers and prisoners a way to disengage from the cycle of hostility that had led to the excessive number of cell extractions under the previous manager, a choice that would permit prisoners to improve their situation. Mutual respect and agency—these are two critical ingredients in any successful preparation for prisoners' return to the community. If prisoners have the opportunity to interact with staff in relations of mutual respect, and if staff offer choices that make prisoners feel that they still have some agency even though they are prisoners, then those prisoners' chances of succeeding when they return to the community will be much improved.[1] In addition, prisoners need to be helped to see themselves as part of the larger community rather than as permanent fixtures in prison culture. At all points along the way, they must be helped to imagine what freedom for them will look like and to sustain a vision of themselves participating again in the larger society.

THE FIRST STEP: ENDING
THE CYCLE OF HOSTILITY

Ending the cycle of hostility is a necessary first step in making prison rehabilitation succeed. The new unit manager at the SHU in Washington knew that. The prisoners in SHU were not enrolled in rehabilitation programs, but he was looking forward to their progressing past their stint in SHU and taking part in programs. He did not want them to prolong their time in SHU by acting out and receiving more disciplinary tickets. I invite all staff to adopt a rehabilitative attitude with prisoners. The classroom teacher and the trainer in woodworking shop can succeed at preparing prisoners to go straight only if the entire staff, including correction officers, adopt a rehabilitative attitude. Each staffer finds his or her own way to break the cycle of hostility.

Officers can be too quick to do cell extractions. The prisoner in a solitary cell refuses to return his food tray, refuses to put his hands through the food port so that cuffs can be applied, or swears at an officer in the hallway outside his cell. The officers become angry and initiate a cell extraction. Often the prisoner has reconsidered his actions by this time and is willing to do what he has been ordered to do, but the officers say it's too late and immediately assemble an extraction team, put on gas masks, and shoot immobilizing gas through the food port in preparation to entering the cell and slamming the prisoner against a wall. If a little time could pass, tempers would likely cool. Often calling in different officers to reason with the prisoner can resolve things without violence.

If the prison had a policy that before a cell extraction could be initiated the shift commander or warden would need to come to the site, talk to the prisoner, and approve of the use of force, there would be far fewer cell extractions and much less use of immobilizing gas and violence. Such a policy would allow several things to happen at once. The time it would take to summon the commander would permit tempers to cool. A different custody person's intervention could lead to a compromise that would make the use of force unnecessary. And then the visit by the commander or warden could allow the recalcitrant prisoner to feel respected and be more amenable to changing his behavior. He might be refusing to return his tray because the food was rotten or had bugs in it and he wanted someone in authority to hear his complaint. When the shift commander came to the unit and the prisoner reported the rotten food, he would feel heard. In any case, this policy could result in far fewer cell extractions taking place. If the prisoner suffered from mental illness, mental health staff could also come to his cell, listen to his complaint, and try to reason with him. Often, when a friendly mental health staffer who is known to the prisoner arrives, the prisoner calms down and becomes more reasonable.

Shaming plays a part in the cycle of hostility. Often staff do not even realize that they are shaming the prisoners they guard, but segregation settings actually multiply occasions of shaming or humiliation through the constant use of chains and shackles, superfluous strip searches, cell searches, and other measures of custodial overkill.[2] The humiliation the prisoner feels as the focus of these practices merely reinforces his tendency to strike out aggressively whenever he feels shamed: he consequently acts even more aggressively to protect himself from humiliation, and the acting out leads to more humiliating forms of punishment.

Prisoners need to find their part in breaking the cycle of hostility too. Todd Ashker was a prisoner at the Pelican Bay SHU for twenty years when, working as his own attorney (*pro se*), he initiated the lawsuit that eventually became the class action *Ashker v. Brown.*[3] He was also one of the leaders of three hunger strikes by California prisoners between 2011 and 2013.[4] And he was one of the initiators of the "Agreement to End Hostilities, August 12, 2012," a document resolving to halt racial animosities in the California prisons. The agreement states, in part: "Therefore, beginning on October 10, 2012, all hostilities between our racial groups . . . in SHU, Ad-Seg, General Population, and County Jails, will officially cease. This means that from this date on, all racial group hostilities need to be at an end . . . and if personal issues arise between individuals, people need to do all they can to exhaust all diplomatic means to settle such disputes; do not allow personal, individual issues to escalate into racial group issues!!"[5] In an article explaining the

Agreement to End Hostilities, Todd wrote, "It's an honor to participate in our collective coalition. For the third time in twenty-nine years I have felt a sense of human connectedness. This collective energy—inside and out— keeps us strong, positive, and alive. It gives us hope of one day having a glimpse of trees; feeling the warmth of the sun."[6]

The hunger strikers at Pelican Bay State Prison deserve credit for shifting attention from the dangerousness of the "worst of the worst" to the prospect for people to grow and change, to have different inclinations and different needs. Keeping prisoners in solitary confinement for over thirty years (the plight of a number of the hunger strikers) is torture, and is absurd. Todd Ashker and all of the hunger strikers at Pelican Bay exhibited an admirable rehabilitative attitude. They fostered respect in all participants, the officers, the courts, the administrators, legislators, and all the various gangs and cliques in prison. They gave all participants their say. They taught prisoners they could still exhibit agency. And their vision always involved a future of greater freedom. They were very connected with the outside world, their community as well as their many supporters. And then, with everyone's attention directed at them, the hunger strike leaders announced a peace agreement between rival gangs.

Ex-prisoners tell me that, on average, the prison staff who had the most positive influence on them were staff who they believed wanted to hear about their experience and sincerely wanted to help them. Such staff have a rehabilitative attitude, in contrast to staff who are exclusively focused on the culture of punishment.

STEP 2: CREATE MUTUAL RESPECT

Concerns about respect are rampant on the streets of our inner cities. Young men become enraged when they feel disrespected, are willing to fight to the death to attain "a little respect," and consider their quest successful only when sufficient outward signs point to their being respected by peers and establishment figures alike. Ironically, this quest to be respected occurs in a social context where low-income youth, especially youth of color, suffer disrespect at every turn. On average, the young men who fight it out on the streets and participate in drive-by shootings are the most disadvantaged in our society. They receive a low-quality education (relative to what the public and private schools provide in middle-class neighborhoods) and then are told that the reason for their academic failure is their own lack of intelligence or laziness. They are the last hired and first fired, they are forced to work for subsistence wages, they are routinely pulled over by police and frisked for no apparent reason, and if they talk back to the officers they are likely to be beaten, arrested, or worse. Mothers of color teach their young sons how to act very subservient with police so they won't be killed. It is as if street toughs and gang members are demanding as fighters precisely what they are systematically denied in the larger society. They are fighting with each other for what they think of as a modicum of respect, but meanwhile they brutalize others and commit crimes that send many to prison.

Several experts on violence have concurred that much of it, in the words of the psychiatrists James Gilligan and Bandy Lee, "is motivated by the fear or the experience of being 'disrespected,' and is resorted to as the only means that is perceived as available by which to maintain or regain respect from others (and, correspondingly, pride and self-respect)." Gilligan and Lee point out that this is "especially likely to be the case when, in the culture in which the individual is living, respect, and non-violent means of gaining respect, are both in short supply."[7] When Gilligan asked prisoners why they had assaulted or killed someone, they would almost always tell him that "it was because 'he disrespected me' (or my mother, wife, girl-friend, fellow gang member, etc.)."[8] James Garbarino, who has spent two decades serving as a psychological expert witness in murder trials, concurs. In his book *Listening to Killers: Lessons Learned from My 20 Years As a Psychological Expert Witness in Murder Cases,* he addresses this same issue. "A respect-based culture in prisons (and youth detention centers)," Garbarino writes, "is a crucial component of a national effort to reduce killing."[9]

In prison, many continue to fight for respect that is denied to them by society at large.[10] In a familiar scenario on the prison yard, one prisoner defeats another in a fight, then yells at him, "You're not a man, you're a pussy." In more than a few cases, rape follows.[11] In my discussions with many prisoners about prisoner-on-prisoner rape I have repeatedly found that it is not really about sex, it's about domination: expressing domination is a desperate way to attain a modicum of respect. But when officers arbitrarily punish prisoners, insult them, and deprive them of the most basic human necessities, the prisoners feel disrespected anew and their resentment mounts.

It would be impossible to chronicle all the instances of disrespect I witness in my tours of prisons as I prepare to testify in court. Let me just say I am repeatedly shocked that some of the practices and abuses I witness can be occurring in the United States today. There is no legitimate "penological objective" in denying prisoners respect while they are doing their time, even in SHU, or especially in SHU. In fact, if rehabilitation is to succeed, prisoners must be respected at every turn and must have reason to respect their warders so they will be prepared to be in mutually respectful relationships after they leave prison.

STEP 3: FOSTER A SENSE OF AGENCY

Another name for a supermaximum security unit is "control unit." The name is justified, because the isolated occupants of supermaximum segregation cells have no control over even the smallest and most personal aspects of their daily lives. They are totally dependent on officers to bring their meals, give them toilet paper and cleaning materials, turn on and off their lights and the water in their cells, take them to shower, bring their mail, tell them what pictures they can have in their cell, and so forth. In other words, the supermaximum security prison unit was designed to entirely eradicate any sense of agency prisoners may have felt in their lives. All control is in the hands of the staff, and prisoners have to adjust to this. But the tendency to isolate prisoners in their cells and diminish their sense of agency is not limited to actual segregation settings such as a supermaximum security unit. At all levels of security, the trend in penology since the 1980s is for staff to maintain relatively more control of prisoners' lives. The hours when prisoners are permitted to roam the facility have been incrementally diminished, the kinds of mail and packages prisoners can receive have been increasingly limited (e.g., families in many states cannot send homemade packages, and they must pay an approved vendor to send in a uniformly packaged set of items), visits have been restricted, and so forth.

Agency is about being the subject of one's own life rather than the object of designs established by others. I do not mean by agency the freedom to write one's own ticket. Rather, agency is the evolving creation of a life by the person who lives it. Of course, many variables affect one's sense of agency, including one's education, earning capacity, financial reserves, personal attractiveness, good friends, and very importantly, personal and family relationships. Personal capacities also play a big part, including the capacity to play, to create, to make friends, to be deeply intimate, even to envision a better future.

Psychotherapists work hard to instill a sense of agency in their patients. Depression is all about a lack of agency. The depressed wife tells her therapist she is mad at her husband because he stays too late at the office, but she is afraid to confront him about his behavior because she is afraid he would desert the family. She has no tenable move to make, no way to alter the unfortunate family dynamic, so she sinks into depression. We look at messages she received as a child from her parents about a wife's role, and we look at ways she can raise the subject with her husband without making him feel criticized and attacked. We talk about some incremental gains that would make her feel she is moving toward an improved situation. She decides on a nonthreatening (i.e., not critical) tack to take with her husband: she will say that if he would select two evenings a week when he would leave work at a decent hour and be home in time to have dinner with the family, she would be okay with his staying late at the office on the other evenings. Her depression lightens. Her dissatisfaction and unhappiness may not be entirely "fixed," but her sense that she can do something to affect her situation is a great improvement over the "stuckness" she has been feeling. Finding a way to move forward is the beginning of restoring a sense of agency, and often in psychotherapy it is the moment when the depression lightens and the patient begins to work on her issues in a new and more effective way.

Similarly, all the people I have spoken with who work with "at risk" or "troubled youth," for example in a school or juvenile court program or juvenile hall, tell me that they are most successful with their wards when what they offer the youths is a choice—about a path forward, a way to complete their schooling, a way to escape from an abusive home situation, a way to take care of a baby as a single mother, some meaningful work, or a way to move away from gang influences and connections. In other words, they offer the youths a greater sense of agency in determining their life trajectory.

Although some loss of agency is inherent in the prison experience, it is nevertheless essential when devising prison policies to also consider how this loss of agency affects a prisoner's chances for effective rehabilitation. In prison, people lose the unique identity they enjoyed in the community, they don prison-issued garb, they are given an identification number, and they are forced to follow orders, lots of orders. There are rules governing almost every miniscule aspect of everyday life, and there are officers watching over the prisoners to make certain they follow every rule, always ready to issue a "ticket" for misconduct. As an expert witness I have had the opportunity to interview well over a thousand prisoners in fifteen states.

Universally they complain about feeling they have little or no agency in their lives.

The ultimate example of the total loss of agency is what I term "dead time" in SHU. By *dead time* I mean an indeterminate sentence to solitary confinement, where the prisoner can do nothing to improve his or her situation. The "snitch, parole, or die" double-bind in California's prisons, described in chapter 4, is an example.[12] Before the settlement of *Ashker v. Brown*, prisoners consigned to SHU would be released from isolation only if they informed on other prisoners as part of a formal "debriefing" procedure ("snitch"), if their prison sentence came to an end ("parole"), or when they died. Even in states where SHU terms are less draconian and prisoners receive a six-month, one-year, or eighteen-month sentence to SHU for specific rule violations, prisoners all too often see a SHU term as a life sentence in the sense that they do not feel capable of avoiding confrontations with officers and tell me that the inevitable confrontation will only result in a sentence to more time in SHU. Release from SHU requires a long period free of disciplinary infractions, and confrontations with officers trigger further disciplinary write-ups. The result is that the prisoner feels hopeless and lacking in agency. And prisoners who feel they have nothing to lose get into a lot of trouble, or self-destruct.

I still think we need to get rid of solitary entirely, and I am not interested in trying to dress up the very damaging practice of solitary confinement with small improvements such as a little more time out of one's cell in congregate activities. But one thing worthy of note that various departments are doing to help with the dead-time problem is to create stepwise improvements in amenities and freedoms. The steps are usually designated "phases," and the period in isolation is divided into a series of phases that are traversed on the path to release. To be effective, the phases need to be very short, the requirements for advancement need to be clear and achievable, and staff need to actively encourage prisoners to advance rather than taunting them with disparaging remarks. In other words, instead of a very long period of stark deprivation without end ("dead time"), prisoners who satisfy clearly specified requirements are granted incremental improvements in their situation— more phone calls, more out-of-cell activities, more commissary, more contact with other prisoners, more liberal recreation opportunities—until they win release from isolation. Advocates of this kind of improvement point to a growing sense of agency in prisoners' ability to advance through the phases and attain greater amenities and freedoms.

Again, I do not support the utilization of solitary confinement at all. The practice of solitary confinement is a human rights abuse and must end, so this very partial addressing of the deadness experienced by current SHU residents does not remedy the harm of solitary confinement. But quite a few departments of corrections are building phases into their SHU policies, and that can provide some transient improvement on the way to ending SHU confinement altogether. I mention this trend as an example, minimal though it is, of fostering greater agency by giving prisoners something they can do to improve their situation, which must be the plan in relation to all treatment and rehabilitation efforts. It is the continual enhancement of a sense of agency, not the continuation of isolation as a management strategy, that I am recommending.

Litigation efforts can also increase a sense of agency on the part of prisoners. In *Cain v. Michigan Department of Corrections*, for example, a group of prisoners served as their own attorneys under the supervision of attorney Sandra Girard, director of Michigan Prison Legal Services. When I testified in this suit in 1998, the jailhouse lawyers who did most of the legal work on the case had official prison jobs as legal assistants to Ms. Girard and worked in a bungalow on the grounds of the large prison in Jackson, Michigan. Ms. Girard would come to the prison to work with them in the office. (The office of Michigan Prison Legal Services would subsequently be removed from the prison.) Raymond Charles Whalen, one of the prisoner plaintiffs, was my "attorney," meaning he worked with me to prepare my testimony and then presented me in court, handling direct examination as well as cross-examination, with Ms. Girard sitting next to him at the attorney bench. I have to say, and I said during the proceedings, that Mr. Whalen was one of the most conscientious, creative, and competent attorneys I have ever worked with, even though he had no law degree and was functioning under Ms. Girard's license and supervision.

Cain v. MDOC was tried in state court, and the issues were many. The plaintiff class was challenging classification procedures in the Michigan DOC, policies about such things as the clothing and possessions permitted prisoners and the conditions in solitary confinement. Because there was much media attention to the case and the group of prisoners who were trying the case had family members and supporters in the community, the judge decided to hold the trial in the gymnasium of a local jail near the prison so that community members would have easier access. The prisoners acting as counsel were transferred from the prison to the jail, and security remained intact. The courtroom was a set of risers in the middle of the jail's basketball court, with benches and chairs for the judge, attorneys, and the jury. The bleachers were open to family and community members, and quite a few attended and cheered at appropriate times. Mr. Whalen called me to the stand in the impromptu courtroom and conducted my testimony and cross-examination with remarkable finesse.

Approximately eight prisoners were acting as counsel in the case, and they all sat at the legal bench with Mr. Whalen and Ms. Girard. It was clear in the facial expressions of the jailhouse lawyers that they were very proud of their legal accomplishment. The pride they evidenced the day I testified was entirely inspiring. The court proceedings were captured on television news, and prisoners throughout the Michigan DOC watched developments very closely. I know, because I toured the prison before and after the trial and talked to many of them, that they also felt great pride having prisoners, their peers, fight for their rights.

I also witnessed this kind of pride in agency on the part of prisoners in another class action lawsuit. Again in Michigan, several years later, the *Neal v. Michigan DOC* class action lawsuit about custodial sexual abuse (perpetrators being staff, women prisoners the victims) went to trial, and I was again asked to testify. Deborah LaBelle and a very able team of attorneys represented five hundred women who had been sexually harassed, assaulted, or out-and-out raped. Several of the women took the stand to testify at trial. This was a very difficult assignment for them. There is a lot of shame in being sexually assaulted, and there is a very reality-based dread of retaliation for reporting sexual assault when the women feel so powerless and the staff who sexually abuse them have so much power over them.[13] It was very moving to see the women take the stand, one after another, to report what happened. Several cried while talking to the jury, but they didn't quit, they kept on telling their stories. The jury decided in their favor and awarded them millions of dollars. There were several trials, each involving subgroups of twelve or fifteen of the women. After the jury for one of the trials ruled in the women's favor, the foreman of the jury read an apology to the women into the record, apologizing that staff representing the state of Michigan had treated them so horribly. Again, the pride the women felt standing up for themselves in court was palpable to onlookers.

I do not mean to imply that the purpose of class action litigation is to foster a sense of agency in the prisoners. There have to be identifiable violations of the Constitution—and this was proven in all the cases for which I have testified as an expert. But the pride prisoners feel when they finally get their day in court is a poignant illustration of agency. When staff control every tiny aspect of prisoners' lives and give them no say in what happens in the prisons, they are stifling agency on the part of prisoners. Staff argue that they need to give the prisoners clear instructions and orders and to punish them if they are to maintain security in the facility. But I have not seen one shred of evidence that treating prisoners disrespectfully and denying them any semblance of agency makes the prisons safer. Staff must instead make every attempt to give prisoners more of a role in deciding how their situation in prison will evolve and to cheer them on as they take more and more control of their lives.

The social psychologist and prison researcher Hans Toch describes in his 2014 book workshops he has led for correctional staff and administrators.[14] He talks about the necessity of creating a humane and responsive system, recruiting prisoners to take part in crisis intervention teams, fostering interdiscipline staff collaboration, and having mental health staff spend more time in the prison's common areas, available to talk. Toch describes his experience helping establish a prison regimen where prisoners and staff collaborate in a democratic process for running the prison. Naturally, the prisoners do not get a say about everything. They are not permitted to change their sentence or to determine whether staff get a raise. But within the parameters that are reasonable in prison—after all, we all know who is still in charge—the prisoners get a small taste of agency as they have their say about, for example, "an attempt to surface and confront the parental nature of staff-inmate transactions at the prison."[15] The officers talk and the prisoners talk. The conversation can sway the way the prison operates.

At Grendon Prison in the United Kingdom, a maximum security facility, very tough prisoners maintain the peace, meanwhile taking part in a large array of decisions that affect their lives.[16] Of course, staff cannot turn all decisions over to the prisoners, but they can foster prisoners' sense of agency everywhere they see it emerging in constructive activities.

STEP 4: EXPAND CONNECTION
WITH THE OUTSIDE WORLD

An important part of any remedy for prisoners' feelings of inertia, social death, and despair is for them to stay connected to a world much larger than the prison culture of punishment, through contacts with loved ones and relevant educational and job training pursuits. A prisoner who sees his mother, his wife, or his child during visiting hours on Sunday is a prisoner who can better withstand the excessive punitiveness of officers on Tuesday.[17] He remembers he is part of a family, he is loved, he has responsibilities as a father. If prisoners can sustain quality contact with loved ones throughout a prison term, take part in educational and training programs, and always think of themselves as solid members of the community at large who are only temporarily spending time in prison, then they can avoid being entirely caught up in the culture of punishment and its cycle of hostility: that is, they can resist the sort of "prisonization" that I discussed back in chapter 8.

It is unfortunate that departments of correction tend to make visiting very difficult. Maximum and supermaximum security prisons tend to be built far from population centers, while most of the prisoners' families live in the big cities. The distance alone makes visiting problematic. Then corrections departments go overboard on limiting and restricting visitation, often by providing scant time for visiting and by requiring family members to wait in long lines to see their loved ones. They may impose very strict rules about clothing, so that family members will be denied visits and will be sent home if they wear the wrong clothes. They may perform increasingly intrusive searches, which dissuade humiliated family members and friends from visiting. They may severely restrict mail and packages from home. Or they may punish prisoners who violate prison rules with loss of visitation—a widespread practice that violates international human rights standards. These obstacles have the overall effect of decreasing the number and quality of prison visits.

In 1986, the California Department of Corrections instituted searches of visitors' automobiles when they parked in the visitor parking lot at San Quentin State Prison and other facilities. San Quentin has a narrow driveway for entry and exit from the visitors' parking lot, and officers would block visitors' automobiles from exiting once they had entered the lot. Then they would thoroughly search the cars, including the trunk and under the chassis, using flashlights and guard dogs and throwing belongings around. Presumably they were looking for drugs and weapons. But the premise for the car searches made no sense. The visitor would have to go through security clearance at the prison gate after parking the car, so one wonders why, if officers found an old, crumpled empty beer can in the recesses of the tire compartment of the trunk, they needed to charge the car's owner with an attempt to smuggle contraband alcohol into a state prison. A class action lawsuit was brought by the Prison Law Office, a public interest law firm that has litigated many prison policies in California and taken some cases as far as the Supreme Court, claiming that the searches were excessive, had no penological objective, and were merely conducted for the unstated purpose of dissuading family members from visiting prisoners. In the declaration that I provided in the *Salazar v. McCarthy* (1986) litigation, I explained the policy's ramifications to the court:

> Visitation by family members and friends is very important to inmates' psychological well-being during confinement and to their ability to adjust to society upon release from confinement. Visits with family and loved ones permit the inmate to maintain a support network and to know that his intimate friends have not deserted him. This diminishes his anxiety and permits him a future to look forward to. Moreover, regular visitation enables an inmate to feel better about his manliness—i.e., he is still a part of the family, looked up to by his children, and able to continue filling the male role of husband, boyfriend or father—and to look forward to continuing intimacies after release. In my experience, men who are denied regular visitation tend to be more belligerent and depressed because of it, and in a significant but smaller number of cases, this kind of social isolation plays a large part in an eventual psychotic decompensation (breakdown) or suicide attempt. It is my opinion that the challenged search procedure is intimidating to visitors, discourages visitation, and is consequently harmful to inmates' mental state.

The court ordered the California Department of Corrections to halt the visitor parking lot searches. Several years later, the department instituted Rapiscan searches of visitors arriving at the prisons.[18] A low-level X-ray machine, similar to those used in airport security today, was installed at the visiting entrance. Individuals wishing to enter the prison to see their husband, father, or son would have to submit to an X-ray scan before being admitted. The imaging device was set low so that the individual being scanned appeared naked on the screen: in other words, the machine would see through their clothes but not their skin as an X-ray machine used in a medical setting would do. In practice, whether or not this was by design, officers began commenting to each other about the body shape of women visitors, saying "nice breasts" and so forth. Or, as several female visitors reported overhearing, one officer would say to another that he would like to have sex with a woman he watched being scanned. Again, the resulting effect of the Rapiscan search was to humiliate and intimidate visitors, making them less likely to visit again. A class action lawsuit charged that this humiliating treatment had the effect of dissuading visits, and as with the parking lot car searches, the settlement of the lawsuit halted the procedure.[19]

Research clearly demonstrates that prisoners who are able to sustain quality contact with loved ones over the length of a prison term are much more likely than others to succeed at "going straight" after they are released.[20] Departments of correction can do much to foster quality contact with loved ones, including placing prisoners in facilities near home (and not sending them to other states to do their time), making visiting procedures and locations attractive and comfortable, providing transportation to prisons for low-income families, and providing families ongoing contact with staff, including mental health staff, who are working with their family member (too often it is next to impossible to reach a medical or mental health clinician in a prison to discuss a relative's crisis or condition).

STEP 5: SUSTAIN A VISION OF A BETTER FUTURE

People who are weighed down by depression do not have a very bright outlook for the future; in fact they often do not think about the future at all. They think about the past: "What have I done wrong?" "Who doesn't like me?" "Why am I so inadequate, so ashamed?" Antidepressant medications have become very popular and seem to have relatively few side effects, so many people with depression seek and find some psychopharmaceutical relief. But to the extent that I have an opportunity to do talking psychotherapy with patients suffering severe depression, I purposely ask about their future, about what hope they have for life taking a better turn later, about what they plan and envision for themselves.

Similarly, prisoners need to envision freedom. They need to imagine themselves in the future as successful members of the community, loving, working, and playing in ways they enjoyed prior to their involvement in the criminal justice system. As they face decisions about using drugs or alcohol, taking part in illegal activities, and getting involved in violent altercations in prison, they need always to be thinking about what effects their choices today will have on their prospects after they leave prison.

As a psychiatrist, I feel that it is essential to never leave prisoners feeling there is nothing they can do to better their situation. Prisoners who feel they have nothing to lose in life can be very destructive. I have visited many SHUs where prisoners were serving an indeterminate sentence, meaning they could be in solitary for years on end and there was little they could do to alter their fate. That was the situation at the SHU at Pelican Bay State Prison when the hunger strikes began there in 2011. Every one of the prisoners I talked to for the *Ashker v. Brown* litigation who had been in SHU at Pelican Bay for over ten years reported having no hope of getting out of SHU, and this led them to feel much despair. I have mentioned the shocking statistic that 50 percent of all completed suicides in a prison system occur among prisoners in solitary confinement. Despair breeds suicide.

Staff with a rehabilitative attitude talk to prisoners about their futures. Instead of saying, "You piece of shit, you'll never amount to anything," staff need to be asking prisoners what loving connections they have now and how can they sustain and improve on those connections while they are in prison so that when they get out they will have deep connections with loved ones. This is especially important when it comes to children. How can prisoners sustain a role as parent and maximize the continuity of their bonds with children during a prison term? How can they plan for work in the community? Should they be taking a course or undergoing a training that might increase their prospects of a good job outside? How can they learn more about what is going on in the world while they are locked away? How can they keep up on developments out there so that when they are released they will be prepared to resume their role as citizens and community members? Thoughts about their future need to be constantly on their minds if they are to succeed at rehabilitation.

RESPECT, AGENCY, SOCIAL CONNECTION, AND
VISION

Respect, agency, connection with the outside world, and vision go together. The counselor or teacher must win the prisoner's respect, and often there is much testing. The prisoner who challenges the counselor is essentially saying, "You're not really interested in my welfare, nobody is." And the counselor has to demonstrate, not with easy words but often with very difficult deeds, that he or she has the prisoner's best interest at heart and deserves the prisoner's respect. When the counselor turns the tide and wins the prisoner's respect, and then provides a path toward greater agency in the larger legal society, the prisoner stands a much better chance of leaving a life of drugs and crime and succeeding at going straight.

The tragedy of contemporary correctional policy is that our prisons breed disrespect, excessively deprive prisoners of agency, excessively cut prisoners off from the outside world, and tend to close down prisoners' vision of freedom. Although some loss of agency is inevitable in incarceration, the current scope of constriction of human agency is both tragic and excessive relative to the requirements for running a safe institution. Further, the disrespect and excessive constriction of prisoners' agency set up an unfortunate vicious cycle: the disrespected prisoner becomes menacing and disruptive or self-defeating and self-harming, further constraints are instituted to contain his or her unacceptable behaviors (for example, greater isolation in a segregation setting), the enhanced constraints further compromise the prisoner's sense of being respected and having agency, as a result the prisoner is more prone to feel there is nothing to lose and to proceed to act out, and the acting out serves as justification for further constraints and encroachments on the prisoner's agency. Addressing this pervasive disrespect and almost total lack of agency for prisoners in correctional settings will almost certainly make prisoners less angry and prison sentences less deadly.

Over the last couple of decades, civil rights attorneys, advocacy groups, and human rights organizations have monitored the state of the prisons and limited the degree to which correctional managers can disrespect prisoners and deny them agency. For example, according to international human rights standards and court determinations of prisoners' constitutional rights, staff are not permitted to disrespect prisoners to the point of sexual abuse or arbitrary beatings, prisoners suffering from serious mental illness are entitled to adequate mental health treatment, and even prisoners in extreme punitive isolation units are entitled to have time out of their cells for recreation and contact with loved ones through the mail and visits. These standards are minimal, and there need to be much larger struggles and victories, but when prisoners are able to stand up for their rights and win class action lawsuits, and when human rights organizations step in to influence correctional managers to honor prisoners' human rights, prisoners have reason to feel more respected and to experience a greater sense of agency in their lives. This is a very positive development. But it barely scratches the surface in terms of what is needed.

Respect and enhancement of the prisoner's sense of agency must be taken further, so that they form the core of a robust effort to rehabilitate prisoners. As I have discussed in this chapter, when prisoners are afforded a greater degree of respect and agency, they are in a better position to maintain a vision of freedom, to sustain hope of one day being accepted back into the company of law-abiding men and women in the community. Being better able to keep that goal in mind, they are less prone to act out in prison and jeopardize the opportunity for a timely release. In fact, mutual respect is the key to healthy relationships in the community, including relationships with family, among friends, among coworkers, and in the community at large—just the kinds of relationships one hopes they will resume after they are released.

At the back end of prison sentences, parole services need to be enriched to include the psychotherapy, counseling, education, and vocational rehabilitation that prisoners will need for successful reentry.[21] Creative programs for prisoners awaiting release from prison include transitional work release, where the prisoner leaves prison during the day to work in the community but returns to sleep in the prison. In California, from the 1940s through the early 1970s, Richard McGee, the head of the California Department of Corrections, created many such programs to help felons reintegrate into the community upon release, including work and training furloughs, weekend sentences, and halfway houses.[22] The success of ex-prisoners depends on community social service agencies making access easy and expanding services for individuals who have served time. And ex-prisoners need to be welcomed into and financially supported at community colleges and universities so they can complete the education that was disrupted when they became involved in the criminal justice system.

STAFF TRAINING IS CRITICAL

Before staff can be expected to adopt an attitude of rehabilitation, they must be trained. This constitutes a culture change, and as Rick Raemisch, the executive director at Colorado Department of Corrections, recently told me in an e-mail, "Culture change takes time." But that would be time well spent.

How can staff be trained to give up the culture of punishment and adopt a rehabilitative attitude? We have a precedent for this type of training in the Prison Rape Elimination Act (PREA).[23] If prison authorities are to effect "zero tolerance" for sexual abuse, as mandated by PREA, they need to provide intensive staff training. But we do not want to have officers sitting through the training sessions only because they are ordered to do so and then scoffing at the entire project with their buddies after the session is over. Trainers on gender issues have become adept at engaging public servants who are mandated to participate in a training that they do not relish. With PREA-mandated trainings, it is always a good idea to have the trainees examine their own personal experiences and how they came to the assumptions they make about women or gays. In order to transform the culture of punishment into a rehabilitative attitude, rigorous training will be needed. If professional selection in hiring weeds out individuals who have proven their ongoing hostility and tendency to abuse prisoners, staff can be trained so that this kind of transformation will become reality.

ABOUT RESILIENCE

While I decry the devastating effects of supermax isolation in both stable prisoners and those with serious mental illness, I periodically meet remarkable people who have spent quite a lot of time in solitary confinement and emerged, not exactly unscathed, but impressively functional and quite admirable human beings. I will mention a few I have met in the community; each has given interviews or written about the experience. My list includes Robert King, Danny Murillo, Brian Nelson, Dolores Canales, Steve Czesla, Sarah Shourd, Shane Bauer, and Five Mualimm-ak.[24] There are too many others to list, but I have named people I have had the privilege and joy of knowing. They are inspiring in person, and their writings and interviews contain much wisdom, even for those of us fortunate enough never to be forced to spend time in a SHU. Sarah Shourd wrote and produced a play about solitary confinement, *The Box,* that is gripping and inspiring.[25]

Robert King was one of the Angola Three, three black prisoners who had formed a chapter of the Black Panther Party inside Angola State Prison.[26] It was the only BPP chapter ever created in prison (many Panthers around the country went to prison, but they were in the BPP before they were arrested). When an officer was killed at the prison in 1972, the warden immediately, with no evidence against the three, had them arrested and consigned to a solitary confinement unit known to be very harsh. And there they remained for thirty years or more. Herman Wallace was finally released in October 2013 and died a few days later of advanced liver cancer; Albert Woodfox was released on February 19, 2016, after forty-three years in solitary and is now in the community. As for King, he was released in 2001 when his conviction was overturned. I met him when he was on a speaking tour. Think about that: he had been in solitary confinement for twenty-nine years. I am very impressed and inspired by the way Robert King, Herman Wallace, and Albert Woodfox have remained strong and committed to social justice work throughout their tenure in isolation and after.

I would very much like to understand what makes Robert King resilient enough to go on a national speaking tour right after being released from twenty-nine years in solitary, maintain focus and a very high intellectual level as he educates people about what's very wrong with the prisons, and remain true to his principles as he kept going back to Louisiana to fight for the freedom of the other two members of the Angola Three. Part of the answer must be his deep, principled caring about social justice. He is very attuned to ugly racial discrimination, the growing movement to improve or abolish the prisons, and the plight of disadvantaged people. He always was concerned about such things, all through his years in prison. So he saw his unfair consignment to isolation as part of a more general racism and inequity. He understood his plight, even if there was little he could do about it. He had also been falsely convicted of the crime that landed him in prison in the first place. (His story of what happened to him in court is very poignant.)[27] And while he remained alone in solitary there was a worldwide movement to free the Angola Three.[28] I don't want to explain away the remarkable strength of character evidenced by Robert King as merely a matter of political consciousness. His strength of character is entirely remarkable, as everyone who has met him can attest.

Mumia Abu-Jamal is another exemplar of resilience and strength. Tried and convicted of the murder of police officer Daniel Faulkner in Philadelphia in 1982, Mumia has spent over thirty years in prison for a crime that he and a huge number of very thoughtful commentators and activists claim he did not commit. Most of his prison time has been on Death Row in solitary confinement. Yet he has written six books and an impressive assortment of articles about current civil rights issues, jazz and the blues, urban life, politics, and culture. I visited Mumia in his solitary confinement unit at the State Correctional Institution in Greene, Pennsylvania, several years ago. The maximum security prison was opened in 1993 and contains one of the state's death rows, where all prisoners are held in solitary confinement. I remember being somewhat frantic because I had a list of prisoners who I was scheduled to see in a very short time frame, but when I entered a contact visiting room where Mumia was sitting I found myself in the presence of a very grounded and wise man who shook my hand warmly and made himself available to converse about his situation as well as the political situation of that time. His groundedness communicated itself to me: in his presence I found myself taking a deep breath, slowing down, and thinking deeply about the questions at hand. How was a man who had spent so many years in solitary confinement able to converse calmly, in erudite fashion, on such a wide variety of topics? When asked by interviewer Marc Lamont Hill, "Who are you?" Mumia responded, "I am a thinker, writer, activist, creative being, man, dad, husband, grandpop and son. But just to keep it simple: I'm a free Black man living in captivity. That's who I am."[29] The journalist Noelle Hanrahan, working with her nonprofit organization Prison Radio, has visited Mumia often, recording him, often across a Lexan window, for broadcast on National Public Radio and other networks, making this courageous and charismatic man's voice known far and wide.[30]

The others I mentioned all have remarkable stories, and each evokes admiration and provides inspiration. All of these individuals, and others like them, are charismatic leaders in the movement to halt the use of supermax isolation. I only wish we could clone their resilience and fierce courage so we could share some of it with other ex-prisoners who are more debilitated by their years in SHU.

A COMMENT ABOUT OUTCOMES

Throughout this book I am focusing on the average prisoner. With the evolution of ever harsher and longer sentences over the last four decades, many more people in prison today than previously are not committed to a life of crime. Many prisoners were caught in the dragnet that followed declaration of the War on Drugs. A large majority of individuals entering prison have never been convicted of a violent crime. The stereotype of the terrifying criminal or violent psychopath is entirely inapplicable to the great majority of prisoners today. Of course, a few murder without remorse or spend their time in prison participating in organized criminal activities and looking forward to the day they can return to the streets to take drugs and commit more crimes. Rehabilitation does not work for everyone. There are failures, and the recidivism rate, the rate of reoffending within three years of release from prison, is between 60 and 80 percent, depending on which subpopulation of prisoners is considered. Those with serious mental illness and those who have spent considerable time in solitary confinement have a much higher than average recidivism rate.[31]

The criminologist Robert Martinson's 1974 essay "What Works? Questions and Answers about Prison Reform" was a landmark in outcome studies for prison rehabilitation.[32] Martinson and a team of researchers had reviewed the entire literature about rehabilitation, run some numbers, and announced that rehabilitation programs had no positive effect on recidivism rates. This was the research that conservative pundits and politicians had been waiting for, and they made Martinson famous as they legislated a drastic turn from rehabilitation to harsher punishments. But the article Martinson published in 1979 qualifying and recanting his 1974 rash overgeneralization never received the media attention that the earlier article had received.[33]

In the 1979 article Martinson confessed there had been serious flaws in his 1974 methodology. He had tried correlating the presence of any kind of rehabilitation program in a prison with the overall recidivism rate and found no significant correlation. But, he said in 1979, a better method would have been to correlate the availability of specific programs with the recidivism rates of prisoners whose needs were matched by those programs: this more nuanced research would clearly show that rehabilitation programs are effective to the extent that they are directed at appropriately motivated and capable subpopulations of prisoners. But it was too late. The argument for longer sentences and harsher punishments had already come to dominate the public discussion about crime, so very little notice was given to Martinson's 1979 recantation. With calls to "stop coddling" prisoners, prison education programs were slashed, weights were removed from the yards, the quality of prison food declined, prisoners were deprived of materials for arts and crafts, and so forth. I remember 1990s discussions at congressional budget hearings about continuing the Pell Grants that permitted prisoners to take college courses. One senator complained he had to pay huge tuition costs to get his son through college, so why should the public pay the tab for criminals to get an education? Of course, that was a foolish argument. The reason to give prisoners the education they didn't receive before going to prison is that educated ex-prisoners are more likely to be successful at holding a job and taking care of a family. Also tragically, in 1979, Martinson, dismayed at how his research had been used to devastate the lives of so many others, actually took his own life.[34]

Let's not be naive. Some prisoners are not interested in education and rehabilitation programs. And I have no illusions about the dangerousness of the much smaller number of prisoners who are incorrigibly inclined to continue their criminal pursuits. But even those unreachable prisoners need to be treated humanely while doing their time: this is not a question of rehabilitation but a question of constitutional safeguards, human rights, and just plain decency. I firmly believe they must not be consigned to solitary confinement for more than fifteen days. But a great majority of prisoners do not fit the stereotype of the heinous criminal. If you take the average prisoner and provide him or her educational and rehabilitative programs behind bars, along with quality contact with loved ones and adequate mental health treatment where relevant, he or she will do much, much better after being released from prison, on average, than another prisoner with similar background and proclivities who spends significant time deprived of programs and quality visits during years in solitary confinement. It is this average and relatively improved outcome I am addressing throughout this book.

The whole notion of "the worst of the worst" was a giant attribution error in the first place. Long-term supermax isolation was designed by prison authorities who were at their wits' end attempting to halt the violence and mayhem in jails and prisons. They threw their net too wide and consigned a large number of prisoners—estimated at one hundred thousand today—to solitary confinement. Although all prisoners in solitary today would not necessarily succeed at going straight if offered meaningful rehabilitation programs, supermax isolation practically guarantees that most who are placed in it will fail at reentry, so that the recidivism rate will continue to rise. On the other hand, although larger transformation of our criminal justice system is still absolutely required, a culture of rehabilitation within prisons would give a large proportion of today's and tomorrow's prisoners very good prospects to make the transition to law-abiding life in the community after they serve their time.

TEN

Mental Health Care in Corrections

A GROWING PROPORTION OF PRISONERS with serious mental illness over several decades has created a huge oversubscription for correctional mental health services and a glaring crisis in correctional mental health care today. For example, many prisoners with serious mental illness are warehoused in prison segregation units, where isolation and idleness greatly exacerbate their mental illness. Others are consigned to general population units where mental health treatment is very scarce and perfunctory, and they are too often victimized. Unfortunately, after being victimized, many are sent to segregation because of a rule violation or a fight, or for their own protection. Even when the prisoner in crisis is identified, and, for instance placed in an observation cell while he or she presents an imminent risk of suicide, on average little actual treatment goes on in observation cells: mental health staff merely come by each day to ask if the patient is still suicidal. Then, because correctional mental health services are so underfunded and oversubscribed, the prisoner in crisis is moved out too fast and is often transferred back to the segregation cell he or she came from, without adequate follow-up. This is why a disproportionate number of prison suicides occur in isolation cells, with prisoners who have cycled through the prison's observation unit.[1]

I met Sam (not his real name), a tall African American man with wide eyes and an intense stare, while conducting an investigation of the ten maximum security prisons in New York in preparation for my testimony in *Disability Advocates, Inc. v. New York State Office of Mental Health* (*DAI, Inc. v. NY OMH*), a lawsuit brought by New York's disability rights advocates and prison law offices claiming that mental health care in New York's prisons was inadequate and that that was why so many prisoners with serious mental illness were finding their way into solitary confinement. Sam's situation illustrated the deficiencies of treatment and the harm of solitary confinement for prisoners with serious mental illness. He had been transferred eight months prior to our meeting from one prison composed entirely of solitary confinement cells, Southport Correctional Facility, to another prison composed entirely of solitary confinement cells, Upstate Correctional Facility. The two supermax prisons were approximately the same size, containing 750 cells each. At Southport, prisoners were permitted no television, though they could have radios in their cells. At Upstate, most of the cells contained two cellmates, but 160 cells were single occupancy. There were individualized small recreation areas outside each cell, and showers were in the cells so the prisoners would not even have to traverse a hallway to exercise or shower, thus further minimizing social interactions. Except if he wanted to shout during recreation to a prisoner in a neighboring outdoor recreation area, Sam had no contact with any other prisoners at Upstate.

Sam had been prescribed several strong antipsychotic, antidepressant, and antianxiety medications prior to his admission to the Southport supermax isolation prison, and prior to being incarcerated he had been in a public psychiatric hospital and had been told he suffered from schizophrenia and would have to take medications for the remainder of his life. But his strong antipsychotic medications were stopped when he entered segregation. He told me that since the medications were stopped he had been hearing voices and talking to himself and that recently a correctional officer had given him a ticket for talking to himself. He reported seeing people in the back of his cell who, in his sane moments, he knew were not really there. He told me he believed the correctional officers put ideas in his head and made him do unspeakable things to himself and to them, such as cutting himself. He said he had asked for medications over a month prior to our meeting, and the psychologist had agreed he needed them, but as of our meeting he had still not seen the psychiatrist. With me, he exhibited a bizarre, flat stare, paranoid ideas, and uncertainty as to whether thoughts that came into his head were emanating from someone saying something to him or from his imagination. He experienced command hallucinations telling him to kill himself and to do some of the other things he got tickets for, such as staying up most of the night banging on the walls and shouting. The diagnosis line in his minimal clinical chart contained the term *deferred* in one progress note, *Major Depressive Disorder* in another, and *Adjustment Disorder* in still another—in other words, his ascribed diagnoses shifted, but the psychosis that was obvious to me remained undetected or unnoted. But a few weeks prior to our meeting he had been noted to have thoughts of suicide and had been sent to an observation cell for six days before being returned to his supermaximum isolation cell. There was a note in his chart that he felt hopeless and suicidal, but there was no treatment plan in the chart, and he had not been seen by a mental health clinician since being returned from the observation cell back to his segregation cell.

Sam's situation, tragically, is fairly routine in many of the prisons I have visited. Every time I tour supermaximum security units I meet individuals in similar straits, usually with notes about "suicidal ideation" in their medical charts. Too many of these individuals go on to actually commit suicide. Some do not, however, and instead continue to cycle between stark isolation and an observation cell. Lack of funding for adequate mental health staffing and programs is a large reason why these prisoners live, and die, like this in our prisons.

The high rate of suicide in prison is only one of many indicators that prison mental health services are far from adequate. There is a widely held but erroneous assumption that correctional mental health care is relatively adequate and that the best place for the indigent individual with serious mental illness to receive treatment is behind bars. This grossly incorrect assumption actually serves to rationalize the consignment of even more individuals with serious mental illness to jail and prison. Thus in many states the law provides for a finding in criminal trials that the defendant is "guilty but insane." The jury can find the defendant guilty, not guilty, not guilty by reason of insanity (NGRI), or "guilty but insane."[2] Because many jurors believe that prison is the best place for a severely disturbed individual to receive needed mental health treatment, they opt, when given the choice, for "guilty and insane."[3] Perhaps they also fear that an NGRI finding would result in the defendant eventually being released when the defendant seems too dangerous for that (though in reality most defendants found NGRI remain in locked mental hospitals for many years.)[4] But in the several states where I have investigated correctional mental health care and where "guilty but insane" is an option in jury instructions at trial, prisoners who have been found "guilty but insane" do not receive any mental health care different from that of other prisoners, and for the most part that care is quite substandard.[5]

The oversubscribed mental health staff try to fulfill their professional duty. They may try focusing their energies on the "major mental illnesses," including schizophrenia, bipolar disorder, and major depressive disorder.[6] Or in some states where there is a larger caseload a decision is made to provide psychotropic medications only. Or there is a tendency, neither articulated nor advocated by anyone in particular, to lock up the most seriously disturbed prisoners in some form of isolative confinement, usually punitive segregation but occasionally protective custody (which too often also happens to be an isolative confinement unit). In any case, prisoners with serious mental illness tend to go untreated, undertreated, or treated with medications and little else, and a disproportionate number wind up in isolative confinement.[7] Eventually the isolated prisoners with mental illness complete their prison term and need to return to the community. But the many years of inadequate treatment and harsh conditions, including prison crowding and long-term isolative confinement, have exacerbated their mental disorder and, as I described earlier in chapter 5, have made them even more disabled. Then we read about prisoners with mental illness being released straight out of isolative confinement and perpetrating horrible crimes in the community.

THE COMMUNITY MENTAL HEALTH MODEL

I trained as a community psychiatrist out of commitment to the principle that mental health services should be available to all, according to their needs and regardless of their ability to pay. That was the vision underlying President Kennedy's Community Mental Health Centers Act of 1963. Federal grants to support local governments in building community mental health centers lasted for five years, with a possible three-year extension.[8] Originally, in the 1960s and early 1970s, community mental health services included not only direct treatment in the community but also prevention and consultation to schools, churches, and other community agencies and institutions (including jails) to best support individuals prone to mental illness living in the community.[9] The model was sound, even visionary, but by the mid-1970s community mental health was being decimated by cuts in public budgets until we reached the point where, in many clinics, the main therapeutic modality would be medication with very little in the way of talking therapy, and even case managers would find their caseloads so large that they could not provide optimal care or even adequate monitoring.[10] Meanwhile, the remainder of the social safety net was cut as drastically as public mental health services, and many of those suffering from mental illness found their way into homelessness, and then jails and prisons.

The array of federally required clinical services at community mental health centers (CMHCs) has changed over the years, even as funding for their implementation has shrunk.[11] At first the list included adult outpatient and crisis intervention services, inpatient services, services for children, day treatment (also known as intermediate care or partial hospital), vocational training, and consultation to schools, businesses, and community and government agencies. Later, halfway houses, supported living programs, self-help groups, substance abuse treatment programs, case management, services for individuals with developmental disabilities, psychiatric or psychosocial rehabilitation services, and other worthy programs would be added to the list of required services.[12] CMHCs were encouraged to collaborate with local colleges, vocational training facilities, and low-income housing agencies to provide wraparound services to individuals with serious mental illness. As part of their preventive work, community psychiatrists have advocated quality schools, full employment, low-income housing, vocational training, and access by disabled individuals to work sites as well as education programs. "Safety net" programs are the underpinning of a sound community mental health program.[13] Clients need a place to live and a job or job training opportunity if clinical treatment is to be effective, no matter how targeted and powerful the prescribed medications. The addition of psychiatric or psychosocial rehabilitation since the 1980s enlarges community mental health practitioners' methods for helping individuals with serious mental illness live the best quality lives they can, given their disability.[14]

Community mental health programs prioritize prevention.[15] Of course, prevention begins long before a prison term. The best way to prevent deteriorating mental health is to provide effective alternatives to incarceration in the community, including mental health and substance abuse treatment. In chapter 12 I will discuss diversion, where a behavioral health or substance abuse court offers arrested individuals community treatment as an alternative to jail time. The first step toward applying community mental health principles in correctional mental health care is to radically change sentencing laws and expand prevention and diversion so the prisons do not fill up with individuals suffering from serious mental illness and so prisoners with serious mental illness do not wind up in solitary confinement.

THE COMMUNITY MENTAL HEALTH
MODEL IN CORRECTIONS

Community mental health provides a model for comprehensive mental health treatment inside correctional facilities.[16] When in the 1960s and 1970s we worked to reintegrate into the community individuals who had been hospitalized for mental illness, we relied on community resources (churches, schools, youth centers, community colleges, job-training agencies) to help them succeed in the community. Equivalent resources are needed in jails and prisons. Prisoners with mental illness need to be in classes or in rehabilitation programs. They must also be given a safe place to serve their sentences (safe from victimization, from the unrestrained expression of their own most troubling proclivities, from abuse by staff, and from damaging conditions such as crowding and solitary confinement) and an adequate level of mental health treatment and psychiatric rehabilitation, as well as general rehabilitation, so that they are prepared to succeed in the community after they are released.[17]

How do we define "mental health" in the context of corrections? Traditionally, it has been defined as the absence of mental illness.[18] But that definition is limited in its usefulness in correctional contexts. The definition of what we consider "healthy" must begin with the set of human capacities we believe someone needs to succeed in the community after release from prison without resorting to illicit substances and running afoul of the law. Then, in the process of developing individual treatment plans, correctional mental health staff need to assess patients on the caseload for the capacities that need strengthening if patients are to succeed after being released. Of course, to be healthy one must have one's mental illness under control, so adherence to mental health treatment and the ability to make basic efforts to take care of oneself (diet, dress, regulation of the sleep-wake cycle) would head the list of capacities associated with mental health. Prisoners need to acquire the capacity to be on time for appointments, to act in disciplined fashion, to be reliable and trustworthy, to set and work on goals, to modulate emotions, to perform reality testing when irrational thoughts emerge, and to settle differences peacefully. The list of healthy capacities can be translated into core aims for mental health treatment. Frequent rewards, including expanded privileges and freedoms, can be granted when prisoners reach a new level of emerging healthy capacities. In other words, we would build into all prison mental health programs the learned capacities we consider prerequisites for success in going straight after release.

Several years ago, a collaboration between the San Francisco courts, the Jail Mental Health Program, the Progress Foundation, and several other mental health agencies took place in San Francisco. I was psychiatric consultant to the program. Funding came from a three-year grant from the California Board of Corrections, the agency that performed oversight of jails or local detention facilities. Individuals with serious mental illness and substance abuse who were deemed at great risk of incarceration were visited frequently by case managers, they were accompanied to appointments at the mental health clinic or a recovery (substance abuse) program, and if necessary they were given a room in a nearby SRO (single-room occupancy) hotel, paid for by the Board of Corrections grant. With this kind of ongoing care, 80 percent of the clients in the program remained free of trouble with the criminal justice system. Nevertheless, the grant was ended after two years because the state agency did not have sufficient budget resources to continue the program.

As in the larger society, a community mental health model in corrections requires a spectrum of treatment modalities at different levels of intensity: sufficient screening, assessment, outpatient treatment, inpatient treatment, crisis intervention, intermediate care, and case management for the population being served. Clinicians need to form trusting therapeutic relationships with prisoners suffering from mental illness. This is not so easy to accomplish in correctional settings: too often there is no time to establish an adequate therapeutic relationship, or the prisoner is seen in episodic fashion and shifted from one clinician to another each time he or she asks to be seen. But research shows that the more trusting and caring the therapeutic relationship, and the more continuous it is over time, the more likely the patient is to adhere fully with treatment and function the best he or she can, given the level of psychiatric disorder.[19] This is the rationale for ensuring that a subpopulation of the mental health caseload is assigned to a team of clinicians who have ongoing responsibility for their treatment.[20]

A related requirement is "through care." Provisions need to be made so that prisoners entering the system are able to continue the mental health care they were receiving prior to incarceration, and prisoners being released need to have postrelease community care arranged in advance of their release. Likewise, when prisoners are transferred from one correctional facility to another, including from jail to prison, or from one location to another within a facility, continuity of care must be a high priority. For example, many departments of corrections provide automatic continuation of previously prescribed psychotropic medications (a "bridge prescription") until the prisoner has an opportunity to meet with a psychiatrist after being transferred to a different facility. The Ohio Department of Corrections provides that when a prisoner is sent to segregation the mental health clinician who was treating him in the general population must go to the segregation unit and see him while he is isolated. This is a great improvement over the usual situation where the prisoner with mental illness is forced to see a different mental health clinician who happens to be making rounds in the segregation pod. However, for many of the reasons I have already described, I believe strongly that prisoners with serious mental illness must be entirely excluded from solitary confinement of any kind.

Using as a reference the standard of care that nonprisoners should receive in the community, I want to outline the components of what I believe need to be included in any correctional mental health program. Not all the components would need to be available at the same time in any particular location—for example, prisoners in need of inpatient psychiatric treatment might be transferred to a hospital within the department of corrections or to an outside hospital by prior arrangement. But inpatient care needs to be available, and it is not acceptable to simply isolate an acutely psychotic or suicidal prisoner in a segregation cell, perhaps with psychotropic medications, when inpatient care is needed.

The following would be required components of the program:

1. There must be a mental health screening assessment—including rigorous suicide risk assessment—upon admission to the department of corrections, upon transfer to a prison, and upon admission to segregation; then there must be periodic mental health assessments from that time onward or as needed (for example, when the prisoner evidences a heightened risk of breakdown or suicide).

2. Suicide risk assessments must be rigorous and not superficial. If staff ask prisoners, "Are you suicidal?" most prisoners will answer, "No," simply because they do not know the staff member and do not want to be stigmatized as weak in the prison setting. But if the screening staff member is well trained to recognize clues of suicide risk and asks the prisoner a longer series of questions—"Do you ever feel that nobody would care if you were dead?" "Do you ever feel that life is not worth living?" "Have you ever thought about ending your life?"—then the prisoner may begin to get a sense that this staff member is concerned about him and can be trusted to a certain extent. If that happens, there is then a good chance he will drop his guard and start responding candidly to the questions.[21] Then, while the staff member spends the time necessary to garner answers to the multiple questions, there is an opportunity for sufficient trust to evolve so that the prisoner becomes more forthcoming and more likely to adhere to the treatment plan.

3. Prisoners must have a way to access mental health care when they feel they need it; the confidentiality of the process must be guaranteed so that the

prisoner seeking mental health services does not carry the stigma of being a mental patient; and there must be a timely and adequate response to prisoners' requests for mental health care.

4. Prisoners must be provided confidential and private meetings with mental health staff. In segregated housing, the intervention cannot occur "at cell-front."

5. There must be sufficient staff at every level of care so that prisoners in need of mental health services are evaluated and treated in a reasonable time and with a comprehensive treatment plan. More important than any staff-to-patients ratio is the adequacy of the treatment being provided. Overreliance on psychotropic medication is a clear sign of inadequate staffing levels and inadequate staff training.

6. There must be a psychiatric inpatient hospital within the department of corrections or available by contract for transfer of prisoners requiring an inpatient level of care.

7. There must be an outpatient mental health treatment program.

8. There must be a crisis intervention program, including suicide prevention and intervention.

9. There must be an intermediate level of care, programs that are not staffed as richly as inpatient wards but that have more staff and programs than an outpatient clinic. Step-down programs, or intermediate care, or residential treatment facilities (all three are synonymous), are the equivalent of halfway houses and day treatment or partial hospitalization programs in the community. Here prisoners suffering from mental illness can be safely housed while participating in a variety of mental health services. The importance of intermediate care cannot be stressed too much. These are usually general-population units, so the prisoners are free to leave the unit to mingle with others on the yard and to eat in the cafeteria. But when they get into trouble "out there," they have support from mental health staff on the unit. In the best intermediate care programs, all officers have received special mental health training and have elected to work on the unit. If enough intermediate care beds are provided to serve the population in need, then many prisoners with mental illness will be provided a safe enough environment and sufficient continuous mental health treatment to avoid victimization and stay out of disciplinary trouble and thus will be less likely to wind up in punitive isolation units or to require protective custody.[22] In *DAI v. NY OMH* we testified to finding too many very disturbed prisoners throughout the state of New York warehoused in segregation cells. One of several possible remedies

that the negotiated settlement included was to dedicate 305 additional intermediate care beds, on the premise that prisoners with serious mental illness
who are fortunate enough to be admitted to an intermediate care unit are
much less likely to be written a rule violation ticket and much less likely to
be sent to segregation.[23]

10. When the mixing of certain prisoners involves a high risk of altercations or danger, prisoners, whether potential perpetrators or victims, can be
separated from each other rather than placed in isolation. Separation, in
contrast to isolation, allows all prisoners to enjoy the freedoms, amenities,
and programs mandated by their classification level, but in separate places:
for example, this might involve transferring some prisoners to a different
cellblock.

11. At every level of care, prisoners who break rules and cause disturbances
must be retained within the treatment program instead of being sent to solitary confinement. With the help of social psychologist Hans Toch, we now
know how to provide mental health treatment for "disturbed/disruptive"
prisoners (see chapter 11). If custody staff believe the patient poses a security
risk in congregate activities, he or she can be released from a cell with staff
supervision and permitted to go alone down the hallway to a dayroom or
library. Next, after he succeeds at that level or phase of treatment, he can be
offered the opportunity to be in the dayroom or library or on the recreation
yard with one or two other prisoners, as long as he can prove over a certain
length of time that he can refrain from self-harm, angry verbalizations
toward staff and others, and threats of violence. The best option, to the extent
possible, is to offer positive rewards for appropriate behavior rather than
negative consequences and punishments for unacceptable behavior. More
time in the dayroom, recreation, and so forth can be among the rewards, as
can more possessions including art materials, more commissary, participation in activities and programs the prisoner likes, and opportunities to participate in congregate activities.

12. Mental health programs must be "trauma informed."[24] Since prisoners,
on average, suffered much trauma prior to their incarceration, and since
events in prison can be very traumatizing, it is important for correctional
mental health staff to be very attuned to trauma and very willing to treat
prisoners who need treatment. Nonsuicidal self-harm—for example, teenag-
ers cutting themselves when they get upset—is more about anxiety than
depression. When I hear of a prisoner who is self-harming but not suicidal, I
know we will have to rule out a trauma-related syndrome if not full-blown

posttraumatic stress disorder (PTSD). Very often past trauma plays an important role in nonsuicidal self-harm. The traumas of prison life can add to one's emotional troubles, too often serving as a "reenactment" of earlier traumas or "retraumatization."[25] If adequate screening for past trauma as well as treatment for PTSD were offered to prisoners, there would be far fewer incidents of self-harm. Many of the treated prisoners would more effectively participate in rehabilitation programs and stay out of trouble while incarcerated, and then would be more likely to succeed after being released from prison.[26]

13. Documentation in the form of paper charts or electronic medical records must meet the standard of care in the community. Medical records must include accurate and thorough histories, mental status examinations, test results, case formulations, diagnoses, treatment plans that outline each phase of the treatment, rationales for treatment interventions and changes in treatment, medication monitoring, and provisions for the continuity of care.

14. Treatment at every level of care must include a variety of therapeutic modalities as well as case management. The prescription of psychotropic medications alone is usually not, in itself, adequate mental health treatment. Medications are often part of the needed treatment but do not substitute for staff taking time to talk to prisoners. That is clearly the standard of care in the community. For example, the Task Force on Correctional Mental Health Care of the American Psychiatric Association arrived at this formulation: "Mental health treatment in the correctional setting, like that in any setting, is defined as the use of a variety of mental health therapies, including biological, psychological, and social. In the correctional setting the goal of treatment is to alleviate symptoms of mental disorders that significantly interfere with an inmate's ability to function in the particular criminal justice environment in which the inmate is located. It is obvious, therefore, that mental health treatment is more than the mere prescribing of psychotropic medication, and psychiatrists should resist being limited to this role."[27]

15. There must be meaningful communication and collaboration, including multidisciplinary team meetings, among mental health staff and between mental health, medical, and custody staff. This is especially important when a prisoner is suicidal.[28]

16. There must be adequate training for both mental health and custody staff working in areas where mental health treatment occurs. Training that includes and integrates the issues of security and mental health is necessary for both clinicians and officers—clinicians must engage in discussions of

security issues, and officers who work with prisoners suffering from mental illness need to know about mental illness and suicide.

17. Informed consent must be in place for all treatments, including documented discussion of the patient's right to refuse treatment, including medications. Informed consent is a fundamental ethical consideration in the practice of medicine, including psychiatry. The National Commission on Correctional Health Care defines it as "the agreement by a patient to a treatment, examination, or procedure after the patient receives the material facts about the nature, consequences, and risks of the proposed treatment, examination or procedure; the alternatives to it; and the prognosis if the proposed treatment is not undertaken. . . . If at any point the patient indicates refusal, the medication must not be forced: the right to refuse treatment is inherent in the notion of informed consent."[29]

18. Case managers must track the prisoner's progress and meet with him or her at regular intervals. The case manager is also a crucial component of mental health services, but case management does not substitute for needed individual and group psychotherapy.

19. Psychiatric rehabilitation programs in prison support postrelease success, while social isolation and idleness during a prison term lead to subsequent disability.[30] Psychiatric rehabilitation includes such things as education, social skills training, anger management, substance abuse treatment, and vocational rehabilitation. For example, a prisoner suffering from schizophrenia needs quality contact with mental health clinicians that includes not only individual and group psychotherapy but psychoeducation: he or she must understand the nature and probable life course of the illness, the benefits and side effects of medications, the dangers of nonadherence to treatment, ways to recognize early or "prodromal" symptoms of an impending psychotic episode or suicidal crisis, the value in seeking help early when an episode seems to be evolving, and, importantly, the dangers of using illicit substances. In addition, the patient needs help navigating the ordinary events of life, the activities of daily living (ADLs). All of this takes staff time, and there must be an adequate amount of face-to-face talk at all levels of treatment.

SUICIDE AND SELF-HARM

Long-term consignment to segregation is a major factor in the high suicide rate among prisoners.[31] Currently, however, we are not responding well enough to this crisis. The standards of the National Commission on Correctional Health Care (as of 2014) provide a list of necessary components for effective crisis intervention and suicide prevention.[32] Among these, continuity of care is absolutely essential. Many successful suicides in prison occur in segregation cells, where prisoners who have been released from Observation are returned. Then they are not closely enough monitored, staff do not talk to them about the quality or causes of their despair, and when I examine their medical record I do not find an adequate treatment plan that covers the frequency of observation or the kind of treatment that is planned subsequent to their release from the observation unit.

I interviewed Josh (not his real name), a thirty-seven-year-old African American prisoner in the SHU at the maximum security Great Meadow Correctional Facility in Comstock, New York, several years ago in preparation for my testimony in *DAI v. NY OMH*. Josh had been in prison for seven years. He was diagnosed with schizophrenia and claustrophobia. He had a long history of cycling back and forth between SHU and Observation: being removed from his isolation cell when officers felt he was acutely suicidal, spending a few days in an observation cell while being asked if he still felt suicidal, and then being transferred back to his cell in the SHU when he finally denied suicidal intentions. When I met with him he was hearing hallucinated voices; he also described having delusions, nightmares, and an intense fear that he would be "set up" by staff to be attacked. Several months prior to our meeting he had set a fire in his cell in a serious suicide attempt, after which he spent a few days in Observation. He had attempted to kill himself many times and often would be issued a disciplinary write-up or ticket for "bodily harm" or for destroying state property. He asked me, "What's the state property, me?!" He did not go to recreation because he was afraid "they [officers] will jump me." So he spent all of his time in a cell, either in SHU or in Observation. I discovered from his clinical chart that every time he had been transferred from solitary to Observation and back to solitary, there was no treatment plan for the period following his return to SHU, and the chart contained no notes of meetings with mental health staff beyond cursory rounds in SHU.

An effective crisis intervention and suicide prevention plan would not in most cases permit sending a prisoner back to a segregation cell after he or she was discharged from Observation. Rather, it would require a detailed treatment plan that would include recommendations on housing, the frequency of monitoring, and the kind of ongoing mental health treatment the prisoner would receive. This might include medications and would have to include some talking psychotherapy so that the mental health staff could assess ongoing suicide risk and the prisoner could be helped to become more functional.[33]

Sometimes self-harm involves suicidal intent, sometimes it does not. Both kinds of self-harm are urgent problems in a correctional setting. Nonsuicidal self-harm, especially cutting of some part of the body, is very commonplace in prison segregation units, and in my experience the worse the conditions of confinement and the less the officers attend to prisoners' urgent needs, the more often prisoners cut themselves for nonsuicidal reasons. Often correctional mental health staff view nonsuicidal self-harm as manipulative and consequently pay little or no attention to the prisoners' despair, anxiety, and needs that are expressed in the self-harm. But this can be a deadly mistake.[34]

MEDICATIONS AND MEDICATION OVER OBJECTION

It can be very dangerous to give medications to someone when no other treatment modality is in effect, and this is especially so when the individual is in solitary confinement. Quite often, if there is no other type of intervention to relieve the target symptoms of mental illness, the dosage of the medications will need to be incrementally increased to control the patient's behavior or resolve the worst symptoms. In general, medications alone will not resolve the symptoms, nor will they improve functioning and prognoses; rather, they will likely sedate the prisoner or cause agitation, and can cause great harm. On the other hand, when medications are administered to a prisoner in the context of a full treatment program (i.e., along with individual and group psychotherapy and therapeutic programs such as vocational rehabilitation or art therapy), then they play an important role as part of the treatment.[35]

The excessive use of psychotropic medications was a big problem in the state hospitals of the 1940s and 1950s. Many people in those institutions were merely turned into chronic patients or "zombies" through the administration of high doses of antipsychotic medications.[36] It was the public's outrage about the warehousing and ill treatment of mental patients in the asylums that brought on "deinstitutionalization" and the downsizing of state mental hospitals starting in the 1960s.[37] At that time, the community mental health movement was premised on the notion that if, along with the downsizing of state mental hospitals, the funds could be transferred to community-based programs and sufferers could be treated in the community, their quality of life and level of functioning would be greatly improved.

Medications must be prescribed carefully, and there must be close monitoring by the psychiatrist to gauge effectiveness and tolerance and to prevent negative side effects, including excessive sedation. And there must be informed consent, which of course means patients must have a right to refuse the treatment.

In very rare instances a patient must be involuntarily treated, or prescribed and administered medications over his or her objections. In such cases standards of care must be met, and there are due process requirements. The legal precedent is *Harper v. Washington,* a case decided by the Supreme Court in 1990. Mr. Harper had been in a Washington state prison for over ten years and had taken strong antipsychotic medications for his serious mental illness, diagnosed as bipolar disorder. When he took medications voluntarily he functioned fairly well in the prison setting, but when he halted his medications he was prone to violent outbursts. The mental health team at the Washington DOC's Special Offender Center decided he needed to be medicated over his objection, and subsequently Mr. Harper sued the state to halt the involuntary medications. The Supreme Court ruling in *Harper v. Washington* stipulates that before involuntary medication is administered a due process hearing must be held before an impartial hearing committee that does not include members of the treatment team; that the prisoner must be given advance notice of the hearing; and that the prisoner must have the right to argue against the involuntary medications.

Both the National Commission on Correctional Health Care and the American Psychiatric Association have published standards for the involuntary administration of medications in nonhospital settings, including prisons.[38] Both sets of standards reflect the standard of medical care in the community. For example, the NCCHC Standard on Forced Psychotropic Medication requires that before medication is administered involuntarily, all less restrictive or intrusive measures must be attempted and found to be ineffective; the physician or psychiatrist must clearly document in the medical record the inmate's condition, the threat posed, and the reason for the proposed involuntary medications, including a note about other treatments that were attempted; and the involuntary medications can be given only for a specified and limited time period.[39]

In a prison where psychotropic medications are the only mental health intervention—that is, where there is really no other mental health treatment—involuntary medications should be barred precisely because no less restrictive interventions were available, so they cannot have been tried and found to be ineffective. In fact, clinical research shows that where there is a good therapeutic relationship between the patient and mental health staff, involuntary medications are very rarely needed.[40]

In the vast majority of cases, when mental health clinicians develop a therapeutic relationship with patients through individual and group psychotherapy and other modalities of treatment and psychiatric rehabilitation, staff are in a position to influence patients and motivate them to adhere to treatment, even in emergency situations, so very little or no involuntary action is needed.[41] The converse also is definitely true. When involuntary medications are utilized more often than on rare occasions, this is almost certainly because mental health personnel are understaffed and inadequately trained, with the result that patients are inadequately treated and mental health staff are unable to foster patients' adherence to treatment. This is why, in states where involuntary medications are permitted outside psychiatric hospital settings (i.e., outpatient settings), there is a requirement that comprehensive mental health services be available.[42]

This issue was highlighted in the *Dockery v. Fisher* class action lawsuit involving the East Mississippi Correctional Facility (EMCF) near Meridian.[43] EMCF is a special-needs prison run on contract with the Mississippi Department of Corrections by a private prison company called the Management and Training Corporation. The prison houses 1,500 prisoners, almost every one recognized as suffering from serious mental illness. I toured the facility with a team of experts in 2014 and 2016 and found the conditions of confinement in the solitary confinement Unit 5 to be the worst prison conditions I had ever encountered during my entire career. A great many prisoners with serious mental illness were languishing in the solitary confinement unit. Mental health staffing was very thin, so even though the prison was the designated site of the state's prison mental health program, most prisoners who were not consigned to solitary were left to their own devices in general-population units with very little or no mental health treatment or rehabilitation. But when prisoners acted inappropriately it was common for them to be given "shots" (the prisoners' word for the procedure), often involuntarily. Often custody officers would surround the prisoner and take him down (throw him to the floor); then the nurse would come and administer an intramuscular injection, usually of Haldol, an old-fashioned antipsychotic medication that causes sedation and has other serious side effects. I asked to see documentation for the kind of hearings on involuntary medication that the *Harper v. Washington* ruling required, but there was none. There were no hearings. Worse, since there was little or no mental health treatment aside from the "shots," it could not be argued that other, less restrictive treatments had been tried and proven ineffective (per the NCCHC and APA standards). And because the practice was so widespread over a long period of time, it could not be argued that it was a rare occurrence, or that involuntary medications were administered for the shortest time they would take to attain specified (and documented) treatment aims.

SOME GUIDING PRINCIPLES

When I conduct trainings for correctional mental health staff along with custody officers, I offer seven guiding principles that usefully inform the work of correctional mental health.

1. Confine the prisoners in humane surroundings that would not be held unconstitutional in the face of competent legal challenge. Prisoners with serious mental illness must not be sent to solitary confinement.

2. Treat prisoners with respect, and communicate to them that they will do better and be better people if they likewise treat the staff with respect (see chapter 9).

3. Provide multimodality therapeutic interventions. Individual psychotherapy that fosters a trusting therapeutic relationship is important. Group therapy also is important, as are meaningful educational and vocational programs. The principles of modern psychiatric rehabilitation need to be applied robustly, and prisoners with and without mental illness need help preparing to succeed at "going straight."

4. Emphasize rewards over punishments. This is such a long-established principle in psychology that it needs no further explication.

5. When the prisoner with mental illness is in segregation or at a classification level that is restrictive in terms of freedoms and amenities, create very short and incremental phases whereby the prisoner can rapidly and continually earn increasing freedoms and amenities. Again, I strongly oppose the placement of prisoners with serious mental illness in isolation, but the reality is that many are currently in isolative settings, so this point is an interim measure until a strict prohibition of isolation can be effected. The best of the correctional step-down mental health units I have toured contain many phases, each relatively brief, with advancement to the next phase very attainable with a change in behavior or attitude. The result, and the variable to

measure in assessing success at behavior change, is the proportion of prisoners who are able to achieve each goal and move briskly through the stages of the program. A corollary is that long-term static conditions (dead time) of deprivation must not be imposed on prisoners. Even prisoners consigned to segregation on account of unacceptable or assaultive behaviors should be given attainable goals to reach if they want to increase their freedom and amenities. Having no way to attain more freedom will almost certainly lead to despair and desperate acts; this is a major reason why disciplinary infractions occur so often, why staff so frequently resort to the use of force, and why suicide rates are so high in supermaximum segregation units.

6. Foster close collaboration between custody and mental health staff. There is a very strong consensus in corrections about the need for this, but it is not easy to accomplish. It requires quite a lot of cross-training: security training for mental health staff, and mental health training for custody staff. In some states, it runs afoul of civil service labor arrangements: for example, some union contracts make it difficult for custody staff with an interest in working with prisoners suffering from mental illness to successfully bid for jobs in the mental health unit. And there are concerns about confidentiality: should custody staff be permitted to know about prisoners' psychiatric issues, and how will their vow to maintain patient confidentiality hold up in an officer culture that frowns on special agreements involving select prisoners? These reasonable issues need to be addressed and resolved in the process of establishing step-down mental health units.

7. Handle discipline in the context of a treatment plan created and put in action by a collaborative treatment team. Many correctional systems require that hearing officers check with mental health staff prior to ruling on disciplinary infractions to make certain the unacceptable behavior is not driven by mental illness. Too often that process involves nothing more than a "rubber stamp," with the mental health team responding that there is no reason this prisoner cannot be fully punished. The issue is not whether the behavior at issue is part of the individual's mental illness or merely a "bad behavior." I find that distinction very difficult to make when the prisoner suffers from schizophrenia. Rather, the question needs to be how to manage the disruptive prisoner in a treatment context with a collaborative (mental health and custody staff) treatment team, something I will discuss further in chapter 11. The biggest obstacle to the application of a community mental health model in corrections is the widespread practice of long-term segregation and supermax isolation. Too often prisoners who are involved in mental health treat-

ment, or who should be in treatment, act inappropriately or break rules and find their way into solitary confinement. If the community mental health model is to succeed in corrections, solitary confinement needs to be comprehensively rethought.[44]

Ultimately, we need to decide whether we believe prisoners with serious mental illness are human beings with feelings and rights or whether they are more like animals who should be kept in a cage with no social interactions or productive activities, and then sprayed with immobilizing gas as punishment for behaviors they often cannot control. Under these circumstances, their mental illness worsens, as do their prognosis and potential recidivism rate. The short list of principles outlined in this chapter would be an important part of a better approach to treating mentally ill prisoners. But there also has to be a larger change in attitude on the part of custody staff and mental health staff, as well as on the part of legislators and the public.

ELEVEN

The Disruptive Prisoner

IF WE ARE GOING TO MOVE beyond solitary confinement, we need a plan to manage and treat prisoners whose behavior is unacceptable or disruptive. Central to any successful plan of this nature will be Hans Toch's important conceptualization of the disturbed/disruptive prisoner.[1] Toch intervened in a debate within the correctional community in the 1980s as to whether misbehaving prisoners were "Mad" or "Bad." Typically, corrections authorities believed that if mental illness was thought to be driving prisoners' rule breaking and violence, the intervention needed to include more intensive mental health treatment; if the prisoners were simply willful bad actors, they needed to be punished, harshly, and that is where supermax solitary confinement came in.[2] Of course, there was much disagreement about which prisoners were Mad and which were simply Bad. And it was clear to me and others that one's race had much to do with the designation: prisoners of color were more likely to be viewed as Bad and sent to segregation, while white prisoners were more likely to be viewed as mentally ill and offered more intensive treatment. Part of the problem is the very "either/or" thinking involved. Could it be that the problem of bad behavior and mental illness requires "both/and" thinking instead?[3] Toch argued that the prisoners at issue were both: they were suffering from mental illness and they had become bad actors. What was needed was a management and treatment strategy that would take the entire picture into account, and that would require close collaboration between custody and mental health staff.

I received a lesson in managing the disturbed/disruptive prisoner when I talked to Taimalie Kiwi Tamasese, the Samoan coordinator at the Just Therapy Family Centre in New Zealand, while she was in the United States conducting training workshops.[4] Kiwi presented an impressive array of creative therapeutic interventions at the training workshop I attended, and I went up after her lecture to talk to her about prison. "I work in the local prison," she let me know immediately, "and just before I began this trip I saw my most difficult client, who is doing well." I asked her to tell me about him. She said he was a very large and very angry Samoan man who had been in prison several years, most of them spent in solitary confinement. Not only that, when Kiwi first met him this man was on a back corridor that was reserved for especially recalcitrant prisoners. He was known to assault officers with his fists, throw things at them, and shout belligerently. She told me she thought he suffered from a psychotic condition, but she would not diagnose him. She went to see him daily. She was the only person in the world who talked to him. The officers delivered and retrieved his food trays, and he would often swear at them in the process, and then they left him entirely alone. The longer he stayed on this desolate corridor, the angrier he became. Meanwhile, the more he shouted epithets at them, the more the officers ignored him.

Kiwi explained her therapeutic strategy. She visited this very angry man every day, sitting outside the bars of his cell. She quietly asked him whether he enjoyed shouting epithets so much, and whether he wouldn't rather have staff come and talk to him. He admitted that he felt trapped and did not know how to get out of the extreme isolation where he found himself. But the things they did to him, like putting him on "loaf" (a compressed pellet of leftover food) and performing cell extractions, made him increasingly angry (the cycle of hostility; see chapter 2). She told him she was going to come back each day to see him, she wanted him to speak cordially to her, and if he cooperated she would see if she could help him get out of the hole he was in. He liked that plan and proceeded to greet her with a friendly smile each day. Soon she asked him if he would like to get out of his cell. He told her the officers would never permit that. She told him to let her worry about that, but he had to behave himself. She talked to the officers and arranged for him to be released from his cell to walk up and down the hallway of the pod. She told him he needed to watch his temper and speak civilly to the other prisoners and the officers; if he did that and there was no trouble, she would try to arrange for him to be released to the dayroom. He followed her instructions. Meanwhile, she began negotiating with staff to let him go to the dayroom by himself if he first managed to go a week without raising his voice or swearing at anyone. With her visiting each day and asking how he was getting along, he successfully proved to the officers that he was ready to go to the dayroom and they permitted it. Next she arranged for him be in the dayroom with another prisoner. He told her which prisoner he felt safest with, and staff permitted a trial for him and that prisoner to be in the dayroom together. They played checkers. Step by step, Kiwi was negotiating his release from isolation. It was a three-way negotiation between the prisoner, custody staff, and the mental health specialist.

A management and treatment plan can be created for even the most recalcitrant, angry prisoner in isolation. In fact, this needs to occur. Keeping disturbed/disruptive prisoners in isolation merely worsens their mental condition and makes them angrier. The goal is to move them out of isolation, into a prison environment where they can take advantage of educational programs, rehabilitation programs, and mental health treatment as needed. I will briefly present two cases and then discuss some principles of management and treatment with disturbed/disruptive prisoners.

VIOLENCE DIRECTED OUTWARD

Paul was a twenty-two-year-old African American man when I interviewed him in his prison's SHU. He had been in prison for three years and told me he was due to be released in one month. In further conversation it became clear that he was quite delusional and believed falsely that he would be released because he had performed a heroic act for which officers were grateful. He had been in SHU for two years, interrupted three times by brief stints at the psychiatric hospital serving the prison system. He was actively delusional during our interview, talking about officers putting something in his food that disturbed his sexual function. He believed officers were sexually abusing him and reported more detailed delusional material, mostly sexual in content. He did not go to recreation because there was no equipment and nothing to do in the small, enclosed individual recreation area except to walk around in circles. He was prescribed Zyprexa, an atypical antipsychotic medication. On mental status examination he exhibited flat affect, delusional thinking with strong ideas of reference (paranoia), very poor reality testing, rigid thinking, and slowed cognition. His judgment was poor and he was unable to abstract. All of these signs, taken together, support a diagnosis of psychotic disorder, possibly schizophrenia.

Paul's clinical chart confirmed much of his history. It contained outpatient progress notes describing paranoia, assaultiveness, and refusal to take psychiatric medications. He was assigned the diagnoses of paranoid delusional disorder and intermittent explosive disorder, and he was quoted as saying, "People reading my thoughts with machines, I'm supposed to be a famous rapist." He was also diagnosed on multiple occasions with antisocial personality disorder.

In notes from a disciplinary hearing following an alleged assault on officers, Paul was said to be suffering from "intermittent explosive disorder." But the possibility cannot be ruled out that at the time of the incident he was either suffering from acute symptoms of what would later emerge and be diagnosed as psychosis or having a transient psychosis-like reaction to rapid cessation of psychiatric medications. A month after that disciplinary hearing he suffered a full-blown psychotic episode with hallucinations and delusions. The delusions were organized in a way that requires some time to evolve, so it is likely he was already delusional at the time of the assault on officers and the disciplinary hearing. In fact, a teacher observed just prior to the violent incident that "he seemed to be out of touch, he stared blankly and was unable to participate in class." He may well have been hearing "command hallucinations," imaginary voices telling him to assault the officers. In any case, he had spent quite a lot of time in SHU, and each time that he had to be admitted to the psychiatric hospital he was returned to SHU after he was discharged. I offered the opinion that his condition was made much worse by his continued confinement in SHU, and this was why he cycled repeatedly between the psychiatric hospital and SHU. I recommended dismissal of the disciplinary charges because the assaults were driven by command hallucinations, as well as transfer out of SHU to a long-term mental health treatment program where he could be provided adequate mental health care.

VIOLENCE DIRECTED INWARD: A SELF-MUTILATOR

Andy, a tall, rail-thin twenty-six-year-old Caucasian man, had always been viewed by others as "odd" while growing up. He had no good friends but "hung out" at the periphery of a group of boys in an urban working-class neighborhood. The other boys took note of his eccentricity and considered him simple. He had below-average grades, and after the sixth grade he tended to be absent from school too many days to receive passing grades. He left school in the eighth grade and began to get into trouble on the streets. A pattern emerged. Other boys would draw him into an illegal activity such as robbing a store. Then they would run away, literally leaving him holding the bag. He was arrested for various minor crimes and spent a large amount of time in juvenile correctional settings.

At seventeen, he stole an automobile at the behest of a group of teens he knew on the streets. He was driving with them in the car when a police car spotted the stolen car. He began to speed up to get away, but his "friends" told him to slow down for a minute. They jumped out of the car and then yelled at him to hit the gas. He was pursued, arrested, and convicted of auto theft and resisting arrest. Because of an extensive juvenile record, he was sent to an adult prison. He was terrified.

Because most of his crimes were relatively nonserious, and because he seemed quite the opposite of a tough guy, he was placed in a minimum security correctional facility. There he predictably began "hanging out" with a group of prisoners. Andy was very frightened of possible attacks in prison, and he became even more vulnerable than before to "groupthink," going along with a group of prisoners without carefully considering the repercussions of his actions, even when the group was up to no good. One day the group decided to "walk away" from the facility while in a lightly guarded work platoon outside the gates. Andy dutifully "walked away" with the others and was captured. Now, because of this escape attempt, he was sentenced to a lengthier term and transferred to a supermaximum security unit to serve out the remainder of his sentence.

In isolated confinement he was permitted out of his cell only for showers and for an hour of recreation five times per week in a fenced yard no bigger than a cell, which the prisoners called a "cage." Andy was functionally illiterate, so he could not even read or write and he was reduced to near-total idleness. He paced incessantly in his cell. He had great difficulty sleeping, especially because several prisoners with mental illness in neighboring cells would stay up much of the night screaming and cursing. Andy became increasingly anxious and experienced panic attacks where he had great difficulty catching his breath. He also experienced mounting anger and began to feel aggravated by officers who either would not heed his requests for help or would taunt him as they passed his cell. He had not received many disciplinary tickets prior to being confined in supermax isolation, but soon he began to accumulate disciplinary tickets at an accelerating rate.

Andy began asking to see the prison psychiatrist for help with mounting anxiety and rage. Meanwhile, he was receiving more disciplinary notices, usually for obscene language or for rule violations. For example, he received a ticket for "interfering with observation window and camera" when he tried to hang a sheet up in front of the shower while showering. Each time he received a disciplinary ticket he was punished, first with loss of privileges for thirty days, which could mean loss of yard or commissary privileges. Then he was put on "loaf" (a special diet consisting of ground-up cabbage and leftovers that were baked into a loaf that prisoners claimed was inedible). The psychiatrist who made rounds and talked to prisoners at cell-front did arrange to see Andy in a private office for an evaluation. In his report of that examination the psychiatrist noted his anxiety, panic attacks, and insomnia. He also reviewed the tickets Andy had been accumulating, mostly for swearing and disobeying orders (there were no assaults). The psychiatrist diagnosed intermittent explosive disorder along with antisocial personality disorder. Andy was not placed on the mental health caseload and was not prescribed any medications.

Approximately a year after entering supermaximum confinement, Andy began cutting himself. At first, he scratched himself on the forearm and noticed that after he did so he felt a little less anxious. He did not tell anyone about the self-injuries. He had already tried to arrange sessions with the psychiatrist and had been told several times that he merely needed to calm down and control his temper. He knew that he would get in trouble if he was discovered injuring himself, so he did not seek assistance but began to cut himself more often, usually at night when he was unable to sleep. Eventually he was discovered by a corrections officer with blood running down his arm and was issued a ticket for the rule violation "self-mutilation."

The psychiatrist was called to see Andy at cell-front and decided that he was merely "manipulating" to gain a transfer to the mental health observation unit and to receive medications. He noted that Andy had tried to hang himself with a sheet prior to cutting himself. He again entered a diagnosis of intermittent explosive disorder and antisocial personality disorder, but he also ordered that Andy be placed on "strip cell status" in his cell. This meant that all of his clothes, sheets, and property were taken from him, officers would make visits to his cell-front every thirty minutes to make certain he was not harming himself, and the psychiatrist would return each weekday to his cell-front to ask if he was still feeling like harming himself. After three days Andy convinced the psychiatrist that he no longer felt like cutting himself or trying to hang himself, his property was returned to him, and the thirty-minute checks were discontinued. He was issued a disciplinary notice for "self-mutilation," where the specific act was "attempting to hang himself and cutting his left wrist and arm." He was given a punishment of thirty days' loss of privileges.

Subsequently, Andy proceeded to slice himself repeatedly, at first once or twice a month, then approximately weekly, and sometimes on a daily basis. He would receive a ticket each time it was discovered he had harmed himself, and he accumulated a very long period of loss of privileges, including visits. But there was a new development. The supermaximum security unit where Andy was confined experienced a severe staffing shortage. It was located far from any urban center, and because of the frustrations of the work and low salaries, quite a few corrections officers resigned. New officers were less well trained and because of the staff shortage were assigned to the supermax unit without much experience. Andy and several other prisoners in the unit continued to express anger toward officers, and Andy continued to self-mutilate. The officers kept writing disciplinary tickets, but they also began to spray Andy in his cell with immobilizing gas.

The psychiatrist was called on many occasions to see Andy. He transferred him to the observation unit in a nearby infirmary on several occasions. A pattern became apparent: Andy would cut himself; the officers would spray him and write a disciplinary ticket and then would call the psychiatrist. The psychiatrist would visit him at cell-front, and on several occasions would have him transferred to the observation unit, where he would be placed in a "strip cell" with one wall made of indestructible plexiglass (Lexan) so that staff passing by could observe him and prevent further acts of self-harm. No talking therapy occurred in the observation unit, but after cutting himself and being moved away from the noise and isolation of his supermax tier to the infirmary or to an observation cell, Andy would calm down, and the panic attacks and urge to cut would abate, so that when the psychiatrist saw him for a few minutes during daily rounds he would say Andy was no longer feeling like harming himself. At that point he would be transferred back to his cell in the supermaximum security unit and the cycle would begin again.

At one point, the psychiatrist decided that Andy might be suffering from bipolar disorder and began to prescribe mood-stabilizing medications (lithium, Depakote) that had the beneficial effect of modulating his mood swings. There is evidence in the clinical file that Andy's behavior problems subsided while he was receiving these psychiatric medications. However, during a cell search, it was determined that he sometimes "cheeked" pills and then hoarded them in his cell. The custody staff assumed that he was accumulating contraband pills for sale to other prisoners, and as a result he was issued a disciplinary charge for contraband and his medications were discontinued. Soon thereafter, the psychiatrist changed the diagnoses on Andy's clinical chart. He discarded the diagnosis of bipolar disorder that had been in place while mood-stabilizing medications were being prescribed, and he reverted to the diagnosis of intermittent explosive disorder, a diagnosis that in correctional facilities can have the connotation of "no serious mental illness, merely a behavior problem." He was also diagnosed with antisocial personality disorder.

I had not seen more than a rare case of self-mutilation (i.e., "cutting" or self-inflicted cuts with either suicidal or nonsuicidal aims) among adult men until I began touring isolated confinement units in prisons. In the larger community, self-mutilation is seen mostly in adolescent girls. But there is an epidemic of self-mutilation in prison isolated confinement units today, and most of the prisoners involved, men as well as women, upon reflection, say they began injuring themselves only after they were placed in segregation. Sometimes, if asked, prisoners admit to suicidal intent; at other times they will say the cutting behavior was driven by uncontrollable anxiety or a need to see blood to know that they were human—and in the nonsuicidal instances, there seems to be some momentary relief from anxiety immediately after the act of self-mutilation.

PSYCHOPATHOLOGY AND VIOLENCE

Both Paul and Andy were repeatedly judged to be nondisturbed. Both men were repeatedly diagnosed as having antisocial personality disorder. That diagnosis and its variants (such as psychopathic personality) are frequently deployed with prisoners who have been involved in violence. Toch notes that "because psychopathy is generally equated with untreatability, offenders that clinicians do not want to deal with can be turned away by adjudging them psychopathic, and hence unamenable to treatment. In other words, psychopathy is featured in what Vicky Agee has called the 'diagnostic game'—the use of diagnoses to shuttle clients from one's own turf to other jurisdictions. Psychopathy (or antisocial personality disorder) unsurprisingly becomes a salient diagnosis in the discharge summaries of hospitals who send patients back to prison after cursory review."[5]

Prisoners who are emotionally disturbed or who receive mental health services are disproportionately given disciplinary tickets or citations.[6] They are also disproportionately involved in violent incidents in prison, either because they are victimized by other prisoners or by staff or because they are unable to control their own emotional outbursts.[7] Individuals suffering from mental illness often tend to behave inappropriately in varied settings, and the inappropriateness of their behavior accounts for the fact that some undesirable patterns of conduct (such as Andy's fateful susceptibility to group pressures and contagion) can be imported from the streets into the prison, where the repercussions of coping failures can become increasingly serious.

MAD OR BAD?

Custody staff often view disturbed violent prisoners as "mad," while mental health staff view them as "bad"—management problems, manipulative, malingerers, or personality disordered—and refuse to intervene. In extreme cases the prisoner is transported from prison to the mental health setting and back in a practice that is referred to pejoratively as "bus therapy."[8] Malingering is too often overemphasized, as an excuse not to provide mental health treatment. In other words, when mental health staff judge the prisoner to be malingering, they assume that the prisoner's unacceptable behaviors are not driven by a mental illness and that they can safely deny treatment and turn the prisoner over to custody staff for predictably harsh punishment.

Often, in the process of reviewing custodial records and clinical charts, one discovers such notes as "This prisoner suffers from a chronic psychosis, but the fight that led to the current term in segregation was not a result of his psychiatric difficulty." Yet this same prisoner evidences signs of serious acute psychopathology while in solitary confinement. Whether or not it is possible to distinguish between the unacceptable acts that are caused by a prisoner's psychosis and those that are not directly attributable to a psychiatric condition though they erupt in a prisoner with serious mental illness—and I am skeptical about officers' and clinicians' capacity to accurately make such distinctions—the confinement of such prisoners in punitive segregation units makes it that much more difficult for mental health and custody staff to collaborate in designing an individualized, secure, and therapeutic management plan. And since the environment in this kind of unit exacerbates psychiatric symptoms, the choice to turn "disturbed/disruptive" prisoners over to custody staff to be placed in a lock-up unit very likely means they will receive even less mental health treatment for an increasingly serious condition. In the dozens of supermaximum security units that I have seen, treatment has generally been denied or limited to the prescription of psychiatric medications after very brief visits at the prisoner's cell door, within earshot of the correctional officers and the prisoners in adjacent cells.

When a prisoner is agitated and officers are considering use of force, it is often possible for a mental health clinician to step in and talk the recalcitrant prisoner down so that no force will be needed. In fact, I believe that a preemptive mental health intervention should be a requirement whenever a prisoner known to be suffering from mental illness is the focus of planned use of force. It is always possible that the unacceptable behavior that is triggering the confrontation with staff was driven by the prisoner's mental illness.

In a supermax unit within a maximum security prison in a western state, Jake was shouting obscenities and refusing to come to the door of his cell so that officers could apply handcuffs and move him to another cell. The officers working in the unit were getting fed up with Jake's repeated misbehavior and noncooperation. They decided to assemble a "cell extraction team" to go into his cell, slam him against a wall, and apply handcuffs so they could move him to a cell at the rear of the unit where, at least, they would not hear his shouting. The mental health counselor, who knew Jake because he had been making weekly rounds on that pod, happened to be on the unit at the time. He told the sergeant in charge of the pod that he would like to visit with Jake before they conducted the cell extraction. He went to Jake's cell and asked him what was going on. Jake told him the officers were not taking him to recreation enough and that was why he refused to "cuff up." The counselor asked him to come closer to the cell door so they could talk without other prisoners hearing them, and then talked to Jake for a few minutes about the need for him to control his anger if he wanted to get along better with the officers. He said he would talk to the officers about getting him to recreation more often. Then he asked Jake if he would please cooperate with the officers and "cuff up." Jake complied, there was no cell extraction, and, with Jake cooperating, the officers decided they did not need to change his cell.

Where mental illness even partially figures in the emergence of rule breaking, assaultiveness, or self-harm, the psychiatric condition should be taken into consideration in terms of culpability, competency, vulnerability, and the potential effectiveness of the punishment. The prisoner with serious mental illness facing disciplinary sanctions should be considered less culpable, so the sanctions or punishments should be diminished accordingly. This issue usually does not arise because prison disciplinarians, including hearing officers, usually display little interest in why a prisoner committed his or her transgression. The focus for the prison is on the amount of harm or damage resulting from the offense. The prisoner who sets himself on fire because voices tell him that flames will purify him can expect a hefty sentence because fires in prison are life threatening and property destroying.

Another mostly unasked question is whether the prisoner is competent, which has to do with his or her condition at the time the case is adjudicated. In the community, defendants must be deemed capable of understanding what goes on in the courtroom and assisting in their defense. In most correctional systems, no similar prerequisite exists. The closest thing to a mandated concern is a US Supreme Court ruling relating to prison hearings which says that "where an illiterate inmate is involved . . . he should be free to seek the aid of a fellow inmate, or if that is forbidden, to have adequate substitute aid in the form of help from the staff or from a sufficiently competent inmate designated by the staff."[9] In most prison systems I have investigated, the prisoner's competence to defend himself at a hearing never comes up. In fact, the prisoner is usually not permitted to defend himself. He is not permitted to call witnesses, he is not permitted the presence of counsel (even a jailhouse lawyer, another prisoner acting as a legal advocate), and often, because he feels the disciplinary hearing is a mockery, the prisoner does not even show up.

Next, the hearing officer or disciplinary panel should consider the vulnerability of the prisoner who is being punished. I know of no rule that tells prison staff that they must think about the consequences of punitive dispositions. Disturbed prisoners are sent to solitary confinement, where they predictably fall apart. To get help, they must wait until their condition deteriorates. If a segregated inmate is sent to an observation/crisis unit or is committed to a hospital, he returns to segregation when he is discharged. Andy's plight is in this respect illustrative.

Another critical question prison authorities too rarely consider is the effectiveness of punitive measures. If the demonstrable ineffectiveness of various punitive sanctions for unacceptable and assaultive behaviors were to become an important consideration, and if authorities were to notice that an exclusively punitive approach on the part of staff transparently fails to lead to rehabilitation, then the issue of whether serious mental illness or "merely a personality disorder" is driving a prisoner's assaultive behavior would become less important than the question of whether the harsh conditions of isolated confinement make a prisoner's tendency toward rule breaking and violence greater, and whether sessions with a mental health clinician might reduce the unacceptable behaviors.

USE OF FORCE

Not only is the use of force unlikely to improve inmate behavior, but it also is very likely to cause serious harm. Of course, there are times when the use of force is required, but in a well-managed correctional facility those times are relatively rare. The use of immobilizing gas, or actually any form of force, on inmates with mental illness is likely to have very damaging effects on their psychiatric condition, disability, and prognosis.[10] A delusional inmate will likely incorporate into his delusional system the intrusion into his cell of deputies wearing padding and gas masks: for example, he will believe that the same external enemies who he already knew were out to harm him are now responsible for his being attacked and sprayed with gas. And just about any inmate who is subjected to multiple sprayings with immobilizing gas and other uses of force will be traumatized by the incidents. Since prisoners as a group have suffered many more prior traumas than the general population, they are very vulnerable to "retraumatization" and even the emergence of PTSD following a new trauma such as a cell extraction with the use of immobilizing gas.

The best way to ward off incidents of excessive force with prisoners suffering from serious mental illness is to have in place adequate mental health treatment, and then, in the immediate prelude to officers' use of force, to call on mental health staff to interact with the prisoner. In too many cases, the prisoner who is eventually the target of the use of force has not been receiving adequate mental health treatment in the period just prior to the use-of-force incident. Had the prisoner been receiving adequate treatment, he or she likely would have been taking prescribed medications that would lessen the severity of symptoms and would have formed a therapeutic relationship with mental health staff, who would then be in a better position to talk him or her into complying with an order, such as the order to cuff up. This is why officers considering use of force with prisoners who are suffering from serious mental illness should ask mental health staff to talk to the prisoner first. Mental health staff's specialized training makes them better equipped than officers to handle inmates suffering from mental illness. Where possible, the mental health staff assigned to the particular module should be tasked with talking to the prisoner, as individuals with severe mental illnesses are more likely to cooperate with mental health staff members with whom they have a preexisting therapeutic relationship.

THE MISSISSIPPI EXPERIENCE

Following two class action lawsuits in Mississippi brought by the ACLU's National Prison Project on behalf of the prisoners (see chapter 2), the Mississippi Department of Corrections was required to greatly reduce the population in administrative segregation at supermax Unit 32 and to establish a step-down mental health treatment unit for the prisoners excluded from administrative segregation.[11] The step-down program inside Unit 32 consisted of three graduated phases with increasing freedoms and amenities, and the prisoners would meet with mental health staff in therapy groups designed to help them attain each phase. The "step-down" program became a route for prisoners to leave Unit 32.

After the majority of prisoners were removed from the supermax unit, the violence rate in the entire DOC decreased significantly. In other words, the prisoners who had been consigned to segregation did not resort to violence after being released from Unit 32, and the yards, on average, became more peaceful. The prisoners suffering from serious mental illness who had been relegated to solitary confinement and then were transferred to the step-down unit and eventually to general population received far fewer disciplinary infractions after they were transferred out of the supermax unit. After eight hundred of the approximately one thousand prisoners in the supermaximum security unit were transferred out of isolated confinement, there was a large reduction in the rates of misconduct and violence, not only among the prisoners transferred out of supermax, but in the entire Mississippi DOC. Eventually, the number of prisoners remaining in Unit 32 dipped beneath two hundred, and the DOC decided to close the unit.[12]

There is no hard evidence that supermaximum security facilities ever reliably reduced systemwide prison violence or enhanced public safety. Fears that a significant reduction in the supermax population or the outright closure of a facility will result in heightened security threats and prison violence have not been borne out by experience, including that of Unit 32. In fact, the Mississippi example supports the theory that the presence of a supermaximum solitary confinement unit within a DOC may actually increase the violence rate in the entire prison system. Contrary to early claims that super-maximum security units were needed to reduce violence in the prisons, evidence is accruing that the rate of violence in prison has not changed, or has risen, since the advent of the supermaximum security prison.[13] It has even more definitely risen when violence against the self is factored in. Alison Liebling, England's leading authority on prison suicides, has written that "under no circumstances should the response to a suicide attempt be punitive: isolation in stripped conditions is sometimes assumed by inmates to be punishment for their behavior. . . . To contribute a unitary meaning to these acts (i.e., attention seeking) is potentially dangerous and misleading. Training should be aimed to encourage all staff to appreciate the complexity of such behavior and its possible causes and motivations, which are multiple."[14] Staff training of the sort that Liebling mentions has to respond individually to individual prisoners (such as Andy and Paul).

ADDRESSING A VIOLENCE PATTERN

In staff training such as that described by Liebling, the first step to effective intervention is to trace the prisoner's pattern of violence or self-destructiveness. As Hans Toch has noted, this requires custody officers, mental health staff, teachers, and other staff members to spend more time with problematic prisoners, getting to know them and gaining their confidence, as well as time conferring with each other to devise a collaborative strategy for managing and treating them.[15] The more severe a prisoner's pattern of violence, the more time will be required to attain good outcomes.[16] But I have found that these efforts save money in the long run by making prisoners more likely to behave acceptably and to adhere to the treatment and management plan. Problems are effectively addressed only if those who work with an individual trust and respect each other and get the benefit of each other's knowledge, wisdom, and expertise. All parties gain in the process. Mental health staff have much to learn from custody staff because they see the prisoners only a fraction of the time that officers see them and have limited control over the prisoners' environment.

According to Toch, looking for a pattern in the violent episodes requires asking when the violence began and looking at possible associations with both situational and individual factors. With regard to situational factors, the prisoner might become assaultive only on a certain shift when certain staff are present, or certain parties might be typically involved in the prisoners' altercations. The team should create an inventory of the circumstances in which the person aggresses, such as the common characteristics of individuals the prisoner selects as victims.[17] Then there are individual factors. Does the prisoner become assaultive only when experiencing a manic mood swing or only after refusing to take psychiatric medications? Is something troubling and irritating going on with the prisoner's family, such as a child who is in trouble or a spouse who is unfaithful? Is the prisoner worried about something happening in court that affects his or her situation?

Interventions can be created to improve the situational variables. For example, the prisoner can be moved out of solitary confinement and into a secure mental health treatment unit. A young prisoner may be involved in a great deal of violence in an age-homogeneous prison for younger inmates but may reduce his violent behavior in a prison that contains an older population (this scenario provides clues about the peer temptations and pressures to which young prisoners react). Or, if there are particular prisoners or officers with whom the prisoner has a difficult time remaining peaceful, the prisoner can be moved to another pod or cellblock where there will be different personalities. If it is noticed that a particular officer gets along very well with hot-headed youthful prisoners, those prisoners can be moved to a unit where they will interact with that officer, or that officer can become involved in training his peers on handling young, rowdy individuals.

Of course, staff must always keep an eye on security and safety. The challenge is to help staff understand motives and dynamics in the violent behavior of offenders so that they discover ways to interrupt violent careers, as opposed to locking the offenders up, thus exacerbating their predispositions or leaving them unchanged. Clinicians can assist custody staff in this enterprise, assuming they are themselves willing to take risks by understanding, engaging, and reforming violent prisoners.

SECURE INTERMEDIATE TREATMENT PROGRAMS

Intermediate mental health treatment programs have an important preventative effect, as I explained in chapter 10. Prisoners with serious mental illness are more likely to adhere to and benefit from treatment when they are in an intermediate treatment program where they can get to know and trust the staff. Their emotional breakdowns are more likely to be noticed early, and more intensive interventions can be initiated. One very helpful form of treatment is dialectical behavior therapy, a therapeutic approach to some very dysfunctional character disorders that was pioneered by Marsha Linehan.[18] I have advised correctional mental health clinicians to get training in dialectical behavior therapy and apply it with their difficult patients. With adequate treatment, prisoners with serious mental illness will be much less likely to get into disciplinary trouble and be sent to administrative segregation or solitary confinement.

Disability Advocates v. New York State Office of Mental Health (*DAI, Inc. v. NY OMH*), a lawsuit on which I served as a psychiatric expert, was brought on behalf of all New York prisoners who suffered from serious mental illness, the issue being the adequacy of their mental health treatment. Sure enough, we found a great many prisoners suffering from serious mental illness in New York's SHUs. We demanded that they be removed from isolation and provided better mental health treatment. But rather than instating a ban on placing prisoners with serious mental illness in the SHUs, the state of New York agreed to expand out-of-cell time in the solitary confinement units for prisoners with serious mental illness so that prisoners would be released from their cells for ten hours per week of educational and therapeutic programming in addition to a number of hours for recreation and unstructured activities. As I mentioned in chapter 10, the state also agreed to create over three hundred new intermediate mental health care beds. The idea was that the more than three hundred additional prisoners with serious mental illness who were fortunate enough to be admitted to intermediate care would be sheltered from the kinds of altercations that might otherwise lead to their transfer into solitary confinement. For example, if trouble was brewing between a patient and another prisoner, the patient could discuss his options with a staff member in the intermediate treatment unit, who might recommend that the patient stay away from that other prisoner or might arrange a transfer of that other prisoner to a different cellblock.

Guidelines for intermediate care units must include a provision that prisoners who qualify for placement in the unit will not be ejected for misconduct or violence. I am not saying that prisoners in intermediate care units should be immune to punishment. Discipline is important, but it must take place within the intermediate care unit. Otherwise, when a prisoner with serious mental illness gets into a fight, for example, he will be ejected from the intermediate care unit and sent to some form of punitive segregation, with all the ill effects that would trigger. Instead, once a prisoner qualifies for intermediate care, he must be disciplined within the intermediate care unit by custody and mental health staff in collaboration. Perhaps he will lose certain privileges on account of a rule violation or fight, perhaps he will be "top-locked" in his cell on the unit and have to miss unit activities for a specified period of time. But he will continue to be seen by the officers and mental health clinicians on the unit instead of going to segregation and missing out on treatment altogether. This is a very important point. I have toured residential treatment programs in several states that I consider high quality, but then I find that quite a few prisoners with serious mental illness are ejected from the program and transferred to segregation as soon as they get into a fight.

The project of addressing a pattern in the misbehavior of disturbed prisoners is best accomplished in a high-security intermediate treatment program— one that can provide the level of security needed and the quality of custody and mental health staff collaboration needed to retain and treat prisoners even if they become recalcitrant and combative. After all, occasional setbacks and acute breakdowns are part of the waxing and waning course of serious mental illness, and in an institutional setting like a prison staff have the opportunity to consistently follow patients and provide the level and kind of care they need at each point along the way.

PSYCHOTROPIC MEDICATIONS

Psychotropic medications can play an important role in managing disturbed/disruptive prisoners, but like other components of comprehensive mental health treatment, they can become more of an obstacle than an aid to proper treatment and rehabilitation if they are employed to compensate for deficiencies in the program.

If there is no underlying psychotic condition or other psychiatric disorder requiring the prescription of medications, the use of antipsychotic medications can be problematic. No medication diminishes violent outbursts in every clinical situation. Medications can diminish hallucinations, reduce paranoia, or dampen mood swings. But in the absence of an underlying psychiatric condition that is responsive to medications, prescribing these drugs in doses high enough to reduce rage and violent acting out will merely result in sedation and toxic side effects.

That said, some medication strategies can help in the management of disturbed/disruptive prisoners.[19] When a manic state is a significant part of the picture, mood stabilizers such as lithium, Depakote, or Lamictal can provide some long-term stability and decrease the tendency toward violent acting out. When violent incidents are impulsive and sporadic, the group of heart medications called beta blockers can reduce the frequency and severity of outbursts.[20] On the other hand, when tranquilizers are prescribed in strong doses simply to control aggressive behavior in the absence of a complete psychiatric examination and adequate treatment planning, they are easily abused and there is great potential for harm.

MODEL PROGRAMS

At the height of popularity of the punishment paradigm and the heyday of supermaximum prisons, the staff at Grendon Prison in the United Kingdom began experimenting with a very different strategy for managing and rehabilitating assaultive prisoners.[21] Convinced that mutual respect and better communication between staff and prisoners was required for altering the behavior of disruptive and assaultive prisoners, they valued and fostered prisoners' agency and thus viewed prisoners as active participants in decisions that affected them. They also fostered collaborative, cross-staff analysis of violent incidents in order to make interventions maximally effective. Rich programming and well-trained staff are required to deal with long-term residents of segregation settings, who may be self-insulating, bitter, mistrustful, and fearful. And even with the most sophisticated staff, working in a unit for disturbed/disruptive inmates tends to be a crisis-studded adventure.

Grendon Prison has a unique history. As prison managements elsewhere in the United Kingdom and the United States turned to intensified segregation, the staff at Grendon remained true to their plan to run a prison unit for very assaultive prisoners as a therapeutic community. British community psychiatrist Maxwell Jones invented this modality just after World War II.[22] In the community, individuals with serious mental illness live together and meet often to decide upon all sorts of questions, such as what the group will eat, what activities they will support, how they will manage animosities that come up between community members, and so forth. The staff meet with the residents and retain the right to decide on staff hiring and firing, the finances of the house, and which treatment plans will be voluntary and which involuntary. But staff view their job as maximizing the clients' democratic participation in running the therapeutic community, and of course this increases the agency of the clients as well as their skills in living together. At Grendon Prison, groups are the place to talk about the meaning of angry feelings, and there is significant evidence that the approach works. There is far less physical violence at Grendon than at other prisons of comparable maximum security level, there are fewer assaults on staff, disciplinary infractions are fewer, and there is less drug use.[23] Grendon also has a lower reconviction rate for those who are released back to the community.[24] The mental health staff at Grendon, some affiliated with Tavistock Institute, have reintroduced psycho-analytic concepts into the field of forensic mental health—but not in the idealistic way that August Aichorn, Franz Alexander, and Erich Fromm did years earlier when they assumed psychoanalysis could be a cure-all for crimi-nal tendencies.[25] They do not claim that psychoanalysis is better than cogni-tive behavioral therapy or any other modality for prisoners who have trouble managing their tempers, and they are fully aware of research findings that psychodynamic interventions by themselves are not very helpful. So they integrate diverse strategies and rely on evidence-based research to come up with effective treatment.[26]

The staff at Grendon believe that factors in prisoners' lives that make them prone to crime, including antisocial attitudes, procriminal associates, crimi-nal influences in the family, and low levels of personal education, must be identified and countered.[27] But it is the prisoners in the therapeutic com-munity, collaborating with staff, who must point out to participants in the community the criminogenic factors in their personal lives and advocate with each other for change. Thus Grendon features conversations involving prisoners and staff that would never happen in an American supermax prison. The following is a transcript of a conversation that occurred at a therapeutic community meeting at Grendon:

"I think about this all the time, Dave," the only officer in the group joined in. "Say you've got two lads, both abused as children. One turns out to be a sexual abuser, one turns out to be an armed robber. The armed robber's always saying, I could never do that—I couldn't turn out to be an abuser. But the abuser says, no, you are abusing. You're inflicting your pain and control and power over somebody else. The only difference is, you're choosing to do it with that weapon, and I'm using this weapon."

"No way, Tom," Dave erupted angrily. "When I go out robbing, it's for the money! The power is what I do, yeah—but the end goal for me is the money! Sex offenders want the power over the person. Me, I just want the pound note."

"But isn't it all interlinked?" Alex suggested.

"Well, no, it's not! When I'm robbing someone, I'm not thinking to myself, oh this is brilliant, I'm about to come . . ."

"No, but I think that's part of it, isn't it?" Alex smiled. "The actual need to be stronger than somebody else. To be overpowering and overbearing."

This exchange is rich in self-exposure as well as psychological insight, quite a welcome contrast to the kind of talk that occurs among the inmates of supermax isolation units in the United States. In the isolation unit, if prisoners are able to talk with each other at all, they typically keep their cards very close to their chests, frightened that exposing their feelings to each other can endanger them. Open and nondefensive exploration of participants' motivations for committing crimes, as reflected in this excerpt of a group meeting at Grendon Prison, can be an important step along the path to rehabilitation.

There are model programs in other countries. For example, the Scandinavian countries incarcerate one-tenth as many people, per capita, as the United States. With less crowding, prisons in Scandinavian countries are relatively small, usually confining one hundred to two hundred prisoners; the warden knows most of the prisoners; staff attempt to make the environment approximate living situations in the larger community; there are rich educational and vocational training opportunities; everyone has meaningful work; and prisoners approaching release are encouraged to participate in work-release programs in the community, returning to sleep in the prison until their sentence runs out. Of course, with that kind of rich programming, there is almost no solitary confinement in these countries.[28]

There are alternative models for managing, treating, and rehabilitating difficult prisoners in the United States. There is an exciting ongoing experiment in the Colorado Department of Corrections (CDOC). When Rick Raemisch replaced Tom Clement as executive director of the CDOC in 2013, he spent a night in his own supermax solitary confinement unit and wrote an op-ed in the *New York Times* about the experience.[29] He then proceeded to downsize the supermax from a population of 7 percent of Colorado DOC prisoners to 1 percent. He started with prisoners who were suffering from mental illness.[30] With so many prisoners released from SHU, the system had to create alternatives to solitary confinement very rapidly. They are doing so, and from all reports, the results are very promising. In an article Raemisch wrote in 2016 with Kellie Wasko, the two state: "The CDOC facilities and the public were not safer as a result of the continued use of long term Administrative Segregation."[31]

The first step Raemisch undertook in the transition was to establish residential treatment facilities (intermediate care) for prisoners with serious mental illness in three prisons, two for men and one for women. The Colorado DOC ended indeterminate SHU sentences (this was one of the changes won by the *Ashker v. Brown* litigation in California) and established transition units to assist prisoners exiting the SHU to adjust to general population. Prisoners were no longer released directly from SHU into the community. The CDOC established restrictive housing units for the most disruptive prisoners, permitting them to earn their way through phases to release from solitary within twelve months. These changes represent a new philosophy in corrections, and as Raemisch and Wasko have noted, the dire predictions of critics have not been borne out:

> Due to the focused and ambitious efforts of the Colorado DOC to embrace new philosophies and implement new policies to address this growing population, outside groups did not believe the successes of what we were accomplishing. Many stated that we were calling Ad Seg something else. But we have opened our policies and practices to be reviewed and witnessed. We have identified better ways to accomplish our goals and adjusted our practices as we design this manner of managing offenders. We manage offenders through scheduling and opportunities for them to come out of their cells. If they refuse these opportunities, we don't document the refusal. Housing units are structured to manage offenders according to schedules to maximize staff resources. We offer our offenders in Residential Treatment Programs out of cell opportunities for both therapeutic and non-therapeutic time—we don't force them to come out if they don't want to. This has brought us ridicule and critique but we feel that we are reaching these offenders through time and patience and consistent dose and frequency of treatment availability. One seasoned staff member even "warned" executive staff that the reforms were going to get someone hurt or killed. That same staff member, a year later, said they could not believe the changes in the offender behavior and participation in treatment.[32]

Rikers Island is another program that warrants watching. The huge jail for New York City has been in the spotlight because of the frequent use of solitary confinement with juveniles and because of high-profile cases where jail prisoners with serious mental illness, including Kalief Browder, have done very poorly or committed suicide. The commissioner at Rikers, Joseph Ponte, had overseen the department of corrections in Maine after that state's legislature voted to remove prisoners with mental illness from solitary confinement, and now he is taking measures to reduce the use of solitary at Rikers. A recent report from the mental health team at Rikers reflects important progress in that effort.[33] Starting in 2013, they developed a treatment program for prisoners with serious mental illness who were prone to violate jail rules, a program that does not involve solitary confinement, called the Clinical Alternative to Punitive Segregation (CAPS) Unit. Staff in the CAPS Unit provide individual and group psychotherapy, art therapy, medication management, and community meetings. By March, 2015, 195 individuals had passed through the CAPS Unit. In 2016 the mental health staff at Rikers announced that the program was proving valuable enough to "adapt . . . to existing mental health units as a means to promote better clinical outcomes and also help prevent jail-based infractions."[34]

The programs at Grendon Prison, the Colorado DOC, and Rikers Island do not represent the only "correct" way to program disruptive prisoners who formerly would be consigned to very long-term solitary confinement. But all three of these innovative approaches warrant watching and emulating. There is a new spirit in corrections, a move away from the culture of punishment and toward a rehabilitative attitude. When we bar the placement of prisoners with serious mental illness in solitary confinement units—as we must—and we place them instead in settings where they are safe and can receive the mental health treatment and rehabilitation they need, it is stunning how positive the results can be.

TWELVE

Beyond Supermax Isolation

THE MOST EFFECTIVE ALTERNATIVE to long-term solitary confinement would be massive reduction of the prison population with concurrent upgrading of mental health and rehabilitation programming in the community as well as in correctional settings. Many of the worst conditions of confinement today stem directly from the overcrowding of jails and prisons that spiraled out of control beginning in the 1970s and '80s. The boom in construction of supermaximum prisons happened only after prison crowding had caused unprecedented violence in prisons that correctional administrators were at a loss to address. The powers-that-be opted for a historic wrong turn, proceeding to isolate those they deemed "worst of the worst," and the situation deteriorated from there.

The supermax boom did not occur in a vacuum. By the mid-1970s, as the post–World War II economic boom declined and as wealth became more concentrated in fewer hands, the public education system and social programs such as the 1960s' War on Poverty became less of a funding priority and dwindled in scope and reach. Government officials would henceforth focus more on the maintenance of law and order, the dismantling of federal regulations on corporations, and the expansion of corporate markets and profits, even when that meant waging wars. The Reagan years put the retreat from social responsibility into overdrive, as budgets for public education and social welfare programs were slashed. The slashing continues today and even accelerates as foreign wars and homeland security draw heavily upon the state's fiscal resources and as the gap between rich and poor widens.

Meanwhile, many people face dismal employment prospects and have relatively little in the way of social welfare programs; they cannot find affordable housing, and they receive inadequate medical and mental health treatment. Tragically, in all too many cases, they find their way into the criminal justice system. In other words, poor and disenfranchised people are "disappeared" by an increasingly inequitable society that refuses to adequately fund services they need to stay afloat. Then, in the prisons, many of the most disadvantaged and disabled are warehoused in segregation and supermax units, where they are left idle and isolated. The public hears even less about their plight, and, not accidentally, some of the worst abuses in prison occur in secrecy in solitary confinement units.

Craig Haney provides a detailed analysis of how prison conditions evolved over recent decades to cause unnecessary and unacceptable pain and suffering in prisoners. He concludes:

> Very few scholars ever seriously contemplated or anticipated that an already vast system of coercive institutions would be dramatically increased in size and then turned primarily to the task of imposing punishment for the purpose of causing pain. Yet, that is precisely what has happened in the era we have entered, one in which we seem to confront the worst of both worlds: Prisons justified and maintained in the name of benevolent intervention— however well or poorly this goal was realized—have multiplied and then been directed to inflict penal harm. The excessive levels of prison pain now generated by this system must be candidly addressed, carefully analyzed, and effectively limited—in psychological terms as well as others. It is important to begin a thoughtful dialogue about humane alternatives to these painful policies before the damage becomes irreversible and the social, political, and economic accommodations to such widespread practices become so extreme and entrenched that we can no longer turn away from them.[1]

In federal court, after I testify in a class action lawsuit about the harm of solitary confinement, I am asked what remedies I recommend. The court is interested in concrete answers to very narrow questions, the questions at issue in the class action lawsuit. I can provide that kind of remedy. Simply stated, the culture of punishment and control needs to be replaced by a rehabilitative attitude so that when prisoners are transferred out of solitary confinement, as I strongly advise the court to order, they can participate in meaningful activities that will foster a peaceful prison milieu and a better chance at success after they are released from prison. In chapters 9, 10, and 11 I outline the remedies I recommend.

But the court is not set up to consider the larger social issues. It is time to grapple with the critical question of whether the criminal justice system is ever to become just. If we really want to fairly adjudicate crime while establishing alternatives to mass imprisonment and solitary confinement, we need to level the playing field. We need to do major upgrades in our social institutions, including the schools, social services, housing, health care, and public mental health. We need to close the massive and growing gap between rich and poor, and we need to repair the holes in the social safety net where disadvantaged people fall through on their way to jail.

The mechanism for the imprisonment binge of the late twentieth century was sentencing. Laws enacted in those years brought in ever longer sentences, "truth in sentencing" laws that abolish or restrict the granting of parole, mandatory minimums, "three strikes" laws, the practice of trying kids as adults, more prison time for a growing list of crimes, huge increases in the kinds of drug-related behavior that would be prosecuted as felonies, and longer sentences for all crimes. The new sentencing laws multiplied the prison population geometrically and resulted in a growing proportion of prisoners suffering from serious mental illness. After all, dual diagnosis, a mental illness plus substance abuse, is one of the most common presentations of schizophrenia and bipolar disorder.

The trends in sentencing that led to prison crowding, supermax isolation, and the decimation of life skills in so many people need to be reversed. I am not alone in this appraisal. Many state legislatures are enacting laws to shorten prison sentences and mandate diversion to alternative community programs. In 2010 President Obama signed the Fair Sentencing Act, which vastly reduces the disparity between sentences involving crack cocaine abuse (used more by people of color because of its lower price) and powder cocaine (used more by middle-class whites).

The Sentencing Project, a nonprofit agency, has been researching and educating the public for many years on the need for sentencing reform.[2] They recently published a report, *The State of Sentencing 2015: Developments in Policy and Practice*,[3] that summarizes hopeful changes occurring at the legislative level in many states.

> During 2015, lawmakers in at least 30 states adopted changes in policy and practice that may contribute to further declines in incarcerated populations and address the collateral impacts of justice involvement.... Many of the reforms adopted in recent years are likely to have only a modest impact on rates of incarceration, but the continued pace of change in policy and practice suggests strong interest among state of officials in reconsidering sentencing and collateral consequences. More substantial remedies will be required to significantly reduce the nation's high rate of incarceration.... Meaningful

reforms would involve eliminating or repealing mandatory minimum policies; scaling back "three strikes" laws and recidivist statutes; addressing statutory penalties mandating life without the possibility of parole for certain offenses; and reconsidering the length of prison terms in regard to the goal of public safety.

One of the most promising developments in the realm of sentencing has been the implementation of diversion.[4] Defendants with mental illness or substance abuse problems are sent to behavioral health courts or substance abuse courts, where the judge has the authority to assign them to treatment programs in the community as an alternative to serving jail or prison terms.[5] Since a term in jail or prison has the effect, on average, of making the prognoses for mental illness worse, and since individuals entering prison with substance abuse problems are very likely to resort again to substance abuse when they are released, it makes sense to divert them at the front end, one hopes before they plead guilty or not guilty, and to consign them to the relevant mental health or substance abuse treatment in the community under court supervision.[6] Another model, called the sequential intercept model, involves intensive mental health treatment interventions at points in the career of individuals with mental illness when they are at heightened risk of being swept up in the criminal justice system, for example when they are arrested, when they are in jail, and when they are transferred to a forensic hospital for assessment. The hope is that diversion and intensive therapeutic intervention at these points will bump them out of the criminal justice system and into ongoing treatment.[7] Outcome studies of diversion and behavioral health courts are very promising.[8] And for individuals suffering from serious mental illness, the impact of community mental health treatment and substance abuse programs on recidivism and parole violation rates is far superior to the outcomes of incarceration.[9]

There needs to be a robust effort to smooth the path for the prisoner who finishes a sentence or is paroled, to maximize his or her chances of "making it" back in the community. At the back end of prison sentences, creative programs for prisoners awaiting release from prison should include transitional work release, where, for months before they are released from prison, they leave prison during the day to work in the community but return to sleep in the prison. Parole services need to be enriched to include the psychotherapy, counseling, education, and vocational rehabilitation that prisoners will need for successful reentry. And ex-prisoners need to be welcomed into and financially supported at community colleges and universities so they can complete the education that was disrupted when they became involved in the criminal justice system.

I have presented in this book a few of the promising programs I have seen in effect. There are many others, both programs that prepare prisoners for postrelease success and postrelease programs, including halfway houses, that help ex-prisoners adjust in the community. Beefing up all such programs is a major part of the short-term alternative to solitary confinement.

In addition to sentencing reform and efforts to massively downsize prisons and change the culture of prisons from one of punishment to one of rehabilitation, other broader movements are attempting to transform America's criminal justice system. Restorative justice has grown as a movement since its emergence in the 1970s. It involves bringing together the perpetrators of crimes as well as the victims and all other interested parties, talking through what happened, creating a collaborative plan addressing retribution, and attempting to restore the individuals and the community as they were prior to the crime.[10] The perpetrator is required to take responsibility for his or her illegal acts, the victim is present to witness and participate in the invention of appropriate punishments or other consequences, and community members are present throughout the entire procedure. In theory, the government is not involved; this is a civil matter, handled by citizens collectively. In practice thus far, there has been some involvement of government. For example, in some counties where restorative justice is practiced today, the prosecutors, defense attorneys, and courts sponsor the citizen-run adjudication process for relatively minor crimes, but then the civil group adjudicating the crime must seek the approval of the court for the decisions it wants to put in place. It is a promising approach to crime in that the perpetrator takes more responsibility and community members are active agents in the process. On a smaller scale, there are promising attempts in high schools and universities to establish peer processing of rule and law violations. It is quite possible that some form of restorative justice can be established in the prisons. Imagine if, when a fight between individuals or gangs is about to erupt, a charismatic prisoner who is trusted by prisoners and motivated to prevent violence meets with the parties who are about to fight each other and tries to help them work out a peaceful resolution of the issues they were about to fight over.

Transformative justice is a movement that draws on the restorative justice approach but rejects the aim of simply returning the actors (the ones who broke the law and their victims) and the community to their prior state.

Instead, transformative justice seeks to transform both the actors and the social arrangements—the backdrop to the crime itself—for the better.[11] For example, transformative justice would address fixing the public mental health system that was broken when the perpetrator, who suffers from mental illness, committed the crime. The movement for transformative justice aspires to alter institutions and eventually to address all manner of inequity and injustice, including racism and the massive gap between rich and poor. The first thing transformative justice requires is participation, by the citizenry, in the process of adjudicating crimes and levying consequences.

Both restorative justice and transformative justice aim at reconciliation and reparation, with the model being the truth and reconciliation process in South Africa. Nelson Mandela had a choice when he exited prison after serving twenty-seven years: he could turn the African National Congress (ANC) into an army dedicated to the murder of white South Africans who had oppressed blacks so brutally during apartheid, or he could forgive his former oppressors and seek peace in an integrated country where the ANC would hold democratic power. He chose the peaceful route and set up the Truth and Reconciliation Commission. Under the leadership of Rev. Desmond Tutu, it encouraged the testimony of both victims and perpetrators of human rights abuses and offered reparations to victims.

The Critical Resistance Conference in 1998 in Berkeley opened eyes around the world about the terrible abuses occurring in our prisons.[12] Besides calling for the immediate cessation of supermax solitary confinement, Angela Davis and the other organizers of Critical Resistance called for improved and nonrepressive public education, community-run programs of restorative and transformative Justice that could take over the functions of state-run institutions such as courts, drug treatment in the community instead of the incarceration of users, an end to the prosecution of women who had killed men who repeatedly battered them, and quality public health and mental health services.[13] Angela Davis summed up what was needed: "a justice system based on reparation and reconciliation rather than retribution and vengeance."[14] A society planned around such measures would be a great improvement over what we have.

The supermax experiment has failed. Consigning one hundred thousand prisoners to deadening isolation has not remedied the violence and gang problems in our prisons. Rather, it has had devastating effects on those suffering from or prone to serious mental illness and has decimated the life skills even of relatively stable prisoners. It is time to trade the culture of punishment for an attitude of rehabilitation. It is time to provide intensive programming for today's prisoners, including those who are the most troublesome, which means prisons need high-security intensive mental health treatment units.

The imprisonment binge and the love affair with supermax isolation constituted a foolhardy attempt to "disappear" the most troublesome of our social problems. But the more criminals that we lock away, the more those criminals are beaten, raped, and locked up in solitary, where they despair of ever returning to their families or finding meaningful employment. As Dostoevsky cautioned, when we ignore the plight of prisoners, we begin to turn our backs on the harsh realities of our social existence. We go about our ordinary daily activities in comfortable homes, modern offices, and shopping malls, but we cannot quite free our minds of the possibility of future violent incursions into our lives from the dispossessed "dangerous others" who, we hope, are locked up. We are creating the monsters we love to dread. We can do better.

NOTES

INTRODUCTION

1. Haney (2015, 12, 13).
2. Mualimm-ak (2016, 148).
3. Crowding in institutions had been shown to correlate with increased violence, mental breakdown, and suicide. See Paulus (1988); Paulus, McCain, and Cox (1978); Thornberry and Call (1983).
4. The Counter Intelligence Program or COINTELPRO was a federal intelligence and police operation initiated in the 1950s by the FBI to "protect national security." COINTELPRO conducted surveillance and arrests of individuals suspected of being "subversives."
5. D. James and Glaze (2006).
6. Rhodes (2004); Shalev (2009).
7. Beck (2015).
8. I was very pleased to take part recently in a colloquium that criminologist Martin Horn organized at John Jay College of Criminal Justice "to further a national consensus on ending the over-use of extreme isolation in prisons" (Prisoner Reentry Institute 2015).
9. Casella (2015).
10. Cohen (2016). See also Cohen (1998, 2011, 2014b).
11. Obama (2016); Love (2015).
12. Goode (2012); see also Fettig (2016).
13. Torrey et al. (2014).
14. L. Davis et al. (2013).
15. Dostoevsky (1862).

1. SUPERMAX ISOLATION

1. Hirsch (1992).
2. Thibaut (1982).

3. Kidd (2014). The Reading Gaol in England, built in 1842, was designed to be run according to the same Pennsylvania System that was in effect at Eastern State. Prisoners were isolated from each other and were required to wear hoods so they would have no eye contact. There was strict silence and the guards wore felt covering their boots to diminish the ambient noise. Reading Gaol's most famous prisoner, Oscar Wilde, who was confined there from 1895 to 1897 for having sex with men, described the experience in a poem: "And the silence is more awful far / Than the sound of a brazen bell. // And never a human voice comes near / To speak a gentle word: / And the eye that watches through the door / Is pitiless and hard: / And by all forgot, we rot and rot, / With soul and body marred" ([1898] 1964, 210–11). On Wilde's imprisonment, see Buruma (2016).

4. Dickens ([1842] 1913); de Toqueville (1835); see also de Beaumont and de Tocqueville (1833).

5. Dickens ([1842] 1913, 58).

6. Ryder (2007).

7. de Beaumont and de Tocqueville (1833, 5–6).

8. de Beaumont and de Tocqueville (1833, 25).

9. Rothman (1971).

10. Medley, Petitioner, in re Medley (1890).

11. Kohn (1994); Champion (2012); MacDonald and Nadel (2012).

12. Jackson (1969).

13. Yee (1973). See also Cummins (1994).

14. Reiter (2016) details the history of these units.

15. Solitary Watch, "About Solitary Watch," n.d., accessed January 24, 2017; Davies (2016).

16. It is my understanding that the pull-up bar and the ball are recent amenities, improvements obtained as a result of prisoner hunger strikes beginning in 2011.

17. Montgomery (2013); see also Montgomery (2016) and Montgomery and Sambamurphy (2013).

18. Holt and Miller (1972); Bales and Mears (2008).

19. Robertson (2016).

20. Transgender or trans individuals identify as a sex different from the one to which they were assigned at birth. Trans women were born in a body classified at birth as male according to biological characteristics, but they identify, or have an inner sense of themselves, as female; the reverse is true for trans men (Mildred Brown and Rounsley, 1996).

21. Robertson (2016).

22. Slahi (2015).

23. Slahi (2015, 218).

24. I am concerned about the approach to immigration that the Trump administration is adopting at the time of this writing. Not only is it xenophobic, hostile to immigrants, and overtly discriminatory against Muslims, but it will overcrowd US Immigration and Customs Enforcement (ICE) facilities, and, given the federal

government's insistence that states and counties hold detainees for ICE, it is likely to return jails and prisons to the kind of crowding that occurred in the 1980s and ushered in the rapid expansion of supermax isolation. In other words, decades of prison reforms are at risk as the federal government's immigration policies take effect. Fortunately there are already signs of robust popular resistance to this unfortunate development.

25. Jeff Beard, director of California Department of Corrections and Rehabilitation, address at the John Jay Colloquium to further a national consensus on ending the overuse of extreme isolation in prisons; see Prisoner Reentry Institute (2015). See also Fettig (2016).

2. A CULTURE OF PUNISHMENT

1. Presley v. Epps (2005 and 2007).
2. Calavita and Jenness (2015, 183).
3. Calavita and Jenness (2015, 55).
4. The British criminologists Alison Liebling, David Price, and Guy Schefer offer many insights into the dilemma of officers who find that a punitive approach and good staff-prisoner relationships are at odds in their 2011 book *The Prison Officer*.
5. B. Steiner and Woodredge (2015).
6. Irwin and Austin (1994).
7. Rhodes (2004, 57).
8. Martin (2000).
9. Fellner (2015).
10. Walker v. Montana (2003).
11. Gates v. Deukmejian (1994).
12. K. Menninger (1968).
13. Fellner (2015).
14. Haney and Zimbardo (1998); Zimbardo (2007).
15. Bauer (2016).
16. Zimbardo (2007).
17. Rothwell and Baldwin (2007).
18. Morgan, Van Haveren, and Pearson (2002); J. Wells et al. (2009).
19. Arax and Gladstone (1998); Arax (2004).
20. K. Menninger (1968).
21. K. King, Steiner, and Breach (2008).
22. Kupers (2013a).
23. Kupers (2012); for a different perspective, see Metzner (2012).
24. H. Thompson (2016, 558, epilogue).
25. Montgomery (2013, 2016); Montgomery and Sambamurthy (2013).
26. Gang affiliation is an ambiguous notion at best. Largely white officers observe prisoners' behavior and appearance and determine that certain prisoners are

gang members or affiliated with a gang. Mexican American prisoners tell me that when they arrived in prison and encountered former neighbors and schoolmates they had known growing up in the barrio they greeted them with a ritual handshake (tapping fists, etc.). Officers observing two Latino prisoners with tattoos greeting each other with that kind of gesture would assume, when they were pretty confident that one of the men was in a gang, that the other man was also in the gang. So they would have him transferred to SHU. If a prisoner in SHU protested that he was not affiliated with a gang, the gang investigators would say, "That may be, but we don't know that for sure, and if you ever want to get out of here you will need to debrief." In the *Ashker v. Brown* case that eventually abolished the practice of incarcerating people in SHU on the basis of gang affiliation, one critical legal issue was due process. There were hearings to validate (categorize and label) prisoners as gang members, but prisoners universally complained they were not given an opportunity to defend themselves against charges of gang affiliation and that the evidence used to validate them was often entirely bogus.

27. See Reiter (2016); Montgomery (2013).

28. Ruiz (2013); see also Center for Constitutional Rights (2013).

29. Madrid v. Gomez (1995).

30. Foucault (1995, 3–5).

31. Foucault (1995, 8–9).

32. Garland (1985, 2001).

33. Garland (2001, 15).

3. RACE MATTERS A LOT

1. Quigley (2010).

2. *The 13th,* directed by Ava DuVernay, Netflix (2016).

3. Hagler (2016); Sentencing Project (2016).

4. Sentencing Project (2015a); see also Nellis (2016).

5. Hagler (2016).

6. Hagler (2016).

7. This disparity reflects both racial and class bias—both kids of color and low-income kids are more likely to be arrested and convicted than white kids or kids of higher economic classes. But the racial disparity also cuts across the class lines, most dramatically in inner-city populations where people of color bear the brunt of the disparity and even middle-class black youth are disproportionately stopped and frisked, and arrested, by police. See Mauer (1999); Farbota (2015).

8. Stuntz (2011).

9. See the *Washington Post* editorial entitled "The Fair Sentencing Act Corrects a Long-Time Wrong in Cocaine Cases," August 3, 2010, www.washingtonpost.com /wp-dyn/content/article/2010/08/02/AR2010080204360.html.

10. Schlanger (2013); Walsh (2010); Eichelberger (2015).

11. Lowen and Isaacs (2012, 16).

12. Lowen and Isaacs (2012, 15).

13. Law (2014).

14. Schlanger (2013); see also Mears and Bales (2010).

15. Kupers (1999).

16. R. King and Kupers (2010).

17. Mancini (1996); Oshinsky (1996); Lichtenstein (1996).

18. Haney and Zimbardo (2009).

19. Arax (2000, 2004); Arax and Gladstone (1998).

20. Cornwall (1996).

21. Navarro, Quinn, and Weinstein (1997).

22. Human Rights Watch (1997).

23. Jailhouse lawyers like these have brought many human rights abuses in prison to the attention of courts in cases that would never have been filed if the prisoners had to wait for an official attorney to take their case. Mumia Abu-Jamal (2009), while serving as a jailhouse lawyer from his cell on Pennsylvania's Death Row, described the work of jailhouse lawyers.

24. R. King (2012).

25. R. King (2012, 171–72).

4. THE DECIMATION OF LIFE SKILLS

1. Kupers (2008a).

2. Mumola (1997).

3. Arrigo and Bullock (2008); Scharff-Smith (2006); Grassian (1983); Grassian and Friedman (1986); Cloyes, Lovell, and Rhodes (2006); Guy (2016); Kupers (2013b).

4. Amicus Brief to the Supreme Court of the United States (2005).

5. Toch (1975, 54; see also [1975] 1982).

6. Haney (2003a; see also 2006, 2015). Haney was a member of the team who conducted the Stanford mock prison experiments (Haney, Banks, and Zimbardo 1973).

7. Haney (2015, 23–24).

8. Grassian (1983, 2006, 2016); Grassian and Friedman (1986).

9. Mirzaei et al. (2001); Vyas, Bernal, and Chattarji (2003); Bremner (2002); Bremner et al. (2003); Taber and Hurley (2009).

10. Schaeffer (2016).

11. Gendreau, Freedman, and Wilde (1972).

12. Casella and Ridgeway (2012); Makinodan, Rosen, Ito, and Corfas (2012).

13. Schaeffer (2016).

14. O'Keefe et al. (2010).

15. Grassian and Kupers (2011); see also Lovell and Toch (2011); Scharff Smith (2011); Pizarro and Stenius (2004).

16. Villa (2016, 40).

17. Ashker v. Brown (2015); Kupers (2015b).
18. See Toch (2003) on visitation rights.
19. See Reiter (2012, 2016) on this policy.
20. Guenther (2013, xxiii).
21. Weinstein (2000, 122).
22. Lovell, Johnson, and Cain (2007); see also Mears and Bales (2009).
23. Clear (2007).
24. UN Committee against Torture (1984, pt. 1, art. 1, para. 1).
25. Organization of American States (1985).
26. On Abu-Ghraib, see Danner (2004).
27. Russel v. Epps (2005).
28. Mendez (2011).
29. Ojeda (2008).
30. Fields (2008).
31. American Psychiatric Association (2012); American Public Health Association (2001, 2013); American Academy of Child and Adolescent Psychiatry (2012); "Istanbul Statement" (2007); UN Commission on Crime Prevention (2015).
32. Walker v. Montana (2003, 82).
33. "Istanbul Statement" (2007); UN Commission on Crime Prevention and Criminal Justice (2015).

5. ADDING MADNESS TO THE MIX

1. Hudgins and Côté (1991); Casella and Ridgeway (2010); Correctional Association of New York (2004).
2. Human Rights Watch (2003).
3. Kupers (1999, 2008b, 2013b, 2015b).
4. Mears and Watson (2006); Way et al. (2005); Kaba et al. (2014); Patterson and Hughes (2008).
5. Madrid v. Gomez (1995); Jones 'El v. Berge (2001); Presley v. Epps (2005 & 2007).
6. Madrid v. Gomez (1995).
7. Ibid.
8. Kupers (2013a, 2013b).
9. Goffman (1962); Scheff (1966).
10. Human Rights Watch (2001, 2011).
11. Human Rights Watch (1996).
12. American Civil Liberties Union of Texas (2015).
13. Torrey et al. (2014).
14. Rogers (1997); Rogers, Harrell, and Liff (1993). On the issue of malingering in correctional settings, see Kupers (2004).
15. Scully et al. (1997); Wyatt (1991).
16. Mendel (1989); Yung et al. (1998).

17. Kulhara, Banerjee, and Dutt (2008).
18. Kupers (2007).
19. I am indebted to Fred Cohen for this formulation.

6. WOMEN DO NOT DO WELL IN SOLITARY

1. Battle et al. (2003).
2. Herman (1994).
3. Owen, Wells, and Pollack (2017).
4. Beck et al. (1993, 9).
5. Browne, Miller, and Maguin (1999).
6. Greenfeld and Snell (1999).
7. Owen (1998).
8. Richie (2012, 117–18, 118, 119).
9. Greenfeld and Snell (1999).
10. Boyd et al. (1998); Fullilove, Lown, and Fullilove (1992).
11. Pollock (2014); Wright et al (2012).
12. Belknap (2015).
13. Kupers (2010a); Sabo, Kupers, and London (2001).
14. Law (2014b).
15. "Of all successful suicides in corrections, approximately half occur among the 6% to 8% of the prison population that is consigned to segregation at any given time" (Kupers 2008b).
16. American Civil Liberties Union (2014, 2–3 and n. 8).
17. Pearson (2016a).
18. Pearson (2016b).
19. Glowa-Kollisch et al. (2016).
20. Pearson (2016a).
21. Zlotnick et al. (2008); Lord (2008).
22. Kupers (2010a); Human Rights Watch (1996); Amnesty International (1999); Beck et al. (2013).
23. Kupers (2005a).
24. Research by Carmen, Riccard, and Mills (1984), Walker (1979), and Wright et al. (2007) suggests that, while men tend more to respond to abuse by turning outward and expressing themselves angrily, women tend more to turn inward and become depressed.
25. Kupers (2010a).
26. Rothwell and Baldwin (2007).
27. Human Rights Watch (2001); Rose (2001).
28. Giraldo v. Cal. Dep't. of Corr. and Rehab. (2008).
29. Jenness et al. (2007).
30. Prison Rape Elimination Commission (2009).
31. Hastings et al. (2015), especially § 115.43, Protective Custody.

32. Law (2013).

33. Kupers (in press).

34. Allen, Flaherty, and Eli (2010).

35. Law (2014c).

36. Kupers (2005a).

37. Benedict (2014); Bloom and Covington (2008).

7. YOUTH IN ISOLATION

1. On the dismantling of the juvenile justice system, see Gately (2015); Coalition for Juvenile Justice (2016). See interviews with youth in solitary at Human Rights Watch, "Video: Firsthand Accounts," n.d. (accessed February 11, 2017), http://solitarywatch.com/resources/multimedia/video-2/firsthand-accounts/.

2. Carson and Sabol (2012).

3. Kupers (2003).

4. Human Rights Watch (2011).

5. Erikson (1950).

6. Karnik et al. (2009).

7. Teplin et al. (2002); Teplin et al. (2012); Chong (2004).

8. H. Steiner, Garcia, and Matthews (1997).

9. Gonnerman (2015).

10. Memory (1989).

11. Hayes (2004); NCCHC (2012).

12. For newspaper coverage of the case and the trial, go to the list of articles at the website of Helena, Montana's *Independent Record*, http://helenair.com /search/?q=Raistlen+Katka.

13. Katka v. Montana Department of Corrections (2009).

14. Glaser (1995).

15. Ibid.

16. US Dept. of Justice (2014); see also New York Advisory Committee to the US Commission on Civil Rights (2014); and New York Civil Liberties Union (2014).

17. Schwirtz (2014).

18. Kagan, majority in Miller v. Alabama (2012).

19. Amicus Curiae (2012).

8. THE SHU POSTRELEASE SYNDROME

1. Medical Dictionary, Free Dictionary by Farlex, http://medicaldictionary .thefreedictionary.com/syndrome. My description here of a SHU postrelease syndrome is new. Other researchers who have studied the effects of long-term solitary confinement, including Lovell (2008), Haney (2003b), and Lowen and Isaacs (2012),

provide preliminary discussion of approximately equivalent experiences, but they do not employ the term *syndrome* in their descriptions.

2. CBS Denver (2013).
3. Vazquez (2016, 59).
4. Raemisch and Wasko (2016).
5. C. Thompson (2015).
6. C. Thompson (2015).
7. American Psychiatric Association (2013).
8. Greenberg (2015).
9. Haney (2003b, 33, 65); see also Clemmer, who first defined the concept ([1940] 1958).
10. Irwin (1970).
11. Kupers (2005c).
12. Kupers (2015b).

9. A REHABILITATIVE ATTITUDE

1. Kupers (2009).
2. Gilligan (1997).
3. For a more detailed biography of Todd Ashker, see Reiter (2016, 10–33).
4. See Montgomery and Sambamurthy (2013); Montgomery (2016); Reiter (2016).
5. Ashker (2016, 89).
6. Ashker (2016, 88).
7. Gilligan and Lee (2013).
8. See also Gilligan (1997, 2003).
9. Garbarino (2015, 241).
10. Kupers (2005a).
11. Human Rights Watch (2001).
12. Reiter (2012, 2016).
13. Kupers (2010a).
14. Toch (2014).
15. Toch (2014, 92).
16. D. Jones (2004); Aitkenhead (2007).
17. Jorgensen, Hernandez, and Warren (1986).
18. For a description of Rapiscan, go to "Rapiscan 638DV 320KV," Rapiscan Systems, www.rapiscansystems.com/en/products/bpi/rapiscan_638dv_320kv.
19. Harrington-Wisely et al. v. State of California et al., Super. Ct. Case No. BC 227373.
20. Holt and Miller (1972); Bales and Mears (2008); Duwe (2011); Berg and Huebner (2011).
21. L. Davis et al. (2013).
22. McGee (1969, 186); see also Glaser (1995).

23. Prison Rape Elimination Commission (2009).

24. See R. King (2012); on Murillo, Lau (2015); on Nelson, C. Thompson (2015); Canales (2016); on Czesla, Baldassari (2015); Shourd (2011, 2016a); Bauer (2016); Mualimm-ak (2016).

25. See video review of *The Box* at Shourd (2016b).

26. The Angola 3, "About the Case," n.d., 2017, accessed February 11, 2017, http://angola3.org/the-case/. Robert King and I did a series of three video interviews on race, slavery and the psychology of prisons (R. King and Kupers 2009).

27. See R. King (2012, 137–41).

28. For the story of the Angola Three, go to the website The Angola 3, http://angola3.org.

29. Abu-Jamal and Hill (2014).

30. See, for example, the many broadcasts by Abu-Jamal on Prison Radio, listed at www.prisonradio.org/media/audio/mumia.

31. Lovell, Johnson, and Cain (2007); Hughes and Wilson (2004).

32. Martinson (1974).

33. Martinson (1979).

34. Hallinan (2001, 36). Martinson had been known to suffer from depression, possibly bipolar disorder, and his reasons for throwing himself out the window of his fourteenth-floor apartment are not entirely known.

10. MENTAL HEALTH CARE IN CORRECTIONS

1. Patterson and Hughes (2008).
2. Grisso (2003).
3. La Fond (1990).
4. Melton et al. (1997, 188–89).
5. ACLU of Colorado (2013); Cohen (2014a).
6. Kupers (2005b).
7. ACLU of Colorado (2013); Cohen (2014a).
8. Druss et al. (2008); R. Wells (2010).
9. Breakey (1996); Nelson and Prilleltensky (2010); Grob (1991).
10. McQuistion (2003); Torrey (1997, 2010).
11. Breakey (1996).
12. Bataille (1990).
13. Gold (2014).
14. Anthony (2000); Spaniol et al. (1994).
15. Caplan (1970).
16. Kupers (2015a).
17. I had the honor and pleasure of serving on the Committee on Psychiatry and the Community that was established by the Group for the Advancement of Psychiatry (GAP) when that committee wrote a manual on working with persons with serious mental illness in the criminal justice system (GAP 2016).

18. Woods (2011).

19. Teague, Drake, and Ackerson (1995).

20. American Psychiatric Association (2000).

21. Thienhaus (2007); Thienhaus and Piasecki 2007).

22. Lovell et al. (2001).

23. Kupers (2010b).

24. SAMHSA (2014).

25. Bill (1998).

26. Kupers (2005a).

27. American Psychiatric Association (2000, 15–16); see also Cohen (2011); NCCHC (2014); Penal Reform International (1995); Thienhaus and Piasecki (2007); Sowers, Thompson, and Mullins (1999).

28. Hayes (2013).

29. NCCHC (2014).

30. Lovell, Johnson, and Cain (2007).

31. Liebling (1999); Hayes (2013); Reeves and Tamburello (2014).

32. NCCHC (2014). The NCCHC list of necessary components for effective crisis intervention and suicide prevention includes sufficient training of mental health and custody staff; identification of prisoners who might be a suicide risk through regular screening; referral (i.e., to appropriate mental health practitioners); evaluation (i.e., comprehensive mental health examinations that document past suicidal and self-harm crises and incidents as well as current stressors); housing (for example, transfer to an observation cell, or after a period of observation, to a location where the patient will be safe and appropriately monitored); monitoring (this means not only intensive observation during the immediate crisis, but also ongoing monitoring at incrementally less frequent intervals as the prisoner demonstrates diminishing risk of self-harm); communication (between custody and mental health staff and also between the various mental health and medical providers); intervention (including but not limited to observation and monitoring, since meaningful talking psychotherapy must occur if the staff are to get to the issues driving the prisoner to despair and to contemplate or attempt suicide); notification (of family members); reporting in the clinical chart or electronic medical record; review (peer review, quality assurance, etc., with the assumption that where programmatic deficiencies or lapses in staff interventions are discovered they will be corrected); and critical incident debriefing (which are essential if flaws in the mental health program are to be addressed).

33. Schmidt and Ivanoff (2007).

34. Milton Brown, Comtois, and Linehan (2002).

35. Kane et al. (2015).

36. Goffman (1962).

37. Fakhoury and Priebe (2007).

38. NCCHC (2014); American Psychiatric Association (1999).

39. "Emergency medications should work acutely (e.g., neuroleptics and benzodiazepines as opposed to antidepressants and mood stabilizers) and must target the serious presenting symptoms" (J. Menninger 2016, 3).

40. McCabe et al. (2013); Day et al. (2005).

41. McCabe et al. (2013); Day et al. (2005).

42. The American Psychiatric Association, in its 1999 "Mandatory Outpatient Treatment Resource Document," states: "Studies have shown that mandatory outpatient treatment is most effective when it includes services equivalent to the intensity of those provided in the assertive community treatment or intensive case management models. States adopting mandatory outpatient treatment statutes must assure that adequate resources are available to provide effective treatment." For example, the California Welfare and Institutions Code (sections 5325–37) permits assisted outpatient treatment and involuntary medications with due process only in counties that prove they supply a variety of mental health treatment modalities and services, including multiple modalities of psychotherapy, case management, home visits, and so forth, that are available to the population being involuntarily treated, and then only after all less restrictive interventions have been exhausted.

43. Goode (2014); Fettig (2016).

44. Haney (2006); American Psychiatric Association (2012).

II. THE DISRUPTIVE PRISONER

1. Toch (1982, 2014); Toch and Adams (2002); Toch and Kupers (2007).
2. Toch (1992).
3. Wilden (1972).
4. For more on the Just Therapy clinic and its very democratic work environment, see Waldegrave et al. (2003). The theory guiding their therapeutic interventions owed a lot to Michael White's narrative therapy (White and Epston 1990).
5. Toch and Kupers (2007, citing Agee 1979); Toch (1982, 2004).
6. Ditton (1999); James and Glaze (2006); Toch and Adams (2002).
7. Human Rights Watch (2003); Kupers (1999).
8. Wilson (1980); Toch (1982).
9. Wolff v. McDonnell (1974, 26).
10. Fellner (2015).
11. Kupers et al. (2009).
12. Kupers et al. (2009).
13. Briggs, Sundt, and Castellano (2003).
14. Liebling (1999, 337–38).
15. Toch (1982, 2014); Toch and Adams (1987, 2002).
16. Toch and Adams (1987).
17. Monahan (1981).
18. Linehan et al. (1994, 1999).
19. American Psychiatric Association (1999).
20. Kane et al. (2015).
21. Morris (2004); Aitkenhead (2007).
22. M. Jones (1968); Main (1946).

23. D. Jones and Shuker (2004, 191).
24. D. Jones and Shuker (2004, 192).
25. Aichorn ([1935] 1963); F. Alexander and Staub ([1931] 1956); Anderson (1998).
26. Morris (2004).
27. Morris (2004).
28. Hochschild (2016); E. James (2013); Larson (2013).
29. Raemisch (2014).
30. Palazzolo (2014).
31. Raemisch and Wasko (2016).
32. Raemisch and Wasko (2016).
33. Glowa-Kollisch et al. (2016); Ordway and Wihbey (2014).
34. Glowa-Kollisch et al. (2016).

12. BEYOND SUPERMAX ISOLATION

1. Haney (2006, 353); see also Haney (2008).
2. Sentencing Project 2015b.
3. Sentencing Project (2015c). See also Sentencing Project (2015a).
4. Steadman, Morris, and Dennis (1995); Steadman et al. (2011); Kuehn (2007); UN Office on Drugs and Crime (2007).
5. Spaniol et al. (1994); Stettin, Frese, and Lamb (2013); Rivas-Vazquez et al. (2009).
6. Council of State Governments Justice Center (2012); Loveland and Boyle (2007); Liebowitz et al. (2014).
7. Munetz and Griffin (2006).
8. Liefman (2014); McNiel and Binder (2007); Steadman et al. (2011).
9. Durose, Cooper, and Snyder (2014).
10. Braithwaite (1999, 2004); Van Wormer and Walker (2013).
11. Wozniak et al. (2008).
12. Holmquist (1998).
13. A. Davis (2003).
14. A. Davis (2003, 107).

REFERENCES

Abu-Jamal, Mumia. 2009. *Jailhouse Lawyers: Prisoners Defending Prisoners v. the U.S.A.* San Francisco: City Lights Books.

Abu-Jamal, Mumia, and Marc Lamont Hill. 2014. *The Classroom and the Cell: Conversations on Black Life in America.* Chicago: Third World Press.

Agee, Vicki L. 1979. *Treatment of the Violent Incorrigible Adolescent.* Lexington, MA: Heath.

Aichhorn, August. [1935] 1963. *Wayward Youth.* New York: Viking Press.

Aitkenhead, Decca. 2007. "Inside Grendon Prison." *Guardian,* July 14. www/guardian.co.uk/prisons/story/0,,2124716,00.html.

Alexander, Franz, and Hugo Staub. [1931] 1956. *The Criminal, the Judge, and the Public.* Glencoe, IL: Free Press.

Alexander, Michelle. 2010. *The New Jim Crow: Mass Incarceration in the Age of Colorblindness.* New York: New Press.

Allen, Suzanne, Chris Flaherty, and Gretchen E. Ely. 2010. "Throwaway Moms: Maternal Incarceration and the Criminalization of Female Poverty." *Affilia* 25 (2): 160–72.

American Academy of Child and Adolescent Psychiatry. 2012. "Solitary Confinement of Juvenile Offenders." April. www.aacap.org/aacap/policy_statements/2012/solitary_confinement_of_juvenile_offenders.aspx.

American Civil Liberties Union. 2014. *Worse Than Second Class: Solitary Confinement of Women in the United States.* April. New York: ACLU. https://www.aclu.org/sites/default/files/assets/worse_than_second-class.pdf.

American Civil Liberties Union of Colorado. 2013. "Out of Sight, Out of Mind: Colorado's Continued Warehousing of Mentally Ill Prisoners in Solitary Confinement." http://aclu-co.org/wp-content/uploads/files/imce/ACLU-CO%20Report%20on%20Solitary%20Confinement_2.pdf.

American Civil Liberties Union of Texas. 2015. "A Solitary Failure: The Waste, Cost and Harm of Solitary Confinement in Texas." https://www.aclutx.org/sites/default/files/field_documents/SolitaryReport_2015.pdf.

American Psychiatric Association. 1999. "Mandatory Outpatient Treatment Resource Document." rd1999_MandatoryOutpatient.pdf.

———. 2000. "Practice Guidelines for the Treatment of Patients with Schizophrenia." In *Practice Guidelines for the Treatment of Psychiatric Disorders*. Washington, DC: American Psychiatric Association.

———. 2012. "Position Statement on Segregation of Prisoners with Mental Illness." www.psych.org/File%20Library/Learn/Archives/ps2012_PrisonerSegregation .pdf.

———. 2013. *Diagnostic and Statistical Manual of Mental Disorders, Fifth Edition (DSM-V)*. Arlington, VA: American Psychiatric Association.

American Public Health Association. 2001. *Standards for Health Services in Correctional Institutions, Third Edition*. Washington, DC: American Public Health Association.

———. 2013. "Policy No. 201310, Solitary Confinement as a Public Health Issue." https://apha.org/policies-and-advocacy/public-health-policy-statements/policy-database/2014/07/14/13/30/solitary-confinement-as-a-public-health-issue.

Amicus Brief to the Supreme Court of the United States. 2005. Brief of Professors and Practitioners of Psychology and Psychiatry as Amicus Curiae in Support of Respondents, Supreme Court of the United States, No. 04–495.

———. 2012. Brief for the American Psychological Association, American Psychiatric Association and National Association of Social Workers as Amici Curiae in Support of Petitioners, Nos. 10–9646 and 10–9647. http://fairsentencingofyouth .org/wp-content/uploads/2013/01/Brief-for-The-American-Psychological-Association-American-Psychiatric-Association-and-National-Association-of-Social-Workers-in-Support-of-Petitioners4.pdf.

Amnesty International. 1999. *Not a Part of My Sentence: Violations of the Human Rights of Women in Custody*. New York: Amnesty International USA.

Anderson, Kevin. 1998. "The Young Erich Fromm's Contribution to Criminology." *Justice Quarterly* 15 (4): 667–96.

Anthony, William. 2000. "A Recovery-Oriented Service System: Setting Some System Level Standards." *Psychiatric Rehabilitation Journal* 24:159–68.

Arax, Mark. 2000. "Eight Prison Guards Are Acquitted in Corcoran Battles." *Los Angeles Times,* June 10. http://articles.latimes.com/2000/jun/10/news/mn-39555.

———. 2004. "Whistleblower CA Prison Guard Challenges 'Green Wall.'" *Los Angeles Times,* January 20. www.energy-net.org/nuz/hrights/cal/04125106.txt.

Arax, Mark, and Mark Gladstone. 1998. "Prison Officer Breaks Silence on May Slaying." *Los Angeles Times,* December 28. www.worldfreeinternet.net/news /nws162.

Arrigo, Bruce A., and Jennifer Leslie Bullock. 2008. "The Psychological Effects of Solitary Confinement on Prisoners in Supermax Units: Reviewing What We Know and What Should Change." *International Journal of Offender Therapy and Comparative Criminology* 52:622–40.

Ashker, Todd Lewis. 2016. "A Tale of Evolving Resistance." In Casella, Ridgeway, and Shourd 2016, 83–92.

Baldassari, Erin. 2015. "Building a Prison-to-School Pipeline." *East Bay Express,* October 7. www.eastbayexpress.com/oakland/building-a-prison-to-school-pipeline/Content?oid=4526966.

Bales, W. D., and D. P. Mears. 2008. "Inmate Social Ties and the Transition to Society: Does Visitation Reduce Recidivism?" *Journal of Research in Crime and Delinquency* 45:287–321.

Bataille, G. G. 1990. "Psychotherapy and Community Support: Community Mental Health Systems in Transition." *New Directions for Mental Health Services* 9:10–11.

Battle, C., C. Zlotnick, L. Najavits, M. Guttierrez, and C. Winsor 2003. "Posttraumatic Stress Disorder and Substance Use Disorder among Incarcerated Women." In *Trauma and Substance Abuse: Causes, Consequences, and Treatment of Co-morbid Disorders,* edited by Paige Ouimette and Pamela J. Brown, 209–25. Washington, DC: American Psychological Association.

Bauer, Shane. 2016. "My Four Months as a Private Prison Guard." *Mother Jones,* June. www.motherjones.com/politics/2016/06/cca-private-prisons-corrections-corporation-inmates-investigation-bauer.

Beck, Allen J. 2015. *Use of Restrictive Housing in U.S. Prisons and Jails, 2011–2012.* Bureau of Justice Statistics Special Report, NCJ 249209, October. US Department of Justice. https://www.bjs.gov/content/pub/pdf/urhuspj1112.pdf.

Beck, Allen J., Marcus Berzofsky, Rachel Caspar, and Christopher Krebs. 2013. *Sexual Victimization in Prisons and Jails Reported by Inmates, 2011–2012.* Bureau of Justice Statistics Report, NCJ 241399, May. US Department of Justice. https://www.bjs.gov/content/pub/pdf/svpjri1112.pdf.

Beck, Allen, Darrell Gilliard, Lawrence Greenfeld, Caroline Harlow, Thomas Hester, Louis Jankowski, Tracy Snell, James Stephan, and Danielle Morton. 1993. *Survey of State Prison Inmates, 1991.* Bureau of Justice Statistics Report, NCJ 136949, March. US Department of Justice. https://www.bjs.gov/content/pub/pdf/SOSPI91.PDF.

Belknap, Joanne. 2015. *The Invisible Woman: Gender, Crime, and Justice.* Belmont, CA: Wadsworth.

Benedict, Alyssa. 2014. *Using Trauma Informed Practices to Enhance Safety and Security in Women's Correctional Facilities.* Washington, DC: National Resource Center on Justice Involved Women.

Berg, Mark T., and Beth M. Huebner. 2010. "Reentry and the Ties That Bind: An Examination of Social Ties, Employment, and Recidivism." *Justice Quarterly* 28 (2): 382–410.

Bill, Louise. 1998. "The Victimization and Re-victimization of Female Offenders." *Corrections Today* 60 (7): 106–12.

Bloom, Barbara E., and Stephanie S. Covington. 2008. "Addressing the Mental Health Needs of Women Offenders." In *Women's Mental Health Issues across the*

Criminal Justice System, edited by Rosemary L. Gido and Lanette Dalley, chap. 9. Upper Saddle River, NJ: Prentice Hall.

Boyd, C.J., E. Hill, C. Holmes, and R. Purnell. 1998. "Putting Drug Use in Context: Life-Lines of African American Women Who Smoke Crack." *Journal of Substance Abuse Treatment* 15 (3): 235–49.

Braithwaite, John. 1999. "Restorative Justice: Assessing Optimistic and Pessimistic Accounts." *Crime and Justice* 25:1–127.

———. 2004. "Restorative Justice and De-professionalization." *Good Society* 13 (1): 28–31.

Breakey, W.R., ed. 1996. *Integrated Mental Health Services: Modern Community Psychiatry.* New York: Oxford University Press.

Bremner, J.D. 2002. "Neuro-Imaging Studies in Post-traumatic Stress Disorder." *Current Psychiatry Reports* 4 (4): 254–63.

Bremner, J.D., Meena Vythilingam, Eric Vermetten, Steven M. Southwick, Thomas McGlashan, Ahsan Nazeer, Sarfraz Khan, L. Viola Vaccarino, Robert Soufer, Pradeep K. Garg, Chin K. Ng, Lawrence H. Staib, James S. Duncan, and Dennis S. Charney. 2003. "MRI and PET Study of Deficits in Hippocampal Structure and Function in Women with Childhood Sexual Abuse and Posttraumatic Stress Disorder." *American Journal of Psychiatry* 160 (5): 924–32.

Briggs, C., J. Sundt, and T. Castellano. 2003. "The Effect of Supermaximum Security Prisons on Aggregate Levels of Institutional Violence." *Criminology* 41:1341–76.

Brown, Mildred L., and Chloe Ann Rounsley. 1996. *True Selves: Understanding Transsexualism—For Families, Friends, Coworkers, and Helping Professionals.* San Francisco: Jossey-Bass.

Brown, Milton Z., K.A. Comtois, and M.M. Linehan. 2002. "Reasons for Suicide Attempts and Nonsuicidal Self-Injury in Women with Borderline Personality Disorder." *Journal of Abnormal Psychology* 111 (1): 198–202.

Browne, Angela, Brenda Miller, and Eugene Maguin. 1999. "Prevalence and Severity of Lifetime Physical and Sexual Victimization among Incarcerated Women." *International Journal of Law and Psychiatry* 22:301–22.

Buruma, Ian. 2016. "Oscar Wilde's 'Living Death.'" *New York Review of Books,* November 24.

Calavita, Kitty, and Valerie Jenness. 2015. *Appealing to Justice: Prisoner Grievances, Rights, and Carceral Logic.* Oakland: University of California Press.

Canales, Dolores. 2016. "Because I Could Laugh." In Casella, Ridgeway, and Shourd 2016, 137–46.

Caplan, Gerald. 1970. *The Theory and Practice of Mental Health Consultation.* New York: Basic Books.

Carmen, Elaine, P. Riccard, and T. Mills. 1984. "Victims of Violence in Psychiatric Illness." *American Journal of Psychiatry* 141 (3): 378–83.

Carson, E. Ann. 2015. *Prisoners in 2014.* Bureau of Justice Statistics Bulletin, NCJ 248955, September. https://www.bjs.gov/content/pub/pdf/p14.pdf.

Carson, E. Ann, and William J. Sabol. 2012. *Prisoners in 2011.* Bureau of Justice Statistics Bulletin, NCJ 239808, December. http://bjs.ojp.usdoj.gov/content /pub/pdf/p11.pdf.

Casella, Jean. 2015. "Supreme Court Justice Kennedy: 'Solitary Confinement Literally Drives Men Mad.'" *Solitary Watch,* March 25. http://solitarywatch.com /2015/03/25/supreme-court-justice-kennedy-corrections-system-is-broken-and-solitary-confinement-literally-drives-men-mad/.

Casella, Jean, and James Ridgeway. 2010. "Suicide and Solitary Confinement in New York State Prisons." October 18. http://solitarywatch.com/2010/10/18 /suicide-and-solitary-confinement-in-new-york-state-prisons/.

———. 2012. "Scientists Discover How Social Isolation Damages Young Brains." *Solitary Watch,* September 18. http://solitarywatch.com/2012/09/18 /scientists-discover-how-social-isolation-damages-young-brains/.

Casella, Jean, James Ridgeway, and Sarah Shourd, eds. 2016. *Hell Is a Very Small Place: Voices from Solitary Confinement.* New York: New Press.

CBS Denver. 2013. "Colorado Department of Corrections Director Murdered." March 20. http://denver.cbslocal.com/2013/03/20/colorado-department-of-corrections- director-murdered.

Center for Constitutional Rights. 2013. "Pelican Bay Prison Hunger-Strikers." July 9. https://ccrjustice.org/pelican-bay-prison-hunger-strikers.

Champion, Jerry Lewis. 2012. *Alcatraz Unchained.* Bloomington, IN: AuthorHouse.

Chong, J.-R. 2004. "Families of Boys Found Hanged at CYA Facility File Legal Claims." *Los Angeles Times,* February 11. http://articles.latimes.com/2004 /feb/11/local/me-cya11.

Clear, Todd R. 2007. *Imprisoning Communities: How Mass Incarceration Makes Disadvantaged Neighborhoods Worse.* Oxford: Oxford University Press.

Clemmer, Donald. [1940] 1958. "The Process of Prisonization." In *The Criminal in Confinement,* edited by Leon Radzinowicz and Marvin E. Wolfgang, 89–115. New York: Basic Books.

Cloyes, K., D. Lovell, D. Allen, and L. Rhodes. 2006. "Assessment of Psychosocial Impairment in a Supermaximum Security Unit Sample." *Criminal Justice and Behavior* 33:760–81.

Coalition for Juvenile Justice. 2016. "Federal Juvenile Justice Appropriations." www .juvjustice.org/federal-policy/federal-juvenile-justice-appropriations.

Cohen, Fred. 1998. *The Mentally Disordered Inmate and the Law.* Kingston, NJ: Civic Research Institute.

———. 2011. *Practical Guide to Correctional Mental Health and the Law.* Kingston, NJ: Civic Research Institute.

———. 2014a. "Denial of Needed Mental Health Care, Excessive Segregation and Predictable Tragedy: The Nebraska Ombudsman Report." *Correctional Mental Health Report* 16 (1): 3–5.

———, ed. 2014b. "Long-Term Penal Isolation: A Problem Solving Symposium." Special issue. *Correctional Law Report* 26 (1).

———. 2016. Introduction to "Alternatives to Solitary Confinement." Special issue. *Correctional Law Reporter* 28 (3).

Cornwall, Tim. 1996. "Staged Fights, Betting Guards, Gunfire and Death for the Gladiators." *Independent,* August 21.

Correctional Association of New York. 2004. *Mental Health in the House of Corrections: A Study of Mental Health Care in New York State Prisons.* Albany: Correctional Association of New York.

Council of State Governments Justice Center. 2012. *Developing a Mental Health Court: An Interdisciplinary Curriculum.* New York: Council of State Governments Justice Center. http://learning.csgjusticecenter.org.

Cummins, Eric. 1994. *The Rise and Fall of California's Radical Prison Movement.* Stanford, CA: Stanford University Press.

Danner, Mark. 2004. "Abu Ghraib: The Hidden Story." *New York Review of Books,* October. www.nybooks.com/articles/ 2004/10/07/abu-ghraib-the-hiddenstory/.

Davies, Caroline. 2016. "Welcome to Your Virtual Cell: Could You Survive Solitary Confinement?" *Guardian,* April 27. https://www.theguardian.com/world/2016 /apr/27/6x9-could-you-survive-solitary-confinement-vr.

Davis, Angela. 2003. *Are Prisons Obsolete?* New York: Seven Stories.

Davis, Lois M., Robert Bozick, Jennifer L. Steele, Jessica Saunders, and Jeremy N. V. Miles. 2013. "Evaluating the Effectiveness of Correctional Education: A Meta-analysis of Programs That Provide Education to Incarcerated Adults." Research Report RR-266-BJA, RAND Corporation, Santa Monica, CA. www.rand.org /pubs/research_reports/RR266.html.

Day, J. C., R. P. Bentall, C. Roberts, F. Randall, A. Rogers, D. Cattell, D. Healy, P. Rae, and C. Power. 2005. "Attitudes toward Antipsychotic Medication: The Impact of Clinical Variables and Relationships with Health Professionals." *Archives of General Psychiatry* 62 (7): 717–24.

de Beaumont, Gustave, and Alexis de Tocqueville. 1833. *On the Penitentiary System in the United States and Its Application in France.* Translated by Francis Lieber. Philadelphia: Carey, Lea and Blanchard.

de Tocqueville, Alexis. 1835. *Democracy in America: Historical-Critical Edition.* Translated by James Schleifer. 4 vols. Indianapolis: Liberty Fund, 2010.

Dickens, Charles. [1842] 1913. *American Notes for General Circulation.* London: Chapman and Hall. Project Gutenberg eBook. www.gutenberg.org/files/675/675-h /675-h.htm.

Ditton, Paula M. 1999. *Mental Health Treatment of Inmates and Probationers.* Bureau of Justice Statistics Special Report, NCJ 174463, July. US Department of Justice. https://www.prisonlegalnews.org/media/publications/bojs_mental_ health_and_treatment_of_inmates_and_probationers_1999.pdf.

Dostoevsky, Fyodor. 1862. *The House of the Dead.* Translated by Constance Garnett. Quoted in *The Yale Book of Quotations* (2006) by Fred R. Shapiro, 210. New Haven, CT: Yale University Press.

Druss, Benjamin G., Thomas Bornemann, Yvonne W. Fry-Johnson, Harriet G. McCombs, Robert M. Politzer, and George Rust. 2008. "Trends in Mental Health and Substance Abuse Services at the Nation's Community Health Centers, 1998–2003." *American Journal of Public Health* 98, suppl. 1 (September): S126–31.

Durose, Matthew R., Alexia D. Cooper, and Howard N. Snyder. 2014. *Recidivism of Prisoners Released in 30 States in 2005: Patterns from 2005 to 2010—Update.* Bureau of Justice Statistics Special Report, NCJ #244205, April. US Department of Justice. https://www.bjs.gov/content/pub/pdf/rprts05p0510.pdf.

Duwe, Grant. 2011. "Evaluating the Minnesota Comprehensive Offender Reentry Plan (MCORP): Results from a Randomized Experiment." *Justice Quarterly*, March 9. DOI: 10.1080/07418825.2011.555414.

Eichelberger, Erika. 2015. "How Racist Is Solitary Confinement?" *Intercept*, July 16. https://theintercept.com/2015/07/16/rikers-study-black-inmates-250-percent-likely-entersolitary.

Erikson, Erik. 1950. *Childhood and Society.* New York: W. W. Norton.

"The Fair Sentencing Act Corrects a Long-Time Wrong in Cocaine Cases." 2010. *Washington Post*, August 3. www.washingtonpost.com/wp-dyn/content/article/2010/08/02/AR2010080204360.html.

Fakhoury, Walid, and Stefan Priebe. 2007. "Deinstitutionalization and Reinstitutionalization: Major Changes in the Provision of Mental Health Care." *Psychiatry* 6 (8): 313–16.

Farbota, Kim. 2015. "Black Crime Rates: What Happens When Numbers Aren't Neutral?" *Huffington Post,* September 2. www.huffingtonpost.com/kim-farbota/black-crime-rates-your-st_b_8078586.html.

Fellner, Jamie. 2015. *Callous and Cruel: Use of Force against Inmates with Mental Disabilities.* New York: Human Rights Watch. http://hrw.org/node/134861.

Fettig, Amy. 2016. "What Is Driving Solitary Confinement Reform?" *Correctional Law Reporter* 28 (3): 33.

Fields, Rona M. 2008. "The Neurobiological Consequences of Psychological Torture." In Ojeda 2008, 139–62.

Foucault, Michel. 1995. *Discipline and Punish: The Birth of the Prison.* Translated by Alan Sheridan. 2nd ed. New York: Vintage Books.

Fullilove, Mindy Thompson, E. Anne Lown, and Robert Fullilove. 1992. "Crack Ho's and Skeezers: Traumatic Experiences of Women Crack Users." *Journal of Sex Research* 29:275–87.

GAP (Group for the Advancement of Psychiatry). 2016. *People with Mental Illness in the Criminal Justice System.* Committee on Psychiatry and the Community. Washington, DC: American Psychiatric Association.

Garbarino, James. 2015. *Listening to Killers: Lessons Learned from My 20 Years as a Psychological Expert Witness in Murder Cases.* Oakland: University of California Press.

Garland, David. 1985. *Punishment and Welfare: A History of Penal Strategies.* Aldershot: Gower.

————. 2001. *The Culture of Control: Crime and Social Order in Contemporary Society.* Chicago: University of Chicago Press.

Gately, Gary. 2015. "Federal Juvenile Justice Funding Declines Precipitously." Juvenile Justice Information Exchange, February 12. http://jjie.org/federal-juvenile-justice-funding-declines-precipitously/108343/.

Gendreau, P., N. L. Freedman, and G. J. S. Wilde. 1972. "Changes in EEG Alpha Frequency and Evoked Response Latency during Solitary Confinement." *Journal of Abnormal Psychology* 79 (1): 54–59.

Gilligan, James. 1997. *Violence: Our Deadly Epidemic and Its Causes.* New York: Putnam.

————. 2003. "Shame, Guilt and Violence." *Social Research* 70 (4): 1149–80.

Gilligan, James, and Bandy Lee. 2013. *Report to the New York City Board of Correction.* http://solitarywatch.com/wp-content/uploads/2013/11/Gilligan-Report.-Final.pdf.

Glaser, Daniel. 1995. *Preparing Convicts for Law-Abiding Lives: The Pioneering Penology of Richard A. McGee.* Albany: State University of New York Press.

Glowa-Kollisch, S., F. Kaba, A. Waters, Y. Leung, E. Ford, and H. Venters. 2016. "Punishment to Treatment: The Clinical Alternative to Punitive Segregation: (CAPS) Program in New York City Jails." *International Journal of Environmental Research and Public Health* 13 (2): 182–92.

Goffman, Erving. 1962. *Asylums: Essays on the Social Situation of Mental Patients and Other Inmates.* Chicago: Aldine.

Gold, J. 2014. "Mental Health Cops Help Reweave Social Safety Net in San Antonio." Shots: Health News from NPR, August 19, National Public Radio. www.npr.org/blogs/health/2014/08/19/338895262/mental-health-cops-help-reweave-social-safety-net-in-san-antonio.

Gonnerman, Jennifer. 2015. "Kalief Browder, 1993–2015." *New Yorker,* June 7. www.newyorker.com/news/news-desk/kalief-browder-1993-2015.

Goode, Erica. 2012. "Prisons Rethink Isolation: Saving Money, Lives and Sanity." *New York Times,* March 10. www.nytimes.com/2012/03/11/us/rethinking-solitaryconfinement.

————. 2014. "Seeing Squalor and Unconcern in a Mississippi Jail." *New York Times,* June 7. www.nytimes.com/2014/06/08/us/seeing-squalor-and-unconcern-in-southern-jail.html.

Grassian, Stuart. 1983. "Psychopathological Effects of Solitary Confinement." *American Journal of Psychiatry* 140:1450–54.

————. 2006. "Psychiatric Effects of Solitary Confinement." *Washington University Journal of Law and Policy* 22:325–53.

————. 2016. "Psychiatric Effects of Solitary Confinement." In Casella, Ridgeway, and Shourd 2016, 155–61.

Grassian, Stuart, and Nancy Friedman. 1986. "Effects of Sensory Deprivation in Psychiatric Seclusion and Solitary Confinement." *International Journal of Law and Psychiatry* 8:49–65.

Grassian, Stuart, and Terry Allen Kupers. 2011. "The Colorado Study vs. the Reality of Supermax Confinement." *Correctional Mental Health Report* 13 (1): 1–4.

Greenberg, H. R. 2015. "Delayed Suicides of the 'Forgotten Battalion.'" *Psychiatric Times,* December 1. www.psychiatrictimes.com/suicide/delayed-suicides-forgotten-battalion.

Greenfeld, Lawrence A., and Tracy L. Snell. 1999. *Women Offenders.* Bureau of Justice Statistics Special Report, NCJ 175688, December. https://www.bjs.gov/content/pub/pdf/wo.pdf.

Grisso, Thomas. 2003. *Evaluating Competencies: Forensic Assessments and Instruments.* 2nd ed. New York: Springer.

Grob, Gerald N. 1991. *From Asylum to Community: Mental Health Policy in America.* Princeton, NJ: Princeton University Press.

Guenther, Lisa. 2013. *Solitary Confinement: Social Death and Its Afterlives.* Minneapolis: University of Minnesota Press.

Guy, Anna. 2016. "Locked Up and Locked Down: Amplifying Voices of Inmates with Disabilities." AVID Project. September 8. http://avidprisonproject.org/.

Hagler, Jamal. 2016. "Eight Facts You Should Know about the Criminal Justice System and People of Color." Center for American Progress. May 28. https://www.americanprogress.org/issues/criminal-justice/news/2015/05/28/113436/8-facts-you-should-know-about-the-criminal-justice-system-and-people-of-color/.

Hallinan, Joseph T. 2001. *Going up the River: Travels in a Prison Nation.* New York: Random House.

Haney, Craig. 2003a. "Mental Health Issues in Long-Term Solitary and 'Supermax' Confinement." *Crime and Delinquency* 49 (1): 124–56.

———. 2003b. "The Psychological Impact of Incarceration: Implications for Post-prison Adjustment." In *Prisoners Once Removed: The Impact of Incarceration and Reentry on Children, Families, and Communities,* edited by Jeremy Travis and Michelle Waul, 33–65. Washington, DC: Urban Institute Press, 2003.

———. 2006. *Reforming Punishment: Psychological Limits to the Pains of Imprisonment.* Washington, DC: American Psychological Association Books.

———. 2008. "A Culture of Harm: Taming the Dynamics of Cruelty in Supermax Prisons." *Criminal Justice and Behavior* 35 (8): 956–84.

———. 2015. "Redacted Report, Ruiz v. Brown." https://ccrjustice.org/sites/default/files/attach/2015/07/Redacted_Haney%20Expert%20Report.pdf.

Haney, Craig, Curtis Banks, and Philip Zimbardo. 1973. "Interpersonal Dynamics in a Simulated Prison." *International Journal of Criminology and Penology* 1:69–97.

Haney, Craig, and Philip Zimbardo. 1998. "The Past and Future of U.S. Prison Policy: Twenty-Five Years after the Stanford Prison Experiment." *American Psychologist* 53:709–27.

———. 2009. "Persistent Dispositionalism in Interactionist Clothing: Fundamental Attribution Error in Explaining Prison Abuse." *Personality and Social Psychology Bulletin* 35:807–14.

Hastings, Allison, Angela Browne, Kaitlin Kall, and Margaret diZerega. 2015. *Keeping Vulnerable Populations Safe under PREA: Alternative Strategies to the Use of Segregation in Prisons and Jails.* April. National PREA Resource Center. https://

www.prearesourcecenter.org/sites/default/files/library/housingvulnerable
populationsfinalmarch.pdf.

Hayes, Lindsay M. 2004. *Juvenile Suicide in Confinement: A National Survey.* NCJ
206354. Report to the Office of Juvenile Justice and Delinquency Prevention, US
Department of Justice. https://www.ncjrs.gov/pdffiles1/ojjdp/grants/206354.pdf.

———. 2013. "Suicide Prevention in Correctional Facilities: Reflections and Next
Steps." *International Journal of Law and Psychiatry* 36 (2013) 188–94. www
.ncianet.org/suicide-prevention-in-correctional-facilities-reflections-and-next-
steps/.

Herman, Judith Lewis. 1994. *Trauma and Recovery: The Aftermath of Violence—
From Domestic Abuse to Political Terror.* New York: Basic Books.

Hirsch, Adam J. 1992. *The Rise of the Penitentiary: Prisons and Punishment in Early
America.* New Haven, CT: Yale University Press.

Hochschild, Adam. 2016. "Our Awful Prisons: How They Can Be Changed." *New
York Review of Books,* May 26.

Holmquist, Micah. 1998. "Critical Resistance: A Step Forward." *Prison Legal News,*
December15.https://www.prisonlegalnews.org/news/1998/dec/15/critical-resistance-a-
step-forward/.

Holt, Norman, and Donald Miller. 1972. *Explorations in Inmate-Family Relationships.* Research Report No. 46. Sacramento: California Department of
Corrections.

Hudgins, Sheilagh, and Gilles Côté. 1991. "The Mental Health of Penitentiary
Inmates in Isolation." *Canadian Journal of Criminology* 33:177–82.

Hughes, Timothy, and Doris James Wilson. 2004. "Reentry Trends in the United
States." Bureau of Justice Statistics. Page last revised August 20. www.bjs.gov
/content/pub/pdf/reentry.pdf.

Human Rights Watch. 1996. *All Too Familiar: Sexual Abuse of Women in U.S. State
Prisons.* New York: Human Rights Watch.

———. 1997. *Cold Storage: Super-maximum Security Confinement in Indiana.* New
York: Human Rights Watch.

———. 2001. *No Escape: Male Rape in U.S. Prisons.* New York: Human Rights Watch.

———. 2003. *Ill-Prepared: U.S. Prisons and Offenders with Mental Illness.* New
York: Human Rights Watch.

———. 2011. *Nation behind Bars: A Human Rights Solution.* New York: Human
Rights Watch.

Irwin, John. 1970. *The Felon.* Berkeley: University of California Press.

Irwin, John, and James Austin. 1994. *It's About Time: America's Imprisonment
Binge.* Belmont, CA: Wadsworth.

"Istanbul Statement on the Use and Effects of Solitary Confinement." 2007. International Psychological Trauma Symposium, Istanbul, Turkey. December 9.
http://solitaryconfinement.org/uploads/Istanbul_expert_statement_on_sc.pdf.

Jackson, George. 1969. *Soledad Brother: The Prison Letters of George Jackson.* Chicago: Lawrence Hill.

James, Doris J., and Lauren E. Glaze. 2006. *Mental Health Problems of Prison and Jail Inmates.* Bureau of Justice Statistics Special Report, NCJ 213600, September. US Department of Justice. www.bjs.gov/content/pub/pdf/mhppji.pdf.

James, Erwin. 2013. "The Norwegian Prison Where People are Treated Like People." *Guardian,* February 25.

Jenness, Valerie, Cheryl L. Maxson, Kristy N. Matsuda, and Jennifer Macy Sumner. 2007. "Violence in California Correctional Facilities: An Empirical Examination of Sexual Assault." Center for Evidence-Based Corrections, University of California, Irvine. May 16. http://ucicorrections.seweb.uci.edu/files/2013/06/PREA_Presentation_PREA_Report_UCI_Jenness_et_al.pdf.

Jones, David, ed. 2004. *Working with Dangerous People: The Psychotherapy of Violence.* Oxford: Radcliffe Medical Press.

Jones, David, and Richard Shuker. 2004. "A Humane Approach to Working with Dangerous People." In D. Jones 2004, 191–98.

Jones, Maxwell. 1968. *Social Psychiatry in Practice. The Idea of a Therapeutic Community.* Harmondsworth, Middlesex: Penguin Books.

Jorgensen, J. D., S. H. Hernandez, and R. C. Warren. 1986. "Addressing the Social Needs of Families and Prisoners: A Tool for Inmate Rehabilitation." *Federal Probation* 38:47–52.

Kaba, Fatos, Andrea Lewis, Sarah Glowa-Kollisch, James Hadler, David Lee, Howard Alper, Daniel Selling, Ross MacDonald, Angela Solimo, Amanda Parsons, and Homer Venters. 2014. "Solitary Confinement and Risk of Self-Harm among Jail Inmates." *American Journal of Public Health* 104:442–47.

Kane, John M., Delbert G. Robinson, Nina R. Schooler, Kim T. Mueser, David L. Penn, Robert A. Rosenheck, Jean Addington, Mary F. Brunette, Christoph U. Correll, Sue E. Estroff, Patricia Marcy, James Robinson, Piper S. Meyer-Kalos, Jennifer D. Gottlieb, Shirley M. Glynn, David W. Lynde, Ronny Pipes, Benji T. Kurian, Alexander L. Miller, Susan T. Azrin, Amy B. Goldstein, Joanne B. Severe, Haiqun Lin, Kyaw J. Sint, Majnu John, and Robert K. Heinssen. 2015. "Comprehensive versus Usual Community Care for First-Episode Psychosis: Two-Year Outcomes from the NIMH RAISE Early Treatment Program." *American Journal of Psychiatry* 173 (4): 362–72.

Karnik, N. S., M. Soller, A. Redlich, M. Silverman, H. C. Kraemer, R. Haapanen, and H. Steiner. 2009. "Prevalence of and Gender Differences in Psychiatric Disorders among Juvenile Delinquents Incarcerated for Nine Months." *Psychiatric Services* 60 (6): 838–41.

Kidd, David. 2014. "The Sounds of Silence." *Governing* magazine, March. www.governing.com/topics/public-justice-safety/gov-prison-sounds-of-silence.html.

King, Kate, Benjamin Steiner, and Stephanie Ritchie Breach. 2008. "Violence in the Supermax: A Self-Fulfilling Prophecy." *Prison Journal* 88 (1): 144–68.

King, Robert Hillary. 2012. *From the Bottom of the Heap: The Autobiography of Robert Hillary King.* Oakland, CA: PM Press.

King, Robert Hillary, and Terry Kupers. 2009. *Robert King and Terry Kupers: The Psychological Impact of Imprisonment.* Video interview by Angola3.org. Uploaded November 20. www.youtube.com/watch?v=ty6UJycHk9M.

———. 2010. *Slavery in US Prisons—Interview with Robert King & Terry Kupers.* Video. Uploaded January 24. https://www.youtube.com/watch?v=8crPbPH428c.

Kohn, Stephen M. 1994. *American Political Prisoners: Prosecutions under the Espionage and Sedition Acts.* Santa Barbara, CA: Greenwood.

Kuehn, B. M. 2007. "Mental Health Courts Show Promise." *Journal of the American Medical Association* 297:1641–43.

Kulhara, P., A. Banerjee, and A. Dutt. 2008. "Early Intervention in Schizophrenia." *Indian Journal of Psychiatry* 50 (2): 128–34. www.ncbi.nlm.nih.gov/pmc/articles /PMC2738348/.

Kupers, Terry Allen. 1999. *Prison Madness: The Mental Health Crisis behind Bars and What We Must Do about It.* San Francisco: Jossey-Bass/Wiley.

———. 2003. "Rape and the Prison Code." In *Prison Masculinities,* edited by Donald F. Sabo, Terry Allen Kupers, and Willie James London, 111–17. Philadelphia: Temple University Press.

———. 2004. "Malingering in Correctional Settings." *Correctional Mental Health Report* 5 (6): 81–95.

———. 2005a. "Posttraumatic Stress Disorder (PTSD) in Prisoners." In Stojkovic 2005, chap. 10.

———. 2005b. "Schizophrenia, Its Treatment and Prison Adjustment." In Stojkovic 2005, chap. 9.

———. 2005c. "Toxic Masculinity as a Barrier to Mental Health Treatment in Prison." *Journal of Clinical Psychology* 61 (6): 13–24.

———. 2007. "How to Create Madness in Prison." In *Humane Prisons,* edited by David Jones, 47–58. Oxford: Radcliffe, 2006.

———. 2008a. "Prison and the Decimation of Pro-social Life Skills." In Ojeda 2008, 127–38.

———. 2008b. "What to Do with the Survivors? Coping with the Long-Term Effects of Isolated Confinement." *Criminal Justice and Behavior* 35 (8): 1005–16.

———. 2009. "Mutual Respect and Effective Prison Management." In *Transforming Corrections: Humanistic Approaches to Corrections and Offender Treatment,* edited by David Polizzi and Michael Braswell, 121–34. Durham, NC: Carolina Academic Press.

———. 2010a. "The Role of Misogyny and Homophobia in Prison Sexual Abuse." *UCLA Women's Law Journal* 18 (1): 107–30.

———. 2010b. "Treating Those Excluded from the SHU." *Correctional Mental Health Report* 12 (4): 49–54.

———. 2012. "Programming Cells Are Neither the Problem nor the Solution." *Correctional Mental Health Report* 13 (6): 83–85.

———. 2013a. "Expert Report of Terry Kupers, Dockery v. Epps, No. 3:13-cv-326 TSL-JCG (S.D. Miss. 2013)." https://www.aclu.org/prisoners-rights/dockery-v-epps-expert-report-terry-kupers.

————. 2013b. "Isolated Confinement: Effective Method for Behavior Change or Punishment for Punishment's Sake?" In *The Routledge Handbook of International Crime and Justice Studies*, edited by Bruce Arrigo and Heather Bersot, 213–32. Oxford: Routledge.

————. 2015a. "A Community Mental Health Model in Corrections." *Stanford Law and Policy Review* 26:119–58.

————. 2015b. "Redacted Report, Ruiz v. Brown." https://ccrjustice.org/sites/default/files/attach/2015/07/Redacted_Kupers%20Expert%20Report.pdf.

————. In press. "Gender and Domination in Prison." *Western New England University Law Review*.

Kupers, Terry Allen, Theresa Dronet, Margaret Winter, James Austin, Lawrence Kelly, William Cartier, Timothy J. Morris, Stephen F. Hanlon, Emmitt L. Sparkman, Parveen Kumar, Leonard C. Vincent, Jim Norris, Kim Nagel, and Jennifer McBride. 2009. "Beyond Supermax Administrative Segregation: Mississippi's Experience Rethinking Prison Classification and Creating Alternative Mental Health Programs." *Criminal Justice and Behavior* 36:1037–50.

La Fond, John Q. 1990. "Mental Health Law and Policy: Future Trends Affecting Forensic Psychiatrists." American Journal of Forensic Psychiatry 5:10–11.

Larson, Doron. 2013. "Why Scandinavian Prisons Are Superior." *Atlantic*, September 24.

Lau, J. 2015. "Incarceration to Convocation." *Daily Californian*, May 10. www.dailycal.org/2015/05/10/incarceration-to-convocation/.

Law, Victoria. 2013. "Women in Solitary Confinement: Sent to Solitary for Reporting Sexual Assault." Solitary Watch, December 12. http://solitarywatch.com/2013/12/12/women-solitary-confinement-sent-solitary-reporting-sexual-assault/.

————. 2014a. "Advisers to the U.S. Civil Rights Commission Hold Briefing on Juvenile Solitary Confinement New York." Solitary Watch, July 14. http://solitarywatch.com/2014/07/14/teens-isolation-state-advisory-committee-u-s-human-rights-commission-holds-briefing-juvenile-solitary-confinement-new-york/.

————. 2014b. "On the Way to Solitary, Women in Massachusetts Jail Get Strip Searched and Videotaped." Solitary Watch, May 15. http://solitarywatch.com/2014/05/15/way-solitary-women-massachusetts-jail-get-strip-searched-videotaped/.

————. 2014c. "Women in Solitary Confinement: Buried inside the Federal Prison System." Solitary Watch, January 24. http://solitarywatch.com/2014/01/24/women-solitary-confinement-buried-inside-federal-prison-system/.

Lichtenstein, Alexander C. 1996. *Twice the Work of Free Labor: The Political Economy of Convict Labor in the New South*. London: Verso.

Liebling, Alison. 1999. "Prison Suicide and Prisoner Coping." In *Prisons*, edited by Michael Tonry and Joan Petersilia, 283–359. Chicago: University of Chicago Press.

Liebling, Alison, David Price, and Guy Schefer. 2011. *The Prison Officer*. New York: Willan.

Liebowitz, Sarah, Peter J. Eliasberg, Ira A. Burnim, and Emily B. Read. 2014. *A Way Forward: Diverting People with Mental Illness from Inhumane and Expensive Jails into Community-Based Treatment That Works*. July. https://www.prisonlegalnews .org/media/publications/A%20Way%20Forward%20-%20Diverting% 20People%20with%20Mental%20Illness%20from%20Inhumane%20and%20 Expensive%20Jails%20into%20Community-Based%20Treatment%20that%20 Works,%20ACLU%20%26%20Bazelon,%202014.pdf.

Liefman, Steve. 2014. "Statement of Judge Steve Leifman Concerning People with Mental Illnesses Involved in the Criminal Justice System." US House of Representatives. http://docs.house.gov/meetings/IF/IF02/20140326/101980/HHRG-113-IF02-Wstate-LeifmanS-20140326.pdf.

Linehan, Marcia M., Henry Schmidt, Linda A. Dimeff, J. Christopher Craft, Jonathan Kanter, and Katherine A. Comtois. 1999. "Dialectical Behavior Therapy for Patients with Borderline Personality Disorder and Drug-Dependence." *American Journal of Addictions* 8 (4): 279–92.

Linehan, Marcia M., Darren A. Tutek, Heidi L. Heard, and Hubert E. Armstrong. 1994. "Interpersonal Outcome of Cognitive Behavioral Treatment for Chronically Suicidal Borderline Patients." *American Journal of Psychiatry* 151 (12): 1771–76.

Lord, Elaine. 2008. "The Challenges of Mentally Ill Female Offenders in Prison." *Criminal Justice and Behavior* 35 (8): 928–42.

Love, David. 2015. "President Obama's Review of Solitary Confinement Signals Possible Reform of America's Dungeons." *Atlanta Black Star*, July 24. http:// atlantablackstar.com/2015/07/24/president-obamas-review-of-solitary-confinement-signals-possible-reform-of-americas-dungeons/.

Loveland, David, and Michael Boyle. 2007. "Intensive Case Management as a Jail Diversion Program for People with a Serious Mental Illness: A Review of the Literature." *International Journal of Offender Therapy and Comparative Criminology* 51 (2): 130–50.

Lovell, David. 2008. "Patterns of Disturbed Behaviour in a Supermax Population." *Criminal Justice and Behavior* 35 (8): 985–1004.

Lovell, David, David Allen, Clark Johnson, and Ron Jemelka. 2001. "Evaluating the Effectiveness of Residential Treatment for Prisoners with Mental Illness." *Criminal Justice and Behavior* 28 (1): 83–104.

Lovell, David, L. C. Johnson, and K. C. Cain. 2007. "Recidivism of Supermax Prisoners in Washington." *Crime and Delinquency* 52 (4): 633–56.

Lovell, David, and Hans Toch. 2011. "Some Observations about the Colorado Segregation Study." *Correctional Mental Health Report* 13 (1): 3–6.

Lowen, Matthew, and Caroline Isaacs. 2012. *Lifetime Lockdown: How Isolation Conditions Impact Prisoner Reentry*. Phoenix, AZ: American Friends Service Committee. http://afsc.org/sites/afsc.civicactions.net/files/documents/AFSC-Lifetime-Lockdown-Report_0.pdf.

MacDonald, Donald, and Ira Bruce Nadel. 2012. *Alcatraz: History and Design of a Landmark*. San Francisco: Chronicle Books.

Main, Thomas. 1946. "The Hospital as a Therapeutic Institution." *Bulletin of the Menninger Clinic* 10:66–70.

Makinodan, Manabu, Kenneth M. Rosen, Susumu Ito, and Gabriel Corfas. 2012. "A Critical Period for Social Experience–Dependent Oligodendrocyte Maturation and Myelination." *Science* 337 (6100): 1357–60.

Mancini, Matthew J. 1996. *One Dies, Get Another: Convict Leasing in the American South, 1866–1928.* Columbia: University of South Carolina Press.

Martin, Steve J. 2000. "Sanctioned Violence in American Prisons." In May and Pitts 2000, 113–17.

Martinson, Robert. 1974. "What Works? Questions and Answers about Prison Reform." *Public Interest* 3 (5): 22–54.

———. 1979. "New Findings, New Views: A Note of Caution Regarding Sentencing Reform." *Hofstra Law Review* 7 (2): 243–58.

Mauer, Marc. 1999. *Race to Incarcerate.* New York: New Press.

May, John P., and Khalid R. Pitts, eds. 2000. *Building Violence: How America's Rush to Incarcerate Creates More Violence.* Thousand Oaks, CA: Sage Publications.

McCabe, Rosemarie, Jens Bullenkamp, Lars Hansson, Christoph Lauber, Rafael Martinez-Leal, Wulf Rössler, Hans Joachim Salize, Bengt Svensson, Francisco Torres-Gonzalez, Rob van den Brink, Durk Wiersma, and Stefan Priebe. 2013. "The Therapeutic Relationship and Adherence to Antipsychotic Medication in Schizophrenia." *PLOS ONE* 7 (4). http://journals.plos.org/plosone/article?id=10.1371/journal.pone.0036080.

McGee, Richard A. 1969. "What's Past Is Prologue." *Annals of the American Academy of Political and Social Science* 381 (1): 1–10.

McNiel, Dale E., and Renée L. Binder. 2007. "Effectiveness of a Mental Health Court in Reducing Criminal Recidivism and Violence." *American Journal of Psychiatry* 164:1395–1403.

McQuistion, H. L. 2003. "Challenges for Psychiatry in Serving Homeless People with Psychiatric Disorders." *American Journal of Psychiatry* 164 (9): 1395–1403.

Mears, Daniel P., and William D. Bales. 2009. "Supermax Incarceration and Recidivism." *Criminology* 47 (4): 1131–66.

———. 2010. "Supermax Housing: Placement, Duration, and Time to Reentry." *Journal of Criminal Justice* 38 (4): 545–54.

Mears, Daniel P., and Jamie Watson. 2006. "Towards a Fair and Balanced Assessment of Supermax Prisons." *Justice Quarterly* 23 (2): 232–70.

Melton, Gary B., John Petrila, Norman G. Poythress, and Christopher Slobogin. 1997. *Psychological Evaluations for the Courts: A Handbook for Mental Health Professionals and Lawyers.* New York: Guilford Press.

Memory, J. M. 1989. "Juvenile Suicides in Secure Detention Facilities: Correction of Published Rates." *Death Studies* 13:455–63.

Mendel, Werner M. 1989. *Treating Schizophrenia.* San Francisco: Jossey-Bass.

Mendez, Juan E. 2011. "Interim Report Prepared by the Special Rapporteur of the Human Rights Council on Torture and Other Cruel, Inhuman or Degrading

Treatment or Punishment." United Nations, A/66/268, August 5. https://archive.org/stream/452639-un-report-on-torture/452639-un-report-on-torture_djvu.txt.

Menninger, John A. 2016. "Involuntary Treatment: Hospitalization and Medications." Brown University Department of Psychiatry. www.brown.edu/Courses/BI_278/Other/Clerkship/Didactics/Readings/INVOLUNTARY%20TREATMENT.pdf.

Menninger, Karl. 1968. *The Crime of Punishment*. New York: Penguin.

Metzner, Jeffrey. 2012. "The Use of Programming Cells in the Treatment of Seriously Mentally Ill Inmates in Supermax Prisons: Response to Kupers." *Correctional Mental Health Report* 13 (6): 90–91.

Mirzaei, S., P. Knoll, A. Keck, B. Preitler, E. Gutierrez, H. Umek, H. Köhn, and M. Pecherstorfer. 2001. "Regional Cerebral Blood Flow in Patients Suffering from Post-traumatic Stress Disorder." *Neuropsychobiology* 43 (4): 260–64.

Monahan, John. 1981. *Predicting Violent Behavior: An Assessment of Clinical Techniques*. Beverly Hills, CA: Sage Publications.

Montgomery, Michael. 2013. "Hunger Strikes Lead to Changes in California Prisons." KQED Public Radio, July 29. www.npr.org/2013/07/29/206555385/hunger-strikes-lead-to- changes-in-california-prison-units.

———. 2016. "Locked Down: Gangs in the Supermax." American Radio Works. http://americanradioworks.publicradio.org/features/prisongangs/notebook.html.

Montgomery, Michael, and Adithya Sambamurthy. 2013. "Video: Indefinite Isolation." Center for Investigative Reporting, Reveal News, July 26. https://www.revealnews.org/article/video-indefinite-isolation/.

Morgan, Robert D., Richard A. Van Haveren, and Christy A. Pearson. 2002. "Correctional Officer Burnout: Further Analyses." *Criminal Justice and Behavior* 29:144–60.

Morris, Mark. 2004. *Dangerous and Severe: Process, Programme and Person: Grendon's Work*. London: Jessica Kingsley.

Mualimm-ak, Five. 2016. "Invisible." In Casella, Ridgeway, and Shourd 2016, 147–52.

Mumola, Christopher J. 1997. *Substance Abuse and Treatment, State and Federal Prisoners*. Bureau of Justice Statistics Special Report, NCJ 172871, January. http://csdp.org/research/satsfp97.pdf.

Munetz, M. R., and P. A. Griffin. 2006. "Use of the Sequential Intercept Model as an Approach to Decriminalization of People with Serious Mental Illness." *Psychiatric Services* 57 (4): 544–49.

Navarro, Robert, Thomas Quinn, and Corey Weinstein. 1997. *Maximum Security University*. Video. San Francisco: California Prison Focus. https://www.youtube.com/watch?v=jg_qI4F_IfU.

NCCHC (National Commission on Correctional Health Care). 2012. "Prevention of Juvenile Suicide in Correctional Settings." www.ncchc.org/prevention-of-juvenile-suicide-in-correctional-settings.

———. 2014. *Standards for Health Services in Prisons*. Chicago: National Commission on Correctional Health Care.

Nellis, Ashley. 2016. *The Color of Justice: Racial and Ethnic Disparity in State Prisons*. Washington, DC: Sentencing Project. www.sentencingproject.org/wp-content/uploads/2016/06/The-Color-of-Justice-Racial-and-Ethnic-Disparity-in-State-Prisons.pdf.

Nelson, Geoffrey B., and Isaac Prilleltensky, eds. 2010. *Community Psychology: In Pursuit of Liberation and Well-Being*. New York: Palgrave Macmillan.

New York Advisory Committee to the US Commission on Civil Rights. 2014. *The Solitary Confinement of Youth in New York: A Civil Rights Violation*. December. www.usccr.gov/pubs/NY-SAC-Solitary-Confinement-Report-without-Cover.pdf.

New York Civil Liberties Union. 2014. "Testimony Regarding the Treatment of Adolescents in NYC Jails and at Rikers Island." October 8. www.nyclu.org/content/testimony-regarding-treatment-of-adolescents-nyc-jails-and-rikers-island.

Obama, Barack. 2016. "Why We Must Re-think Solitary Confinement." *Washington Post,* February 22.

Ojeda, Almerindo, ed. 2008. *The Trauma of Psychological Torture*. Disaster and Trauma Psychology 5. Westport, CT: Praeger.

O'Keefe, Maureen L., Kelli J. Klebe, Alysha Stucker, Kristin Strum, and William Leggett. 2010. *One Year Longitudinal Study of the Psychological Effects of Administrative Segregation*. Colorado Department of Corrections. www.ncjrs.gov/pdffiles1/nij/grants/232973.pdf.

Ordway, Denise Marie, and John Wihbey. 2014. "Solitary Confinement in Prisons: Key Data and Research Findings." *Journalist's Resource*, last updated January 26, 2016. http://journalistsresource.org/studies/government/criminal-justice/solitary-confinement-prisons-key-data-research-findings#sthash.eyPEQAMI.dpuf.

Organization of American States. 1985. Inter-American Convention to Prevent and Punish Torture. www.oas.org/juridico/english/treaties/a-51.html.

Oshinsky, David M. 1996. *Worse Than Slavery: Parchman Farm and the Ordeal of Jim Crow Justice*. New York: Free Press.

Owen, Barbara A. 1998. *In the Mix: Struggle and Survival in a Women's Prison*. Albany: State University of New York Press.

Owen, Barbara, James Wells, and Joycelyn Pollack. 2017. *In Search of Safety: Confronting Inequality in Women's Prisons*. Berkeley: University of California Press.

Palazzolo, Joe. 2014. "Colorado Becomes Latest to Back Ban on Solitary Confinement of Mentally Ill." *Wall Street Journal,* June 6. http://blogs.wsj.com/law/2014/06/06/colorado-becomes-latest-to-back-ban-on-solitary-confinement-of-mentally-ill.

Patterson, Raymond F., and Kerry Hughes. 2008. "Review of Completed Suicides in the California Department of Corrections and Rehabilitation, 1999 to 2004." *Psychiatric Services* 59 (6): 676–84.

Paulus, Paul B. 1988. *Prison Crowding: A Psychological Perspective*. New York: Springer-Verlag.

Paulus, P. B., G. McCain, and V. C. Cox. 1978. "Death Rates, Psychiatric Commitments, Blood Pressure and Perceived Crowding as a Function of Institutional Crowding." *Environmental Psychology and Nonverbal Behavior* 3:107–17.

Pearson, Jake. 2016a. "After Years in Solitary at Rikers, a Woman Struggles to Carry On." *Ledger,* February 16. www.theledger.com/news/20160216/after-years-in-solitary-at-rikers-a-woman-struggles-to-carry-on.

———. 2016b. "A Woman Found Innocent after 3 Years in Rikers Could Be Sent Back for Things That Happened in Jail." *Business Insider,* March 21. www.businessinsider.com/ap-freed-after-years-in-solitary-woman-faces-jailhouse-charges-2016-3.

Penal Reform International. 1995. *Making Standards Work: An International Handbook on Good Prison Practice.* The Hague: Penal Reform International and the Ministry of Justice of the Netherlands.

Pizarro, Jesenia, and Vanja M. K. Stenius. 2004. "Supermax Prisons: Their Rise, Current Practices, and Effect on Inmates." *Prison Journal* 84 (2): 248–64.

Pollock, Jocelyn M. 2014. *Women's Crimes, Criminology and Corrections.* Long Grove, IL: Waveland Press.

Prisoner Reentry Institute. 2015. "Proceedings of a Colloquium to Further a National Consensus on Ending the Over-use of Extreme Isolation in Prisons." John Jay College of Criminal Justice, September 30-October 1. http://thecrimereport.s3.amazonaws.com/2/4a/d/3344/approaches_to_reforming_solitary.pdf.

Prison Rape Elimination Commission. 2009. *National Prison Rape Elimination Commission Report.* June. https://www.ncjrs.gov/pdffiles1/226680.pdf.

Quigley, Bill. 2010. "Fourteen Examples of Racism in Criminal Justice System." *Huffington Post,* July 26. www.huffingtonpost.com/bill-quigley/fourteen-examples-of-raci_b_658947.html.

Raemisch, Rick. 2014. "My Night in Solitary." *New York Times,* February 20.

Raemisch, Rick, and Kellie Wasko. 2016. "Open the Door: Segregation Reforms in Colorado." Corrections.com, January 4. www.corrections.com/news/article/42045.

Reeves, Rusty, and Anthony Tamburello. 2014. "Single Cells, Segregated Housing, and Suicide in the New Jersey Department of Corrections." *American Academy of Psychiatry and Law* 42:484–88.

Reiter, Keramet A. 2012. "Parole, Snitch, or Die: California's Supermax Prisons and Prisoners, 1997–2007." *Punishment and Society* 14 (5): 530–63.

———. 2016. *23/7: Pelican Bay Prison and the Rise of Long-Term Solitary Confinement.* New Haven, CT: Yale University Press.

Rhodes, Lorna. 2004. *Total Confinement: Madness and Reason in the Maximum Security Prison.* Berkeley: University of California Press.

Richie, B. E. 2012. *Arrested Justice: Black Women, Violence, and America's Prison Nation.* New York: New York University Press.

Rivas-Vazquez, Rafael A., Manuel Sarria, Gustavo Rey, Ana A. Rivas-Vazquez, Julissa Rodriguez, and Mario E. Jardon. 2009. "A Relationship-Based Care Model for Jail Diversion." *Psychiatric Services* 60 (6): 766–71.

Robertson, James E. 2016. "Alternatives to Solitary Confinement for Protective Custody Inmates." *Correctional Law Reporter* 28 (3): 41–44.

Rogers, Richard. 1997. *Clinical Assessment of Malingering and Deception*. New York: Guilford.

Rogers, Richard, Ernest H. Harrell, and Christine D. Liff. 1993. "Feigning Neuropsychological Impairment: A Critical Review of Methodological and Clinical Considerations." *Clinical Psychology Review* 13:255–74.

Rose, Katrina C. 2001. "When Is an Attempted Rape Not an Attempted Rape? When the Victim Is Transsexual: *Schwenk v. Hartford*, The Intersection of Prison Rape, Title VII and Societal Willingness to Dehumanize Transsexuals." *American University Journal of Gender, Social Policy and the Law* 9 (3): 505–40.

Rothman, David J. 1971. *The Discovery of the Asylum: Social Order and Disorder in the New Republic*. Toronto: Little, Brown.

Rothwell, Gary R., and J. Norman Baldwin. 2007. "Whistle-Blowing and the Code of Silence in Police Agencies: Policy and Structural Predictors." *Crime and Delinquency* 53 (4): 605–32. http://cad.sagepub.com/cgi/content/abstract/53/4/605.

Ruiz, George. 2013. "Pelican Bay Hunger Strikers." *Truthout*, July 11. www.truthout.org/opinion/item/17524-pelican-bay-profiles-george-ruiz.

Ryder, Judith Anne. 2007. "Auburn State Prison." In *Encyclopedia of Governance*, edited by Mark Bevir. Los Angeles: SAGE Publications. http://dx.doi.org/10.4135/9781412952613.

Sabo, Donald F., Terry Allen Kupers, and Willie James London, eds. 2001. *Prison Masculinities*. Philadelphia: Temple University Press.

SAMHSA (Substance Abuse and Mental Health Services Administration). 2014. "TIP 57: Trauma Informed Care in Behavioral Health Services." http://store.samhsa.gov/product/TIP-57-Trauma-Informed-Care-in-Behavioral-Health-Services/SMA14-4816.

Schaeffer, Carol. 2016. "'Isolation Devastates the Brain': The Neuroscience of Solitary Confinement." Solitary Watch, May 11. http://solitarywatch.com/2016/05/11/isolation-devastates-the-brain-the-neuroscience-of-solitary-confinement/.

Scharff Smith, Peter. 2006. "The Effects of Solitary Confinement on Prison Inmates: A Brief History and Review of the Literature." *Crime and Justice* 34:441–528.

———. 2011. "The Effects of Solitary Confinement: Commentary on One Year Longitudinal Study of the Psychological Effects of Administrative Segregation." *Corrections and Mental Health*, June 21, 1–11. http://community.nicic.gov/cfsfile/.ashx/__key/CommunityServe.

Scheff, Thomas J. 1966. *Being Mentally Ill: A Sociological Theory*. Chicago: Aldine.

Schlanger, Margo. 2013. "Prison Segregation: Symposium Introduction and Preliminary Data on Racial Disparities." *Michigan Journal of Race and Law* 18 (2): 241–50.

Schmidt, Henry, and Andre Ivanoff. 2007. "Behavioral Prescriptions for Treating Self Injurious and Suicidal Behaviors." In Thienhaus and Piasecki 2007, 7-1 to 7–21.

Schwirtz, Michael. 2014. "Solitary Confinement to End for Youngest at Rikers Island." *New York Times*, September 28. www.nytimes.com/2014/09/29/nyregion/solitary-confinement-to-end-for-youngest-at-rikers-island.html?_r=0.

Scully, P. J., G. Coakley, A. Kinsella, and J. L. Waddington. 1997. "Psychopathology, Executive (Frontal) and General Cognitive Impairment in Relation to Duration of Initially Untreated versus Subsequently Treated Psychosis in Chronic Schizophrenia." *Psychological Medicine* 27 (6): 1303–10.

Sentencing Project. 2015a. "Issues: Racial Disparity." N.d. Accessed January 16, 2017. www.sentencingproject.org/template/page.cfm?id=122.

———. 2015b. "Issues: Sentencing Policy." N.d. Accessed January 16, 2017. www.sentencingproject.org/issues/sentencing-policy/.

———. 2015c. *The State of Sentencing 2015: Developments in Policy and Practice.* Washington, DC: Sentencing Project. http://sentencingproject.org/doc/publications/State-of-Sentencing-2015.pdf.

———. 2016. "Criminal Justice Facts." 2016. www.sentencingproject.org/criminal-justice-facts/.

Shalev, Sharon. 2009. *Supermax: Controlling Risk through Solitary Confinement.* Portland, OR: Willan.

Shourd, Sarah. 2011. "In an Iranian Prison: Tortured by Solitude." *New York Times,* November 5.

———. 2016a. "Preface: A Human Forever." In Casella, Ridgeway, and Shourd 2016, vii–xii.

———. 2016b. "Wrapping Up *The Box.*" Video. October. https://vimeo.com/187301582.

Slahi, M. O. 2015. *Guantanamo Diary.* Edited by Larry Siems. New York: Little, Brown.

Sowers, Wesley, Kenneth Thompson, and Stephen Mullins. 1999. *Mental Health in Corrections: An Overview for Correctional Staff.* Lanham, MD: American Correctional Association.

Spaniol, LeRoy, Mary Alice Brown, Laura Blankertz, Darrell J. Burnham, Jerry Dincin, Kathy Furlong-Norman, Noel Nesbitt, Paul Ottenstein, Kathy Prieve, Irvin Rutman, and Anthony Zipple. 1994. *An Introduction to Psychiatric Rehabilitation.* Columbia, MD: International Association of Psychosocial Rehabilitation Services, Publications Committee.

Steadman, Henry J., S. M. Morris, and D. L. Dennis. 1995. "The Diversion of Mentally Ill Persons from Jail to Community-Based Services: A Profile of Programs." *American Journal of Public Health* 85:1630–35.

Steadman, Henry J., Allison Redlich, Lisa Callahan, Pamela Clark Robbins, and Roumen Vesselinov. 2011. "Effect of Mental Health Courts on Arrests and Jail Days." *Archives of General Psychiatry* 68 (2): 167–72.

Steiner, Benjamin, and John Wooldredge. 2015. "Individual and Environmental Sources of Work Stress among Prison Officers." *Criminal Justice and Behavior* 42 (8): 800–818.

Steiner, H., I. Garcia, and Z. Matthews. 1997. "Posttraumatic Stress Disorder in Incarcerated Juvenile Delinquents." *Journal of the Academy of Child and Adolescent Psychiatry* 36 (3): 357–65.

Stettin, Brian, Frederick J. Frese, and H. Richard Lamb. 2013. *Mental Health Diversion Practices: A Survey of the States*. August. Arlington, VA: Treatment Advocacy Center. http://ww1.prweb.com/prfiles/2013/08/13/11024983/Diversion-study.pdf.

Stojkovic, Stan, ed. 2005. *Managing Special Populations in Jails and Prisons*. Kingston, NJ: Civic Research Institute.

Stuntz, William J. 2011. *The Collapse of American Criminal Justice*. Cambridge, MA: Harvard University Press.

Taber, Katherine H., and Robin A. Hurley. 2009. "PTSD and Combat-Related Injuries: Functional Neuroanatomy." *Journal of Neuropsychiatry and Clinical Neurosciences* 21 (1): 1–4. http://neuro.psychiatryonline.org/doi/full/10.1176/jnp.2009.21.1.iv.

Teague, G. B., R. E. Drake, and T. H. Ackerson. 1995. "Evaluating Use of Continuous Treatment Teams for Persons with Mental Illness and Substance Abuse." *Psychiatric Services* 46 (7): 689–95.

Teplin, Linda A., Karen M. Abram, Gary M. McClelland, Mina K. Dulcan, and Amy A. Mericle. 2002. "Psychiatric Disorders in Youth in Juvenile Detention." *Archives of General Psychiatry* 59 (12): 1133–43.

Teplin, Linda A., Leah J. Welty, Karen M. Abram, Mina K. Dulcan, and Jason J. Washburn. 2012. "Prevalence and Persistence of Psychiatric Disorders in Youth after Detention: A Prospective Longitudinal Study." *Archives of General Psychiatry* 69, (10): 1031–43.

Thibaut, Jacqueline. 1982. "'To Pave the Way to Penitence': Prisoners and Discipline at the Eastern State Penitentiary." *Pennsylvania Magazine of History and Biography*, April, 187–222.

Thienhaus, Ole J. 2007. "Suicide Risk Management in the Correctional Setting." In Thienhaus and Piasecki 2007, 6–1 to 6–10.

Thienhaus, Ole J., and Melissa Piasecki, eds. 2007. *Correctional Psychiatry: Practice Guidelines and Strategies*. Kingston, NJ: Civic Research Institute.

Thompson, Christie. 2015. "From Solitary to the Street: What Happens When Prisoners Go from Complete Isolation to Complete Freedom in One Day?" Marshall Project. June 11. https://www.themarshallproject.org/2015/06/11/from-solitary-to-the-street#.xjYEmomna.

Thompson, Heather Ann. 2016. *Blood in the Water: The Attica Prison Uprising of 1971 and Its Legacy*. New York: Penguin/Random House.

Thornberry, Terence P., and Jack E. Call. 1983. "Constitutional Challenges to Prison Overcrowding: The Scientific Evidence of Harmful Effects." *Hastings Law Journal* 35:313–53.

Toch, Hans. 1975. *Men in Crisis: Human Breakdowns in Prisons*. Chicago: Aldine.

———. [1975] 1992. *Mosaic of Despair: Human Breakdown in Prison*. Washington, DC: American Psychological Association.

———. 1982. "The Disturbed Disruptive Inmate: Where Does the Bus Stop?" *Journal of Psychiatry and Law* 10:327–49.

———. 1992. *Violent Men: An Inquiry into the Psychology of Violence.* Washington, DC: American Psychological Association.

———. 2003. "Prison Walls Do a Prison Make: The Untimely Demise of Visitation Rights." *Criminal Law Bulletin* 39:647–58.

———. 2004. "The Disturbed Disruptive." In D. Jones 2004, 9–14.

———. 2014. *Organizational Change through Individual Empowerment: Applying Social Psychology in Prisons and Policing.* Washington, DC: American Psychological Association.

Toch, Hans, and Kenneth Adams. 1987. "The Prison as Dumping Ground: Mainlining Disturbed Offenders." *Journal of Psychiatry and Law* 15:539–53.

———. 2002. *Acting Out: Maladaptive Behavior in Confinement.* Washington, DC: American Psychological Association.

Toch, Hans, and Terry Allen Kupers. 2007. "Violence in Prisons, Revisited." *Journal of Offender Rehabilitation* 45 (3/4): 1–28.

Torrey, E. Fuller. 1997. *Out of the Shadows: Confronting America's Mental Illness Crisis.* New York: John Wiley and Sons.

———. 2010. "Documenting the Failure of Deinstitutionalization." *Psychiatry: Interpersonal and Biological Processes* 73 (2): 122–24.

Torrey, E. Fuller, Mary T. Zdanowicz, Aaron D. Kennard, H. Richard Lamb, Donald F. Eslinger, Michael C. Biasotti, and Doris A. Fuller. 2014. *The Treatment of Persons with Mental Illness in Prisons and Jails: A State Survey. A Joint Report of the Treatment Advocacy Center and the National Sheriffs' Association.* April 8. www.calea.org/sites/default/files/treatment-behind-barsReport.pdf.

United Nations Commission on Crime Prevention and Criminal Justice. 2015. *United Nations Standard Minimum Rules for the Treatment of Prisoners (the Mandela Rules).* www.unodc.org/documents/commissions/CCPCJ/CCPCJ_Sessions/CCPCJ_24/resolutions/L6_Rev1/ECN152015_L6Rev1_e_V1503585.pdf.

United Nations Committee against Torture. 1984. Convention against Torture and Other Cruel, Inhuman or Degrading Treatment or Punishment. New York, December 10. www.un.org/ga/search/view_doc.asp?symbol=a/res/39/46.

United Nations Office on Drugs and Crime. 2007. *Handbook of Basic Principles and Promising Practices on Alternatives to Imprisonment.* Vienna: United Nations. www.unodc.org/pdf/criminal_justice/Handbook_of_Basic_Principles_and_Promising_Practices_on_Alternatives_to_Imprisonment.pdf.

US Department of Justice. 2014. Letter to Bill de Blasio, Joseph Ponte, and Zachary Carter re: CRIPA Investigation of the New York City Department of Correction Jails on Rikers Island. August 4. https://www.justice.gov/sites/default/files/usao-sdny/legacy/2015/03/25/SDNY%20Rikers%20Report.pdf.

Van Wormer, Katherine S., and Lorenn Walker, eds. 2013. *Restorative Justice Today: Practical Applications.* Thousand Oaks, CA: Sage Publications.

Vazquez, Judith. 2016. "On the Verge of Hell." In Casella, Ridgeway, and Shourd 2016, 55–60.

Villa, C. F. 2016. "Living in the SHU." In Casella, Ridgeway, and Shourd 2016, 35–41.

Vyas, A., S. Bernal, and S. Chattarji. 2003. "Effect of Chronic Stress on Dendritic Arborization in the Central and Extended Amygdala." *Brain Research* 965 (1–2): 290–94.

Waldegrave, Charles, Kiwi Tamasese, Flora Tuhaka, and Warihi Campbell. 2003. *Just Therapy: A Journey. A Collection of Papers from the Just Therapy Team, New Zealand.* Adelaide, South Australia: Dulwich Centre Publications.

Walker, Lenore E. 1979. *The Battered Woman.* New York: Harper and Row.

Walsh, Denny. 2010. "Appeals Court Revives Suit over California Prison Lockdowns." *Sacramento Bee,* January 13. www.mcclatchydc.com/news/crime /article24570382.html.

Way, Bruce B., Richard Miraglia, Donald A. Sawyer, Richard Beer, and John Eddy. 2005. "Factors Related to Suicide in New York State Prisons." *International Journal of Law and Psychiatry* 28 (3): 207–21.

Weinstein, Corey. 2000. "Even Dogs Confined to Cages for Long Periods of Time Go Berserk." In May and Pitts 2000, 118–23.

Wells, James B., Kevin I. Minor, Earl Angel, Adam K. Matz, and Nick Amato 2009. "Predictors of Job Stress among Staff in Juvenile Correctional Facilities." *Criminal Justice and Behavior* 36 (3): 245–58.

Wells, R., J. P. Morrissey, I. H. Lee, and A. Radford. 2010. "Trends in Behavioral Health Care Service Provision by Community Health Centers, 1998–2007." *Psychiatric Services* 61 (8): 759–64.

White, Michael, and David Epston. 1990. *Narrative Means to Therapeutic Ends.* New York: W. W. Norton.

Wilde, Oscar. [1898] 1964. "The Ballad of Reading Gaol." In *De Profundis.* New York: Avon Books.

Wilden, Anthony. 1972. *System and Structure: Essays in Communication and Exchange.* London: Tavistock Publications.

Wilson, Rob. 1980. "Who Will Care for the Mad and Bad?" *Corrections Magazine,* February, 5–17.

Woods, Patricia. 2011. "Mental Health: More Than the Absence of Mental Illness." Rochester Health. Healthcare Resource Guide (November). www.rochesterhealth .com/healthnotes/articles/mental-health-more-than-the-absence-of-mental-illness.

Wozniak, John F., Michael C. Braswell, Ronald E. Vogel, and Kristie R. Blevins. 2008. Introduction to *Transformative Justice: Critical and Peacemaking Themes Influenced by Richard Quinney,* edited by John F. Wozniak, Michael C. Braswell, Ronald E. Vogel, and Kristie R. Blevins. Lanham, MD: Rowman and Littlefield.

Wright, Emily M., Emily J. Salisbury, and Patricia Van Voorhis. 2007. "Predicting the Prison Misconducts of Women Offenders: The Importance of Gender-Responsive Needs." *Journal of Contemporary Criminal Justice* 23:310–40.

Wright, Emily M., Patricia Van Voorhis, Emily J. Salisbury, and Ashley Bauman. 2012. "Gender-Responsive Lessons Learned and Policy Implications for Women in Prison." *Criminal Justice and Behavior* 39 (12): 1612–32.

Wyatt, R. J. 1991. "Neuroleptics and the Natural Course of Schizophrenia." *Schizophrenia Bulletin* 17:325–51.

Yee, Min S. 1973. *The Melancholy History of Soledad Prison*. New York: Harper's Magazine Press.

Yung, A. R., L. J. Phillips, P. D. McGorry, C. A. McFarlane, S. Francey, S. Harrigan, G. C. Patton, and H. J. Jackson. 1998. "Prediction of Psychosis: A Step towards Indicated Prevention of Schizophrenia." *British Journal of Psychiatry*, suppl. 172 (33): 14–20.

Zimbardo, Philip. 2007. *The Lucifer Effect: Understanding How Good People Turn Evil*. New York: Random House.

Zlotnick, C., J. Clarke, P. Friedmann, M. Roberts, S. Sacks, and G. Melnick. 2008. "Gender Differences in Comorbid Disorders among Offenders in Prison Substance Abuse Treatment Programs." *Behavioral Sciences and the Law* 26:403–12.

LEGAL CASES

Ashker v. Brown, 4:09-cv-05796-CW (N.D. Cal., 2014).

Brown v. Plata, 131 S. Ct. 1910 (2011).

Cain v. Michigan Dept. of Corrections, No. 88–61119-AZ (State Court, 1995–2005).

Coleman v. Wilson, 912 F. Supp. 1282, U.S. Dist. Ct., E.D. Cal. (1993).

Disability Advocates, Inc. v. New York State Office of Mental Health (S.D. N.Y. Apr. 27, 2007), No. 02 Civ. 4002 (GEL).

Dockery v. Fisher, No. 3:13-CV-00326-TSL-JMR.

Farrell v. Harper, Cal. Super. Ct., Alameda County, No. RG 03079344 (filed 2003).

Gates v. Deukmejian/ Rowland 39 F. 3d 1439; 63 USLW 2318, 7 A.D.D. 1, 5 NDLR P 458 (1994).

Giraldo v. Cal. Dep't of Corr. and Rehab., 168 Cal.App.4th 231 (Ca. 2008).

Graham v. Florida, 560 U.S. 48 (2010).

Harper v. Washington, 494 U.S. 210 (1990).

Harrington-Wisely et al. v. State of California et al., Super. Ct. Case No. BC 227373.

Jones 'El v. Berge, 164 F. Supp. 2d 1096 (W.D. Wis. 2001).

Katka v. Montana DOC, Mont. 1st Judicial Dist., No BDV (2009), 1163.

Madrid v. Gomez, 889 F. Supp. 1146 (N.D. Cal., 1995).

Medley, Petitioner, in re Medley, 134 U.S. 160 (1890).

Miller v. Alabama, No. 10–9646, S. Ct., 2012.

Montgomery v. Louisiana, 577 U.S., S. Ct., 2016.

Neal v. Michigan DOC, Case No. 96–6986-CZ, State Court, 22nd Cir., Washtenaw County (1998, 2005).

Presley v. Epps, No. 4:05CV148-JAD (N.D. Miss., 2005, 2007).

Roper v. Simmons, S. Ct., No. 03–633. Argued October 13, 2004—Decided March 1, 2005.

Russell et al. v. Epps/Mississippi Department of Corrections, U.S. Dist. Ct., N.D. Miss., E. Div., Civ. No. 1:02CV261-D-D (2004).

Rutherford v. Pitchess, 626 F. 2d 866, slip op. at 2–3 (9th Cir. 1980).
Salazar v. McCarthy (Super. Court, County of Marin, 1986).
Walker v. Montana, MT 134 (S. Ct. of Montana, April 29, 2003).
Westefer v. Snyder, U.S. Dist. Ct. S.D. Ill., No. 00–162-GPM (2004).
Wolff v. McDonnell, 418 U.S. 539 (1974).

INDEX

Abu Ghraib, 98
Abu-Jamal, Mumia, 189–90, 245n23
activities of daily living (ADLs), 204
Adderal, 75
administrative segregation, 26–27, *29*, 36, 39, 41, *71*, 105, 224, 227
adolescence, 141, 149. *See also* juveniles
ADX (administrative maximum facility), 8, 25
Afghanistan, 37, 163
African American prisoners, 11, 26, 105, 123, 128–30, 140–41, 157–59. *See also* racism; mentally ill, 27, 108–12, 121–22, 193–95, 205, 214
African National Congress, 239
Agee, Vicky, 219
agency, 49–50, 133, 167; fostering sense of, 171–72, 174, 176–81, 185–86, 229–30
Aichorn, August, 230
Akil, Huda, 90
Alcatraz Federal Penitentiary (California), 24
Alexander, Franz, 230
Alexander, Michelle, 70, 83
Allen B. Polunsky Unit (Texas), 78
Al Qaeda, 37
American Academy of Child and Adolescent Psychiatry, 101
American Civil Liberties Union (ACLU), 5, 125, 146; National Prison Project, 27, 56, 224
American Correctional Association, 44
American Encyclopedia, 24

American Friends Service Committee, 72
American Psychiatric Association (APA), 101, 149, 207, 209; Mandatory Outpatient Resource Document, 252n42; Task Force on Correctional Mental Health Care, 203
American Psychological Association, 149
American Public Health Association, 101
Americans with Disabilities Act (1990), 2
anger management, 10, 87, 204
Angola State Prison (Louisiana), 78, 188–89
antidepressants, 27, 121, 184, 194, 251n39
antipsychotic medications, 27–28, 108–10, 113, 117, 127, 194, 206–8, 214; side effects of, 46, 109, 110, 228
anti-Semitism, 82
antisocial personality disorder, 113, 215, 217, 219
anxiety, 2, 11, 32, 47, 88–89, 92–94, 100, 183, 216–17; brain chemistry changes in response to, 89–90; medications to relieve, 194; paranoia and, 92, 122, 133; postrelease, 12–13, 97, 152–54, 159–60; in PTSD, 126; self-harm driven by, 107, 202, 206, 217–19; suicide and, 28, 99
Arizona, 72–73
Arkansas, 73
Aryan Brotherhood, 76, 81
Ashker, Todd, 95, 173–74
Ashker v. Brown (2015), 11, 154, 161, 185, 232, 244n26; named plaintiffs in, 61–62, 93, 162–63, 173; settlement of, 41, 178

assaultiveness, 109, 210, 214–15, 221, 222, 225–26, 229
attention deficit disorder, 75
Attica Correctional Facility (New York), 60
attribution error, 74–75, 116, 192
Auburn Prison (New York), 21–23
auditory hallucinations, 80, 109, 194, 215
Austin, James, 42

Bauer, Shane, 50, 188
Behavior Management Plans (BMPs), 45–46, 144
behavior therapy, 227, 230
Bentham, Jeremy, 65
Berzon, Marsha S., 84
beta blockers, 229
bipolar disorder, 30, 45, 106–7, 195, 207, 218–19, 236, 250n34
Birdman of Alcatraz, The (film), 24
Black Codes, 73
Black Guerilla Family, 76
Black Lives Matter, 71
Black Panther Party, 4–5, 25, 188
Black Power, 78
Blue Code, 50–52, 130
body cavity searches, 124
booty bandits, 104
Bosnia, 65
Box, The (Shourd), 188
brain: adolescent, 150; changes in chemistry of, 89–90, 114; physical injuries to, 47
Browder, Kalief, 142, 232
Brown v. Plata (2011), 6
Bunchy Carter Free Clinic, 4
Bush, George H. W., 74
Bush, George W., 51, 65, 97
bus therapy, 220

cages, 58–59, 221; recreation periods in, 1, 3, 11, 29, 147, 216
Cain v. Michigan Department of Corrections (1996), 179
California, 6–7, 81–82, 123, 178, 232. See also specific prisons; Agreement to End Hostilities, 173–74; Department of Corrections (CDCR), 34, 40–41, 46–48, 61–63, 82, 83, 94, 117–18, 131, 147, 158, 182–83, 187, 198–99; Department of Mental Health,
118; Division of Juvenile Justice, 147; Medical Facility (CMF), 46; mentally disordered offender (MDO) law, 117, 118; Youth Authority (CYA), 142, 147
California Correctional Institution (Tehachapi), 157–58
California Prison Focus, 77
Callous and Cruel (Fellner), 47–48
Canales, Dolores, 188
Carmen, Elaine, 247n24
cell extractions, 116, 124, 147, 171–73, 213, 221; immobilizing gas used in, 2, 43–44, 48–49, 52, 55, 223
cellmates, 1, 36, 194
Center for American Progress, 70
Center for Constitutional Rights, 93
character disorders, 227
Chicago, 4, 156
Childhood and Society (Erikson), 141
childhood trauma, 163
Child Protective Services, 144
civil commitment, 116–19, 146
Civil Rights Act (1964), 71, 83
Civil War, 23, 73
Clear, Todd, 97
Clement, Tom, 152, 231
cognitive behavioral therapy, 230
cognitive impairment, 89, 93. See also disordered thought processes
Cohen, Fred, 9
COINTELPRO, 4, 241, 241n4
Coleman v. Wilson (1993), 30, 48, 63
Colorado, 8, 23–24, 73; Department of Corrections (DOC), 45, 91, 152, 154, 187, 231–33; District Court, 23
command hallucinations, 80, 109, 194, 215
commissary, 43, 105, 178, 202, 217
community mental health, 7, 13, 114, 196–97, 206, 237, 252n42; in corrections, 197–204, 210–11
concentration problems, 34, 89, 91, 94, 96, 100, 130, 137, 153
confidentiality, 15, 53, 110, 122, 200–1, 210
Congress, U.S., 8–9, 71
Connecticut, 26, 73
Constitution, U.S., 71, 83, 101, 180; Eighth Amendment, 2, 7, 12, 41, 44; Thirteenth Amendment, 69

contraband, 41, 78, 182, 218
Corcoran Correctional Facility (California), 76–77, 166, 171
Cornwall, Tim, 77
Corrections Corporation of America, 50
Côté, Gilles, 102
counts, 113, 127
Crime of Punishment, The (Menninger), 46, 53
crisis intervention, 181, 197, 199, 201, 205, 251n32
Critical Resistance Conference, 239
crowding. *See* overcrowding
cruel and unusual punishment, 45, 93, 99. *See also* Constitution, U.S., Eighth Amendment
culture of punishment, 10–11, 13–14, 38–67, 115, 135, 173, 181–82, 187–88, 233, 235; abuse in, 44–48; Blue Code in, 50–52; cycle of hostility in, 55–58, 182; policy violations in, 48–50; prisoner resistance to, 52–55, 59–63; rule enforcement in, 40–43; severity of, 43–44; therapy in, 58–59; vengeance in, 63–67
cutting, *see* self-harm
cycle of hostility, 55–58, 171–73, 182, 213
Czesla, Steve, 188

Davis, Angela, 239
dead time, 178, 210
death penalty, 23, 24, 64, 70, 99, 148. *See also* Death Row
Death Row, 36, 39, 78, 98–99, 189, 245n23
debriefing, 61–62, 94–95, 178
de Havilland, Olivia, 103
deinstitutionalization, 7, 206
delusions, 106, 114, 158, 205, 214–15, 223
Democratic Party, 74
Depakote, 218, 229
depression, 30, 32, 88, 95–97, 100, 183, 202. *See also* antidepressants, bipolar disorder; in PTSD, 151; in SHU postrelease syndrome, 155; suicide and, 22, 145–46; in women, 125–27, 130, 133, 177, 247n24
despair, 2, 30, 61, 94, 139–40, 181, 206, 210, 240; suicide risk and, 11, 143, 145, 185, 251n32
developmental disabilities, 142, 197

Diagnostic and Statistical Manual of Mental Disorders (DSM-V), 162
dialectical behavior therapy, 227
Dickens, Charles, 21
Disability Advocates, Inc. v. New York State Office of Mental Health (DAI, Inc. v. NY OMH) (2002), 122, 193, 201–2, 205, 227
Disability Rights California, 147
disciplinary tickets, 42, 45, 80, 112, 128, 172, 202, 216–19
Discipline and Punish (Foucault), 65
discretion, procedural, 49, 70–71, 79–80, 148
disordered thought processes, 49, 88, 114. *See also* concentration problems
disturbed/disruptive prisoners, 13, 14, 119, 202, 212–33; assaults by, 214–15; effective interventions with, 212–14, 224–33; psychopathology of, 219–20; psychotropic medications for, 228–29; punishment of, 221–23; self-mutilation by, 215–19; use of force against, 223–24
Dockery v. Fisher (2013), 208
dog runs. *See* cages
domestic violence, 51, 121, 123
Dostoevsky, Fyodor, 15, 240
double jeopardy, 118, 122
drive-by shootings, 123, 174
drug use, *see* substance abuse
due process, 207, 244n26, 252n42
Dukakis, Michael, 74

Eastern Mississippi Correctional Facility (EMCF), *29*, 56, 208
Eastern State Prison (Philadelphia), 20–21, 23
Eastwood, Clint, 65
Edna Mahan Correctional Facility (EMCF; New Jersey), 154
education programs, 10, 13, 71, 182, 187, 191–92, 197, 231, 237–39; for juveniles, 136, 139–40, 145, 147, 150; lack of access in SHUs to, 7, 8, 23, 37, 67; mental health benefits of, 87, 204, 209, 214, 227
electroencephalograms (EEGs), 90
Eme, La (Mexican Mafia), 62, 76
emotional numbing, 12, 35, 160

England, 225, 229, 242n3
equal protection, 70–71
Erikson, Erik, 141
Ethiopia, 2
extra disciplinary punishment, 26
extra-pyramidal syndrome (EPS), 110

Fair Sentencing Act (2010), 71, 236
Farrell v. Harper (2003), 147
Faulkner, Daniel, 189
feces, smearing, 55–56, 80, 103–4, 110–11, 114
Federal Bureau of Investigation (FBI), 4, 76, 241
Federal Bureau of Justice Statistics, 8, 73, 123, 136
Federal Bureau of Prisons, 8, 25, 41
Fellner, Jamie, 47–48
Fields, Rona, 100
flashbacks, 89, 121, 122, 125–26, 128, 156, 158, 165–66
flogging, 22
Folsom Prison (California), 83
food trays, 26, 40, 48, 127, 139, 213
forensic psychiatry, 1–3, 5, 51, 79, 112
Foucault, Michel, 64–65
France, punishment practices in, 64
Franklin, Benjamin, 19, 65
Freeman, Morgan, 65
Freud, Sigmund, 87
Fromm, Erich, 230

gag orders, 34
gang members, 8–9, 35–36, 41, 61–63, 93–95, 152, 156, 174–75, 239, 243–44n26; retaliation for rape of, 104, 137; rival, fights between, 76, 238; validation by prison authorities as, 61, 63, 95, 157, 244n26
Garbarino, James, 175
Garland, David, 66
Gates v. Deukmejian (1989), 46
gender issues, 187. *See also* transgender prisoners, women
genocide, 65
Gilligan, James, 175
Girard, Sandra, 179, 180
gladiator fights, 76–77, 84

Goffman, Erving, 103–4
Graham v. Florida (2010), 148, 149
Grassian, Stuart, 88–89
Great Meadow Correctional Facility (New York), 205
Greenberg, Roy H., 163
Grendon Prision, 181, 229–31, 233
Group for the Advancement of Psychiatry, Committee on Psychiatry and the Community, 250–51n17
group therapy, 5, 59, 87, 209
Guanipa, Yraida, 134
Guantanamo detention facility, 37, 98
Guenther, Lisa, 95–96
guilty but insane, 195

Hailey, Candie, 126
Haldol, 27–28, 108–10, 208
hallucinations, 14, 80, 88–89, 106, 112, 113, 158, 228; command, 80, 109, 194, 215
Hampton, Fred, 4
handcuffs, 4, 31, 41, 62, 93, 105, 130, 122, 221; applied through food port, 44, 52
Haney, Craig, 49, 63, 74, 88, 164, 235, 245n6, 248–49n1
Hanrahan, Noelle, 190
Harper v. Washington (1990), 207–9
hearing voices. *See* command hallucinations
Henderson, Felton, 102
High Desert State Prison (California), 83
High Street Jail (Philadelphia), 19
Hill, Marc Lamont, 190
Holder, Eric, 132
homophobia, 131–32
Hoover, J. Edgar, 4
Horn, Martin, 241n8
Horton, Willie, 74
Hudgins, Sheilagh, 102
human rights, 2, 25, 100, 132, 182, 186, 192; abuses of, 56, 68, 179, 239, 245n23
Human Rights Watch, 47, 77, 102
humiliation, 49, 57, 79, 98, 128, 138, 147, 173, 182–84
hunger strikes, x, 31, 41, 60–63, 173, 185, 242n17
hostility, cycle of, 55–58, 171–73, 182, 213
hyperawareness, 34, 81, 94, 153, 157, 159–60

Marion, Illinois, federal penitentiary, 7–8, 25

Marshall Project, 155–56, 161–62

Martin, Steve, 44–45

Martinson, Robert, 190–91, 250n34

Maryland, 73

Massachusetts, 73, 74, 89, 124–25

Mauritania, 37

Maximum Security University (film), 77

McGee, Richard, 187

Medley, James J., 23–24

memory problems, 2, 11, 34, 89–94, 96, 100, 126, 153

Menninger, Karl, 46, 53

mental health treatment, 3, 5–6, 9, 12–14, 57, 109–19, 127, 192–211. *See also* community mental health, psychotherapy, psychotropic medications; to address violence patterns, 225–26; as alternative to incarceration, 13–14; in cages, 58–59, *59;* cell-front, 110–11, 139, 173, 217; class action lawsuits about, 21, 28, 30, 35, 45–46, 55–57, 193, 224; for disturbed/ disruptive prisoners, 14, 119, 202, 212–17, 220–26; guiding principles for, 209–11; juveniles need for, 139, 143, 145–47, 149; malingering concerns and failure to provide, 45, 112–14, 119, 220; minimum standards for, 99, 186; model programs for, 229–33; outpatient, 199, 201, 208, 214, 252n42; public, 13, 14, 194; racism in access to, 73, 80, 84; release of prisoners in need of, 117–19, 196; secure intermediate, 226–28; for self harm, 107, 206, 217–19; staff training to improve, 181, 184, 225, 251n32; for suicidal prisoners, 193–95, 204–6, 225; for women, 125–27

mentally ill prisoners, 6, 9, 26–27, 52, 56–57, 80, 102. *See also* mental health treatment; accused of malingering, 45, 112–14, 119, 220; cell extractions of, 48–49; criminalization of, 12–14, 57, 97; decimation of life skills of, 87, 91–93; deterioration in solitary confinement of, 2–3, 37–38, 63, 101–4, 108–12, 114–17; excessive force against, 40, 45–48; postrelease civil commitment of, 116–20, 146

Mexican Americans, 62, 76, 81, 132–33, 244n. *See also* Latinos

Michigan, 66, 81, 139; Department of Corrections, 71–72, 179–80; State Prison, 72

Michigan Prison Legal Services, 179

Miller v. Alabama (2012), 148, 149

Mills, Alan, 156

Mills, T., 247n24

Mississippi: Department of Corrections (DOC), 40, 49, 208, 224–25; State Penitentiary (Parchman), 35–36, 39–40, 98–99

Monroe Correctional Complex (Washington), 53–55

Montana: Department of Corrections, Behavior Management Plans (BMPs) of, 45–46, 144–46; State Prison, 26, 45–46, 143–44; Supreme Court, 46

Montgomery, Michael, 31

Montgomery v. Louisiana (2016), 148

mood disorders. *See* bipolar disorder, depression, mania

Mualimm-ak, Five, 2–3, 188

Mule Creek State Prison, *6*

multimodality therapy interventions, 209

Murillo, Danny, 187

Muslims, 242n

mutual respect, 171–72, 174–76, 187, 229

narrative therapy, 252n4

National Association of Social Workers, 149

National Commission on Correctional Health Care (NCCHC), 204, 205, 209, 251n32; Standards on Forced Psychotropic Medication, 207

National Public Radio (NPR), 161, 190

National Standards to Prevent, Detect, and Respond to Prison Rape, 132

Native Americans, 72

Navarro, Robert, 77

Nazi Germany, 56, 65

Neal v. Michigan DOC (2012), 180

Nelson, Brian, 155–56, 188

neo-Nazis, 82

New Jersey, 20, 73, 154

New Jim Crow, The (Alexander), 70

New York City Corrections Department, 148. *See also* Rikers Island

New York State, 2, 73, 88, 102, 121–23, 125, 139, 148, 154, 191, 227. *See also specific prisons;* Assembly, 142; Department of Correctional Services (DOCS), 21

New York Times, The, 231

New Zealand, 212

nightmares, 88, 89, 100, 122, 126, 128, 165–66, 205

9/11 terrorist attack, 65

Norteños, 76, 81–83

Northern Correctional Facility (NCI; Connecticut), 26

Northern Ireland, 100

not guilty by reason of insanity (NGRI), 195

Nuestra Familia, 76

Obama, Barack, 71, 142, 236

observation cells, 128, 216–18, 222; suicidal prisoners in, 28, 35, 126–27, 145, 193–95, 205, 251n32

Ohio Department of Corrections, 199

Ojeda, Almerindo, 100

outcome studies, 237

outpatient mental health treatment, 199, 201, 208, 214, 252n42

overcrowding, 3, 5–9, 19–21, 23, 82, 147, 234, 241n3, 242–43n24; mental illness exacerbated by, 46, 104, 108–12, 119, 196, 198; sentencing trends causing, 14, 236

Owen, Barbara, 123

panic, 2, 11, 34, 88, 89, 91, 121, 128, 129, 159, 216–18

Panopticon, 65

paranoia, 2, 11, 47, 49, 89, 91, 94, 105–6, 133, 228; case examples of, 34, 108–12, 122, 133, 194, 214; in previously stable prisoners, 91–92, 104; in SHU postrelease syndrome, 157–60

parenting skills, 10, 87

parole, 70, 74, 94, 96, 127, 162, 187, 236–37; life imprisonment without, 9, 148–49, 237; snitching requisite for, 61–62, 94, 178; of youths, 136, 147

Pelican Bay State Prison (California), 10, *10*, 25, 30–32, *32–34*, 166, 171; hunger strikes at, 60–63, 174, 185; long-term solitary confinement at, 11–12, 32, 34, 88, 91, 93–94, 102, 154, 157–61; severity of punishments at, 43, 48, 100

Pell Grants, 191

penitentiary, origin of word, 19

Pennsylvania State Correctional Institution, Death Row at, 189, 245n23

Pennsylvania System, 20–23, 242n

pepper spray, 28, 40, 47–50

personality disorders, 113, 215, 217, 219, 220, 222

Philadelphia, 19–20, 189

phone calls, rules governing, 1, 26, 36, 41, 43, 94, 105, 178

Pinell, Hugo, 63

Ponte, Joseph, 232

Portugal, 100

positive rewards, 52, 58, 202

positron emission tomograph (PET scan), 90

postrelease syndrome. *See* SHU postrelease syndrome

posttraumatic stress disorder (PTSD), 89–90, 121, 122, 126, 128, 130, 202–3, 223; similarity of SHU postrelease syndrome symptoms and, 151, 154–55, 162–63, 166

Presley v. Epps (2006), 35

Price, David, 243n4

prisonization, 163–65, 182

Prison Law Office, 147, 183

Prison Radio, 190

prison rape, 7, 36, 89, 165, 166, 175; of juveniles in adult facilities, 137–39; legislation to eliminate, 51–52, 131–32, 187–88; of women by male staff, 104, 130–31

Prison Rape Elimination Act (PREA), 51–52, 131–32, 187–88

privately run prisons, 38, 50, 56

privileges, loss of, 43, 105, 145, 217–18, 228

programming modules, 58

Progress Foundation, 198

protective custody, 36, 72, 80, 196, 201

psychiatric hospitals, 43, 71, 103, 108, 110, 113, 194, 208; civil commitment to,

psychiatric hospitals *(continued)*
116–19, 146; deinstitutionalization of, 7,
206; transfers from prison to, 146, 214–15
psychoanalysis, 141, 230
psychopathic personality, 219
psychosis, 47, 89, 103–6, 108–9, 114, 138, 151,
194, 215, 220
psychotherapy, 184, 196, 205–6, 251n32
psychotropic medications, 35, 114, 156, 195,
199–201, 203, 206–9, 228–29. *See also*
antidepressants, antipsychotic medications, *names of specific drugs*

Quakers, 19, 20, 23
Quinn, Tom, 77

racism, 11, 25, 36, 51, 65, 68–84, 95, 189; in
access to rehabilitation and education
programs, 71–72, 84; of gangs, 81–82; in
policing and court practices, 70–71, 79;
in rule enforcement, 79–80; in solitary
confinement units, 76–79, 212
Raemisch, Rick, 187, 231–32
rape, 64, 73. *See also* prison rape
Rapiscan searches, 183
Reading Gaol (England), 242n3
Reagan, Ronald, 234
recidivism, 9, 35, 96, 190–92, 211, 237
Reconstruction, 73
rehabilitation, 5–14, 87, 115, 117–18, 134,
164, 166–67, 171–92. *See also* education
programs, job training, mental health
treatment; connection with outside
world through, 181–84; to end cycle of
hostility, 172; to foster sense of agency,
171–72, 174, 176–81, 185–86, 229–30; of
juveniles, 136, 140, 147–50; mutual
respect in, 174–76; nineteenth century
belief in solitary confinement as method
of, 19–23; outcomes of, 190–92; parole
and, 94; racism in access to, 11, 71, 84;
reasons for lack of, 5–9, 104. *See also*
culture of punishment; resilience and,
188–90; staff training for, 187–88; vision
of better future sustained by, 184–85
Republican Party, 74
Residential Treatment Programs, 232
resilience, 152, 188–90

resistance, 52–55, 58–60, 90. *See also* hunger
strikes
respect, mutual, 171–72, 174–76, 187, 229
restorative justice, 238–39
restraint positions, 22
restraints, 1, 31, 42, 43, 53–55. *See also* handcuffs, shackles
retraumatization, 122, 134, 203, 223
revenge, 52, 64–65
Rhode Island, 73
Rhodes, Lorna, 44
Riccard, P., 247n24
Riches, John, II, 83
Richie, Beth, 123
right to refuse treatment, 204, 207
Rikers Island (New York), 126, 142, 148,
232–33; Clinical Alternative to Punitive
Segregation (CAPS) Unit at, 126–27,
233
riot guns, 47–48, 76
Ritalin, 75
Rockefeller, Nelson, 60
Roper v. Simmons (2005), 148, 149
Rothman, David, 23
Ruiz, George, 61–62, 93
Ruiz v. Brown (2014), 166
rule violations, 8, 35, 73, 116, 122, 152, 178,
238; disciplinary tickets for, 41, 42, 80,
112, 128, 172, 202, 216–19; by mentally ill
prisoners, 14, 45, 106, 113, 193, 216, 228
Rush, Benjamin, 19
Russell, Willie, 98–99
Russia, invasion of Afghanistan by, 37
Rutherford v. Pitchess (1978), 5
Rwanda, 65

San Francisco, 198
San Quentin Prison (California), 24–25,
29, 59, 60, 182
Schefer, Guy, 243n4
Scheff, Thomas, 103–4
schizoaffective disorder, 106
schizophrenia, 30, 36, 102, 106, 112, 128, 195,
205; diagnosis of, 194, 210, 214, 236;
treatment of, 204. *See also* antipsychotic
medications
Schlanger, Margo, 73
Second Wave women's movement, 134

"What Works? Questions and Answers about Prison Reform" (Martinson), 190–91

White, Michael, 252n4

White Is Right, 78

Wilde, Oscar, 242n3

Willie Russell v. Epps (2004), 35

Winn Correctional Center (Louisiana), 50

Wisconsin, 27

women, 121–35, 148, 188, 219, 239, 247n24; mentally ill, 104, 125–28, 232; racism and, 70, 73, 75; sexual abuse by prison staff of, x, 12, 104, 123, 128–33, 180; subordination of, 133–35; trans, 131, 242n20; traumas of, 12, 104, 121–25; visitors, humiliating treatment of, 183–84

Woodfox, Albert, 188–89

work-release programs, 231

Wright, Emily M., 247n24

youthful offenders. *See* juveniles

zero tolerance of abuse, 40, 51–52, 132, 187

Zimbardo, Philip, 49, 51, 74

Zyprexa, 214